ACTION
for Human Settlements

A C T I O N
for Human Settlements

C. A. DOXIADIS

W · W · NORTON & COMPANY · INC · New York

Copyright © 1976 by the Athens Center of Ekistics

All rights Reserved

Published simultaneously in Canada
by George J. McLeod Limited, Toronto

Library of Congress Cataloging in Publication Data
Doxiadēs, Cōnstantinos Apostolou, 1913–1975.
  Action for human settlements.
  Bibliography: p.
  1. Cities and towns—Planning—1945– 2. Housing.
3. Human ecology. I. Title.
HT166.D679 1977   309.2'62   76–25591
ISBN 0–393–08361–6

Printed in the United States of America

1 2 3 4 5 6 7 8 9 0

To the United Nations,
for its efforts on human settlements

Preface

This is the fourth of the four red books which try to help us understand what will happen to our human settlements and what we can do to save them. It deals with the notion of human settlements, with their problems and solutions, and concludes with the radical changes we need for successful action. The first book, *Anthropopolis: City for Human Development*, explores the concept that we need a city for human development or, in a broader sense, the city we need as humans. The second book, *Ecumenopolis: the Inevitable City of the Future*, deals with the evolution of human settlements and the inevitable changes in their scale, from the small polis (town or city of the past) to the present-day megalopolis and to the city of the future. The third book, *Building Entopia*, faces the problem of how we can turn Ecumenopolis into Anthropopolis. Entopia is the city that combines our hopes and goals with reality.

The concept of the fourth book, *Action for Human Settlements*, was born when the United Nations decided to organize the first International Conference on Human Settlements in 1976 in Vancouver. A first draft was presented to the International Federation of Institutes for Advanced Study Workshop in May 1974[1] and to the eleventh Delos Symposion of the World Society for Ekistics.[2] In this way the ideas for the radical changes we need were exposed to two groups of experts, the first group representing several institutions not connected with the science of ekistics, and the second group consisting of experts from many types of nations and professions connected with the idea of the need for a scientific approach to face the problems of human settlements. In this way the dialogue began a year ago with the distribution of the documents containing my proposals. I am now ready to present them in their final form. The dialogue strengthened my views enormously, because I did not hear anything to weaken them, although certainly there were a great many other ideas and views presented. Mine have not changed, however; they are simply more mature.

The whole effort begins with the clarification of the term human settlements. How can you act in any field unless you have clarified its terms? Even the United Nations, which is organizing the conference for 1976, has not yet agreed on what human settlements are. Thus it became an obligation to start with as clear as possible a definition of human settlements. A definition is contained in the first part of this book.

Having achieved a definition we look at the problems of human settlements and their solutions. This is not at all easy because we are dealing with problems and solutions on a global scale. As many international conferences and sometimes even the conclusions resulting from them have proved, there is a great danger of studying all our problems under the influence of a certain type of problem. The last case of this kind was the United Nations population conference in Bucharest in August 1974. Most of the proposals led towards a resolution slowing down the population increase and leading to zero growth. This line of action was attacked by a group of nations in a very different development phase which had different needs, and the final resolution was based on the need to understand all different aspects and views of the population problem. This task is more difficult for human settlements, which are more complex than the population problem, and this is what we have to face.

Identifying the problems of any human settlement and finding their solutions are more complex tasks than dealing with a housing program because human settlements contain so many elements: Nature; Anthropos (not only Man, but all sorts of human individuals);[3] Society as a system; Shells (not only housing but all sorts of Shells); and all sorts of Networks. The difficulty increases when we deal with groups of human settlements. They increase more when we deal with a nation and, of course, they increase enormously when we deal with the whole globe. It is clear that this study cannot present all problems in human settlements and determine all solutions on a global basis. Years of systematic and scientific effort are required. The second part of this book contains a systematic presentation of problems and solutions for basic groups of human settlements, setting the framework for a better understanding of the overall situation and for the necessary systematic effort.

The third part of this book contains specific proposals for measures that should be taken in all types of human settlements. Even if we deal with primitive settlements we must remember that we are in the middle of a great explosion that creates changes everywhere. These changes started several generations ago, but their impact on the healthy development of human settlements has not been understood well and great mistakes are being made almost everywhere. To face them and to solve the problems they are creating we need to make many radical changes in our policies, programs, laws, and plans.

It is clear that this book on action for human settlements deals with three major subjects: the human settlements themselves, the problems and their solutions, and the radical changes we need. Each of these subjects badly needs a multi-volume study, but our task here is to start the process for such a great effort. This is the practical purpose of this book, not to save all human settlements, but to help start the process on a global basis, or at least to help any continent, country, region, or human settlement that has the initiative and courage to begin.

Action on a global scale is needed because no individual country behaves in the proper way. Anything that can initiate such action will be helpful, no matter if the scale be limited. Action in the right direction helps both the people of the human settlement with which it is directly concerned and many others as well, since it becomes an example from which everyone can learn. Thus action develops the system more and more for the benefit of every inhabitant of our globe.

Table of contents

List of illustrations

PART ONE

The Subject of Human Settlements

A. Human settlements

1. Definition

Human settlements are the territorial arrangements made by Anthropos for himself. They are the result of human action and their purposes are human survival; an easier and better life in infancy; happiness and safety, as Aristotle defined them; and human development as we are now beginning to conceive it.[1] To understand them better we must, in both space and time dimensions, begin with the whole cosmos and come down to Nature on earth, the biosphere, Anthropocosmos and, finally, human settlements. They are the latest and smallest of all the preceding units. They do not even cover the whole biosphere, parts of which, such as the oceans, are occupied only by zoocosmos and phytocosmos, or the atmosphere which Anthropos invades only with skyscrapers, airplanes, and spaceships.

Human settlements range from temporary settlements where the ground has only been levelled for a night's sleep, to semi-permanent and permanent settlements; from nomadic settlements like tents or spaceships, to immobile, huge structures. They start as temporary, small settlements grow to become permanent, constant, and now once again growing settlements. They grow so much that we are beginning to see millions of human settlements merging into one human settlement, Ecumenopolis.[2] The air and water, even the Pacific Ocean, show signs of pollution coming from all over our globe. Is this not a sign of global human aggression that must end in one human settlement? In 1972 the United Nations began this recognition in Stockholm and continued it in 1974 in Nairobi by agreeing that the first two pollutants to be monitored should be sulphur dioxide and oxone in the air.[3]

The chief cause of confusion concerning the term human settlements is the lack of a clear definition. What exactly are human settlements — are they cities, villages, housing, people, society, buildings, or something else? In 1964 I proposed the term "human settlements" instead of "housing, building, and planning" to the United Nations New Committee on Housing, Building, and Planning, but it was rejected. A few years later, however, it was adopted, and now is accepted as the correct term, but its meaning is still unclear. Even within the United Nations there is no "agreed-upon definition."[4] This is so because human settlements are the most complex systems on our globe, two orders higher than cells and one order higher than bodies, if we are to follow Sir Julian Huxley's classification of individuals, but with a degree of complexity many times higher than their component bodies.[5]

1. *Human settlements are the territorial arrangements made by Anthropos for himself.*

1. Human settlements in Rio de Janeiro, Brazil

A comparable uncertainty in definition also exists for the basic types of human settlements and their parts, concerning which there is no agreement. I have, however, been using a framework for a scale of human settlements for many years, and am now ready to transmit this experience which has undergone many tests and experiments. The whole global system of human settlements can be classified on the basis of an ekistic logarithmic scale composed of fifteen units, beginning with the smallest unit of the individual human being, or Anthropos, and ending with the total global system of human settlements, or Ecumenopolis. This scale, which can be seen in Figure 2, is the result of various tests (See Appendix 1). In order to simplify the presentation in this book, however, I will deal with the basic types or parts of human settlements as shown in Figure 3.

Ekistic unit	1	2	3	4	5	6	7	8	9	10	11	12	13	14	15
Com. class				I	II	III	IV	V	VI	VII	VIII	IX	X	XI	XII
Kinetic field	a	b	c	d	e	f	g	A	B	C	D	E	F	G	H
population range			3 - 15	15 - 100	100 - 750	750 - 5,000	5,000 - 30,000	30,000 - 200,000	200,000 - 1.5 M	1.5 M - 10 M	10 M - 75 M	75 M - 500 M	500 M - 3,000 M	3,000 M - 20,000 M	20,000 M and more
name of unit	Anthropos	room	house	housegroup	small neighborhood	neighborhood	small polis	polis	small metropolis	metropolis	small megalopolis	megalopolis	small eperopolis	eperopolis	Ecumenopolis
ekistic population scale	1	2	5	40	250	1,500	10,000	75,000	500,000	4 M	25 M	150 M	1,000 M	7,500 M	50,000 M

2. The ekistic units

Figure 3 shows that, when dealing with small numbers of people, one human settlement can be very different from another human settlement of the same size (a village is very different from an urban neighborhood), but when we deal with larger units we always have the same units. A metropolis can be a completely separate human settlement while at the same time being part of a megalopolis.

What percentage of the world population lives in the various types of human settlements? There is no official study concerning this problem, as many countries have their own systems of statistics, and others have none. When studying the City of the Future in the Athens Center of Ekistics we tried to make some reasonable assumptions which led us to several tentative conclusions about the global situation, given in Appendix 2. More than half the global population, 51.3%, live in very small human settlements, including temporary settlements (43.6% live in human settlements recognized as villages). The next group, 22.4%, lives in towns and smaller groups live in metropolises and megalopolises. I mention these figures to remind us that we constantly speak of urbanization and its great problems, forgetting that almost three-fourths of the global population still live in the old and traditional sizes of human settlements.

2. *To proceed with a proper understanding of human settlements we must accept the ekistic logarithmic scale for their international classification and understanding.*

Types of Human Settlements	Parts of Human Settlements	Population
temporary human settlements	house and housegroup	3 - 100
villages	neighborhoods	100 - 5,000
town or polis	town or polis	5,000 - 200,000
metropolis	metropolis	200,000 - 10 million
megalopolis	megalopolis	10 million - 500 million
national systems of human settlements	national systems of human settlements	500 million - 20,000 million
international systems of human settlements	international systems of human settlements.	20,000 million and more

3. Basic types of human settlements and parts of human settlements, by population

After clarifying the types and parts of the human settlements, we must clearly understand their elements, about which there is much confusion, especially since the development of the environment question. By the word environment most people only mean the natural environment. But the environment is composed of the same five elements as compose human settlements. The first is Nature itself, what is commonly called the environment. The second is Anthropos, which we used to call Man, leaving unclear whether we meant one sex and age or all possible ones. Anthropos means all possible human beings as individuals. The third element is Society as a system of human interaction. The fourth element is Shells (or buildings of all kinds). The fifth element is Networks, beginning with roads and ending with telecommunications. When dealing with any type of human settlement and any aspect or problem relating to it we have to be certain that we clearly know the elements involved. In dealing with a village we cannot limit ourselves to its buildings; we must deal also with its fields and forests, the roads connecting them, and its people, from the individual to the operation of the village society.

3. *When dealing with human settlements we must always be aware that they consist of five elements, Nature, Anthropos, Society, Shells, and Networks, without any of which they cannot exist.*

To think, however, that once we know the elements we can be specific about human settlements is also wrong because any individual dealing with them can express himself in a different way. One person can say that this town is very beautiful, while another may hate it because it is run on a feudal system. Others can speak of its great economic problems, its efficient administration, its beautiful parks, or its historic importance. It is imperative that we clarify the different ways in which we look at human settlements when we speak and work for them, whether as individual citizens or as experts.

As this clarification can be done in many ways we must do so by basic categories. This has already been done and we have tested the study of every possible aspect by looking at human settlements in five ways: economic, social, political or administrative, technological, and cultural. Every special aspect or view can be classified under one of these categories as a subsection. Someday we will have a model incorporating every single aspect, even the strangest. At present the use of the five basic ways is enough to help us out of the confusion.

4. *We look at human settlements in so many different ways that we become confused. We must classify them in five basic ways: economic, social, political or administrative, technological, and cultural. We must then classify any special aspect under these sections as subsections.*

Even if we use all possible definitions of the types, parts, elements, and ways of looking at human settlements we may forget the dimension of time. Human settlements are living organisms, and any reference to them as static and unchanging is completely wrong. It is inadequate to speak of a city and its present-day problems of lack of funds for its amelioration without mentioning that it is in the phase of population and economic growth. Only the dynamics of increase of costs and incomes can give us an idea of whether there really is a serious problem or whether, on the contrary, it is in a normal phase of growth during which there are normal problems, as with a young person entering the phase of adulthood, which can be very naturally solved. Time is a basic dimension in the study of human settlements and without it there is no hope for progress. I mention this aspect because there are many studies of cities which do not show the dynamics of human settlements, as though they were medieval cities enclosed by walls. As a result the studies do not really open our eyes to existing situations, their dynamics, and how they can be faced.

5.   *To understand human settlements properly as living organisms we must study their evolution from past to future, that is, their time dimension.*

Although these aspects cover all the types, parts, elements, views, and dynamic changes of human settlements, we still lack an understanding of the principles and laws governing them. If we do not know whether a human being, or Anthropos, can die without oxygen and a proper temperature, how can we hope to build a human settlement for him in the right place? If we do not know where towns should be created and why, how can we hope to select the right place? We must understand many principles and laws, particularly if we remember the existence of the five elements, their own principles and laws, and the more complicated situation created by their interaction within the total system of a human settlement. This is not the occasion to speak of all of them, because it would require many long volumes but, as we must understand the role played by principles and laws, I will speak here of the five basic principles of human settlements which guide their existence.

The first principle is the maximization of potential contacts. A hunter will settle within a reasonable distance from the paths of the animals he hunts, from water resources and timber which he needs for his fire, etc. The urban dweller today will prefer the house which is reasonably close to his job, to the market, and to his children's school, etc.

The second principle is the minimization of the effort required for all possible contacts as expressed in energy, time, money, etc. Even animals learn how to climb a hill by the easiest road in terms of energy.

The third principle is the optimization of space and energy for reasons of safety. The first two principles may well be influenced by this third one; a shorter road may be avoided because it is unsafe.

The fourth principle is the optimization of the balance of the five elements. This principle has often been forgotten during the last generations, and this is why we have had so many problems with the natural environment (Nature).

In the past, even the most primitive people managed to keep this principle and to achieve a healthy ecological balance between their actions and Nature. This is how they survived. Experts who investigate bands of primitive people admit today that their knowledge of local ecology is perfect.

The fifth principle, the most difficult to apply, is the balance among the previous four principles. We cannot maximize our potential contacts in the middle of a crossroads; we may easily be extinguished by speeding machines. For every solution that we seek we need a balance of the four principles to keep contacts, to make them economic and safe, and to be sure about the balance of the five elements.

6.   *To understand the existence and dynamic evolution of human settlements we must be aware of the five principles which have always guided them.*

In the spirit of what has already been said about human settlements we must now try to understand them better, and this is why we must examine the five elements and the seven basic types of human settlements we selected. This is the task of chapter one. First, however, we must look at one aspect of human settlements that has been overlooked to our cost during the last few generations: it is aspect of the changing human settlements.

2. Change

We are passing through an era that must be called the era of changing human settlements, an era which began 10,000 years ago when hunters became cultivators and settled permanently in villages. At first this fundamental change only occurred locally. It took 10,000 years to spread all over the globe and has not yet been completed. Until recently this change proceeded at a very low rate on a global basis. Thus it does not resemble what is happening today. We expect this long era of development from hunting and nomadic life to cultivation to be completed in a few generations. So it is really a very long era of development. Human settlements were changing, but very slowly.

7.   *The one great change in human settlements from hunting bands to villages of cultivators began 10,000 years ago, is still going on, and will be completed in a few generations.*

Unlike this long era of development, in which everything happened at a slow speed, the present era is an era of great change. This is so because in 1825 a major revolution took place. In northern England, for the first time, people were moved by machine, the first train. This event turned the city into a multi-speed city and influenced all human settlements. Previously, the only speeds inside human settlements were human speed and, in the few cases of large and rich human settlements, animal speed (horses, etc.), but this animal speed did not

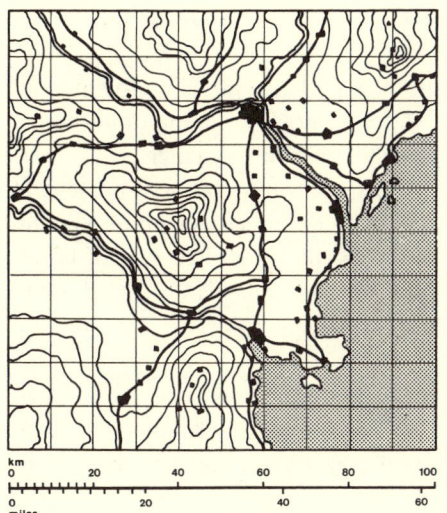

km
0   20   40   60   80   100

0   20   40   60
miles

Beginning of the urban era: polises

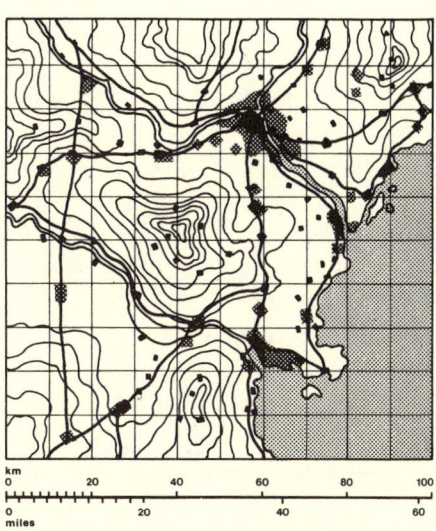

km
0   20   40   60   80   100

0   20   40   60
miles

Early dynapolis: expansion as the static city becomes the center of larger political units

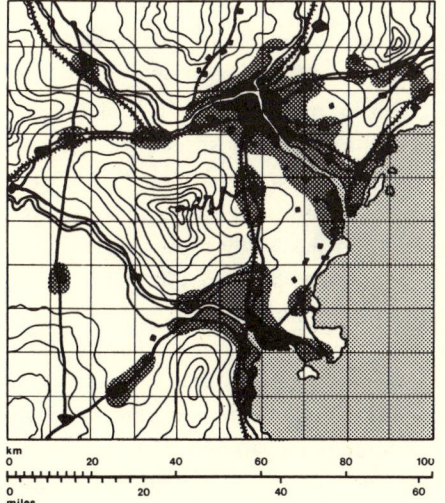

km
0   20   40   60   80   100

0   20   40   60
miles

Dynapolis: expansion in the industrial and railroad era

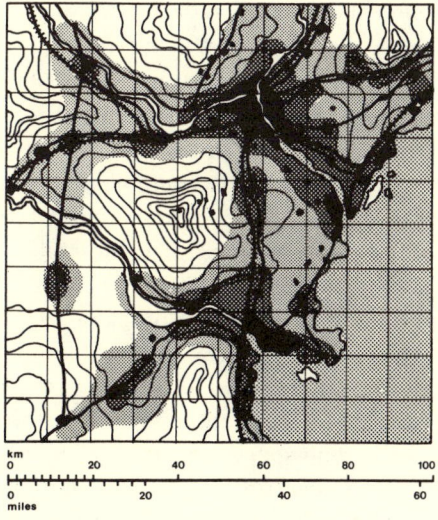

km
0   20   40   60   80   100

0   20   40   60
miles

Dynametropolis: expansion in the automobile era

4.   The changing structure of human settlements

influence to any important degree the formation of cities. The invasion of speed generated by artificial rather than natural forms of energy created a genuine revolution. The fate of human settlements changed completely. The people who really participate in city life live at a distance no greater than one hour's travel from its center. With the invention of the train this distance, which was 5 km for pedestrians and up to 10 km for horse-drawn carts, became several tens of kilometers. The radius, then, of the real city, as an operating system, was multiplied several times and the real city area was multiplied tens of times. Another change also occurred. The inhabitant of the villages around the city became real citizens if the train passed through their territories. This was the beginning.

Thereafter, the change became much more important because the railroad was utilized in more and more countries, and technology and speed developed increasingly. At the beginning of our century this change became revolutionary because, in addition to trains, automobiles invaded the city and countryside. This additional change gave faster speeds and greater mobility to the people who no longer depended on railway stations but could use their automobiles to reach any point in human settlements. Train and automobile speeds increased and then the airplane brought in completely new speeds. Thus human settlements changed radically for the first time in history. They became multi-speed settlements, greatly enlarged, capable of sudden bursts of growth. The opening of a new highway can turn a village into an urban suburb overnight.

These changes created a major revolution in human settlements which started 150 years ago, accelerated 75 years ago, and has by now spread to all countries by plane and automobile and I would say that in areas where incomes remain below $200 per capita most of the villages have not been influenced. This may well mean about half the global population, or slightly more. But even if only half the global population has suffered such a change in 150 years, it is a revolutionary one. It is probable that we are in the middle of this era of change, which started in 1825 and may end by 2125 A.D., as the City of the Future study demonstrates.[6] In the next 150 years all human settlements will have emerged from the era of hunters, which began changing 10,000 years ago, and from the era of one-speed human settlements, which began changing 150 years ago. We are now in the middle of the era of greatest change in human settlements that has ever occurred.

8. *We are now in the middle of an era of the greatest change that has occurred in human settlements, the era of changing from one-speed to multi-speed human settlements.*

We do not understand the fast change we are witnessing, as we can see by examining two examples. Human settlements were created for humans only or, in some areas, like the Champs Elysées in Paris, for horse-drawn carts, but not for machines. Then we brought in machines as invaders and pushed people to the side, onto the sidewalks. Human settlements became machine settlements in which humans also live. The solutions gradually adopted are highways, which cut human settlements into pieces. Another example is the creation of industrial plants serving production and profits, but not the environment. Machines and technology work both for and against humans. There is no indication that we understand the radical change that has occurred. It is time for us to open our eyes, to understand what happens and why, and to prepare ourselves for the new types of human settlements we need, settlements that will be served by machines and technology without being invaded by them. This means human settlements served by machines in the best possible way. If we understand this task we will see that the era of changing human settlements, instead of being an era of great problems, can become an era of proper development. If we understand the inevitable changes in time we can guide them for the sake of humans, instead of letting them happen against the interest of humans, as we do today.

9. *We must understand the great changes happening in human settlements so we can react in the proper ways to all their problems.*

B. Ekistic elements

1. Nature

Nature is the first of the five elements of human settlements for many reasons. First, it is almost a million times older than human settlements. Second, human settlements are products of Nature, which created a system, bore Anthropos, and helped in his development into human beings able to start human settlements. Theoretically, we could also say that human settlements are part of Nature, but, since it is human settlements we must understand as well as possible, we must consider Nature an element of human settlements (Fig. 5).

Recently Nature has been called environment or, more accurately, natural environment. This expression, however, sometimes limits the dimensions of the total natural system, so it is preferable to use the term Nature in general and then distinguish the territorial dimensions with which we are dealing or its parts, such as land, water, etc. In terms of territorial dimensions, Nature begins with the smallest dimension in human settlements, Anthropos, and expands to include our entire global system (See Appendix 1). Nature, in terms of human settlements, starts with ekistic unit 1 and ends with ekistic unit 15. Although the breadth of Nature extends from much smaller units, as we learn in physics,

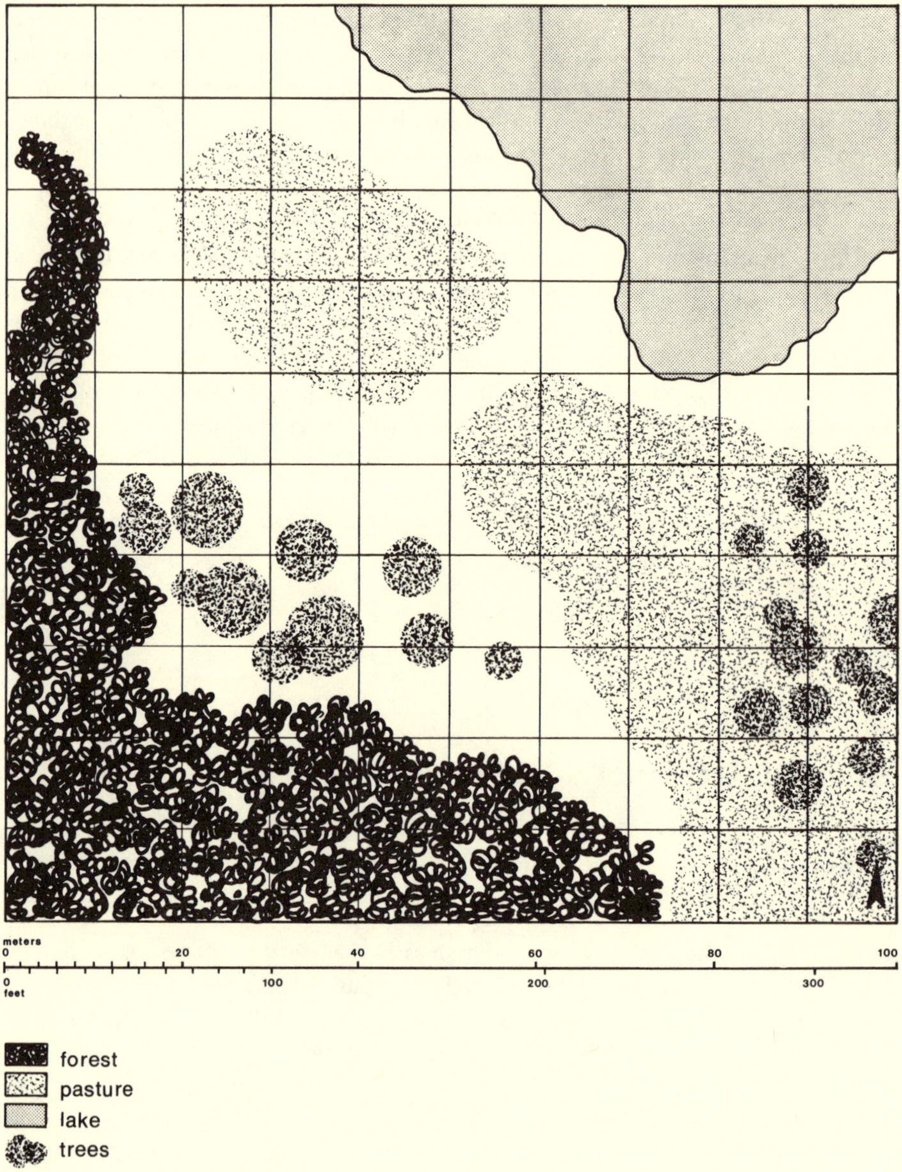

meters				
0	20	40	60	80	100
0 feet	100	200	300

- forest
- pasture
- lake
- trees

Shading indicates intensity of activity.

5. Nature

to much larger units, as we learn in cosmology, in the field of human settlements we limit our interest to the 15 units.

The best way to study Nature as an element of human settlements is to consider its basic parts and then look at them all together as a system. The basic parts for our purposes are, in the following order: land, water, air, climate, flora, and fauna.

We begin with land, without which no human settlement exists. Some people do live in small boats, as in many places in southern Asia, but they depend to a certain extent on the land near which they live. Often they live permanently in one port, the boats being simply a kind of housing for which they did not have to buy land. Land is fundamental to human settlements, and its extent and type determine whether the human settlement will be suitable for hunters or nomads, land cultivators or urban dwellers, or whether no human settlement will be possible at all. For example, the inclination of the land surface may be so steep, let us say more than 20%, that it is very difficult to build roads and houses on it, or a more than 50% slope, in which case it is impossible.

Water comes second, and its quantities and quality determine, together with land, the type of human settlement, especially if humans cannot control its existence and movement. No water means no human settlements, with the exception of temporary nomadic settlements. Too much water may mean very special types of farming settlements, as in many parts of Bangladesh where people build their homes on poles to remain above the water's surface, sometimes for long periods.

Air is often forgotten, or simply mentioned in terms of pollution, when we speak of human settlements, but the amount of oxygen it contains and its movement can easily limit the formation of human settlements within certain areas.

Climate determines the type of life that can be created within a certain area, and defines the upper and lower limits for the existence of human settlements. Looking at the overall distribution of the global population, we see that climate and the formation of the land surface are the most limiting elements, followed by the availability of water, flora, and fauna. Several of these elements together form the total estimate of habitability in every area of our globe.

The existence of flora and fauna enables hunters and cultivators to establish settlements. The possibilities for flora and fauna to be increased enable other human settlements of different types to be established.

After examining all these parts of the element of Nature we can consider their interrelationships, which form the very complex system of Nature as a whole. This ecological system determines the type of life that can be created in a particular place for any plant or animal, including humans.

10. *Any systematic study of human settlements must start with an analysis of Nature and all its parts: water, air, climate, flora, and fauna, and their interrelationships. Without such a beginning there is no hope of proceeding successfully.*

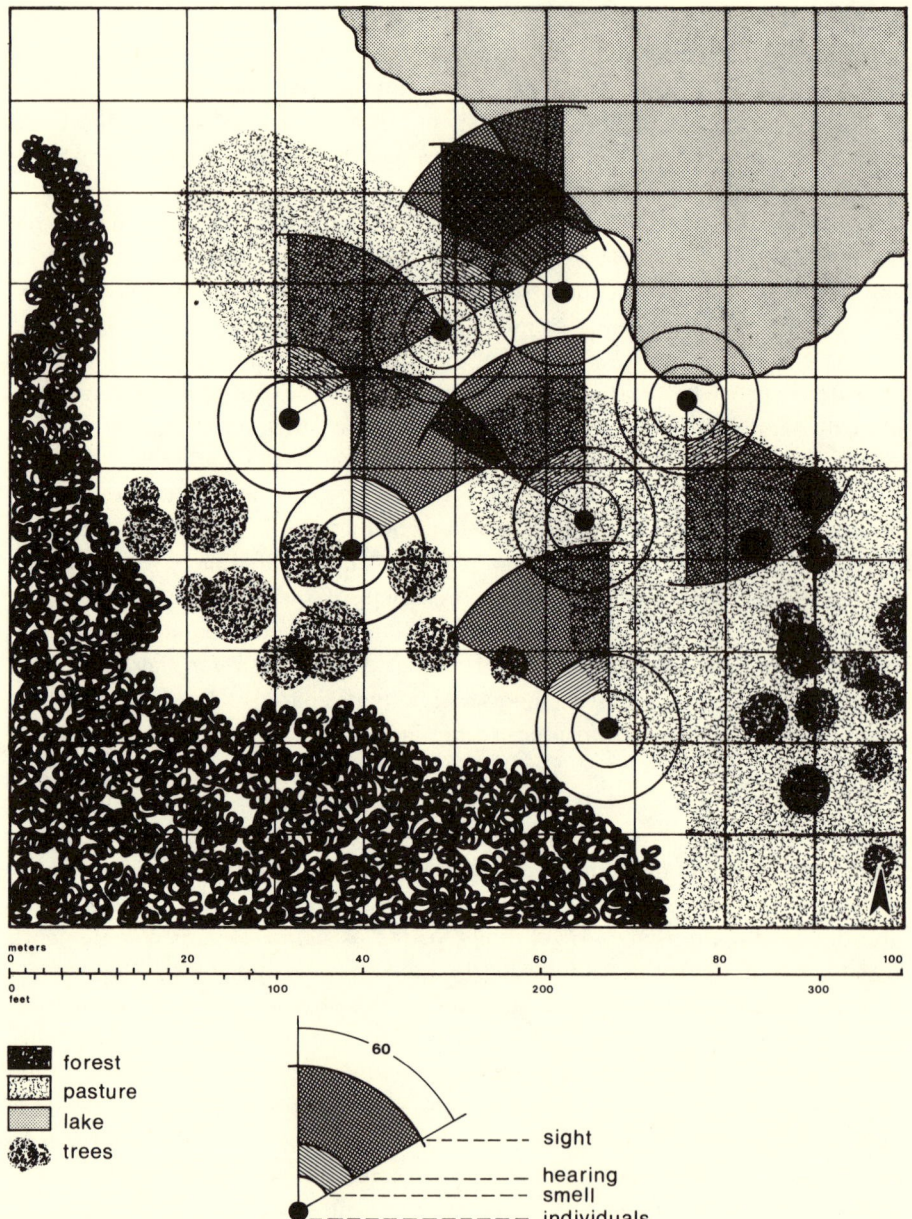

forest
pasture
lake
trees

60

sight
hearing
smell
individuals

6. Anthropos

The dots represent "human bubbles." The concentric circles represent the spheres within which each person can smell, hear, and see in some detail.

2. Anthropos

The second element is Anthropos, the individual human being (which should no longer be called Man because of the apparent confusion of one sex with all human beings). Anthropos is our second element of human settlements because he followed Nature, evolving much later, but preceded the other three elements, Society, Shells, and Networks. Anthropos first adjusted himself to the total natural environment, as did all other animals; he then moved from one type of savannah to almost all types of natural environment in many parts of our globe. In fact we have to move from ecology to human ecology in order to understand the new types of relationships which humans have created in all kinds of environments. Anthropos started changing his natural environment some tens of thousands of years ago by building a few huts. Later, approximately ten thousand years ago, he started the agricultural revolution. This he followed with the creation of all kinds of human settlements.

The agricultural revolution, the creation of human settlements, and then the creation of canals and systems of canals to irrigate large areas led Anthropos to a new phase of his evolution. In this new phase he had to understand the local ecology, relate himself to it and, finally, take the initiative to create revolutionary changes in his environment. In this way Anthropos gradually moved from ecology to ekistics, the science of human settlements.

11. *We must understand how the activities of Anthropos, who changed the natural environment in a revolutionary way, moved from ecology to ekistics.*

Anthropos consists of many parts and can be viewed in many ways. Consider the possible single or combined aspects such as body, senses, mind, and soul or psyche. To understand total Anthropos in space we can proceed as follows: if we consider only his body we can present him as did Leonardo da Vinci by showing the limits of his body alone. But Anthropos needs more space than that occupied by his body. Anthropos really occupies a "human bubble" as Edward T. Hall called it.[7] Such bubbles define the relationships of several people in space (Fig. 6).[8] If we present not only Anthropos's body, but also the four aspects of Anthropos as a sequence of spheres, we can see his real relation to space (Fig. 7). Anthropos's body occupies the smallest sphere; then comes the sphere of his senses; then the sphere of his mind (whether of one person or of all of us — the "noosphere" as Teilhard de Chardin has called it);[9] then the unknown sphere of his soul or psyche which may reach beyond the sphere of the mind.

After referring to the four aspects of Anthropos as a system we must remember that this does not mean that one Anthropos is the same as another. If we study one individual throughout his lifetime we will find that he is never the

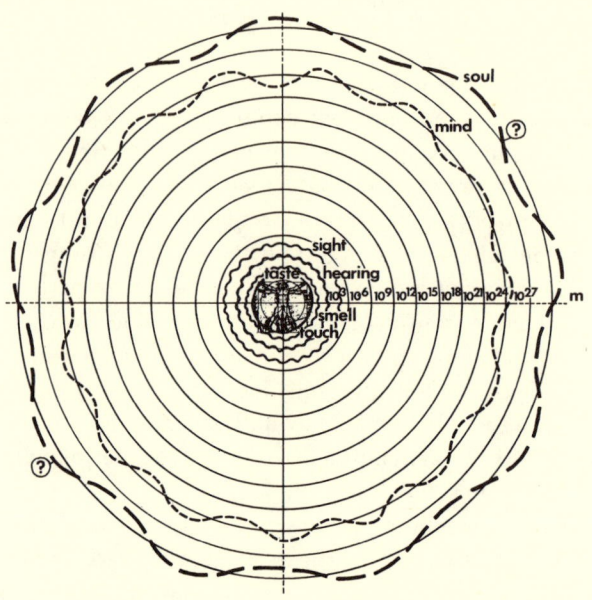

Labels in figure: soul, mind, (?), sight, taste, hearing, smell, touch, m

Scale: 10^3 10^6 10^9 10^{12} 10^{15} 10^{18} 10^{21} 10^{24} 10^{27}

7. Anthropos's relation to space

Development phases	Name of phase	Ages
12	old age	76 – 100
11	early old age	61 – 75
10	real adulthood	41 – 60
9	middle adulthood	26 – 40
8	young adulthood	19 – 25
7	adolescence	13 – 18
6	school age	6 – 12
5	preschool (play age, strider, early childhood)	2.5 – 5
4	toddler	16 – 30 months
3	infant	7 – 15 months
2	breast dependence	0 – 6 months
1	prenatal or fetal	-9 months – 0

8. Tentative scale for human development measurements

same. All his needs, activities, energy, etc., constantly change, starting from zero, gradually reaching the highest possible demands and accomplishments, and then gradually decreasing. We must look at each individual in relation to the phase of his life through which he is passing. A village or neighborhood inhabited by young families with many children should be very different from a neighborhood inhabited only by old people. There is no overall agreement on the definition of the development phases but, as such a definition is necessary in order to achieve a method for understanding our subject and to enter the substance of the human relationship to human settlements, I have looked into the proposals made by medical doctors, psychiatrists, and others and tried to create a scale coordinating all their different views into a unifying system that can serve our goals for a proper study of Anthropos in human settlements. This tentative scale divides human lifetime into twelve development phases (Fig. 8).[10]

We must study each human settlement on the basis of this scale, considering the numbers and percentages of people in each phase. Only such an analysis will give us a proper image of the biological conditions of a given population. A human settlement with a high percentage of its population in the prenatal or fetal phase needs special care in its public spaces for expectant mothers. Such a settlement will grow very quickly, unless the percentage of the population in the next phases is much smaller, which implies a high mortality rate and all kinds of other problems.

Studying the next two phases, the breast dependence phase and the infant phase, will help us understand the problems which exist at home since these children cannot move about by themselves. In contrast, the next two phases, the toddler and preschool phases, show the need for safe streets where these children can communicate and play and the need for special centers where they can be cared for while their mothers are at work, especially if their mothers work in outlying fields or factories.

Studying the school age phase will help us understand what Anthropos needs between his sixth and twelfth year in terms of public space for movement, play, and schools. A study of the adolescent phase will have to be on a completely different scale because, although a good elementary school at the level of a small polis may well satisfy all needs during the school age phase, it cannot do so during the adolescent phase. The secondary or professional school must guide the adolescent's mind into much broader possibilities. The location and type of school, secondary or professional, must, therefore, be determined with this broader goal in mind.

In a similar way we have to face the revolutionary phase of young adulthood, for in this phase basic decisions are taken and requirements for a great number of choices are extensive. The phases of middle and real adulthood guide us to understand the basic conditions of the governing periods in terms of economy, politics, etc. The two phases of old age define many of the problems of human character. There are many questions concerning this phase, such as whether the community is aging or remains balanced or what social policies are needed for those abandoned by the younger generations, as happens often in our changing human settlements.

12. *Understanding the relationships between Anthropos and the total environment is incomplete unless we study them in the twelve development phases through which humans pass.*

While studying each development phase we need to cover many aspects, such as the total human development system consisting of body, senses, mind, and soul or psyche; the freedom and the ability to move inside and outside human settlements; human contacts; and the safety and quality of life. We must conclude with questions, such as the ultimate goals of the humans under study, their creativity, and many other matters.

13. *To understand the relationships between humans and the total environment we must study them through the element Anthropos, which consists of four parts: body, senses, mind, and soul or psyche.*

3. Society

The meaning of the term Society is difficult to clarify because many disciplines deal with Society and each discipline supplies its own definition. I will study this problem as a non-expert in Society who attempts to connect it with the other four elements of human settlements.

I consider Society a total system of relationships, visible or invisible, among people which forms Networks (Fig. 9). Society does not consist only of people, because if we take all the people of London into a desert they will no longer form a Society and will be in a chaotic situation; the particles will be there, but Society will not exist. Society can be considered the "total network of relations between human beings," as Toynbee, stated so well in his *Study of History*,[11] and I follow him when he quotes F.A. Hayek stating that "individuals are merely the foci in the network of relationships."[12]

14. *To understand Society properly as an element of human settlements we must look at all its relationships with the total physical environment consisting of Nature, Shells, and Networks.*

We have many types of societies, and their definition depends on the parts of Society being considered. If we study races, as is still fashionable in several areas of our globe, we will find that the study must be broken down into many categories. Similarly, we can look at different income levels, nationalities, or religions. We can also study such phenomena as social contacts, aggression, safety and security, and how the society is organized. Once we have defined the parts and categories of Society we can proceed to measurements, which

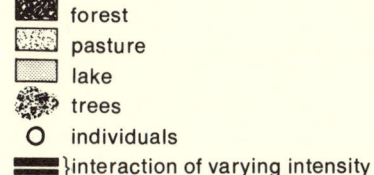

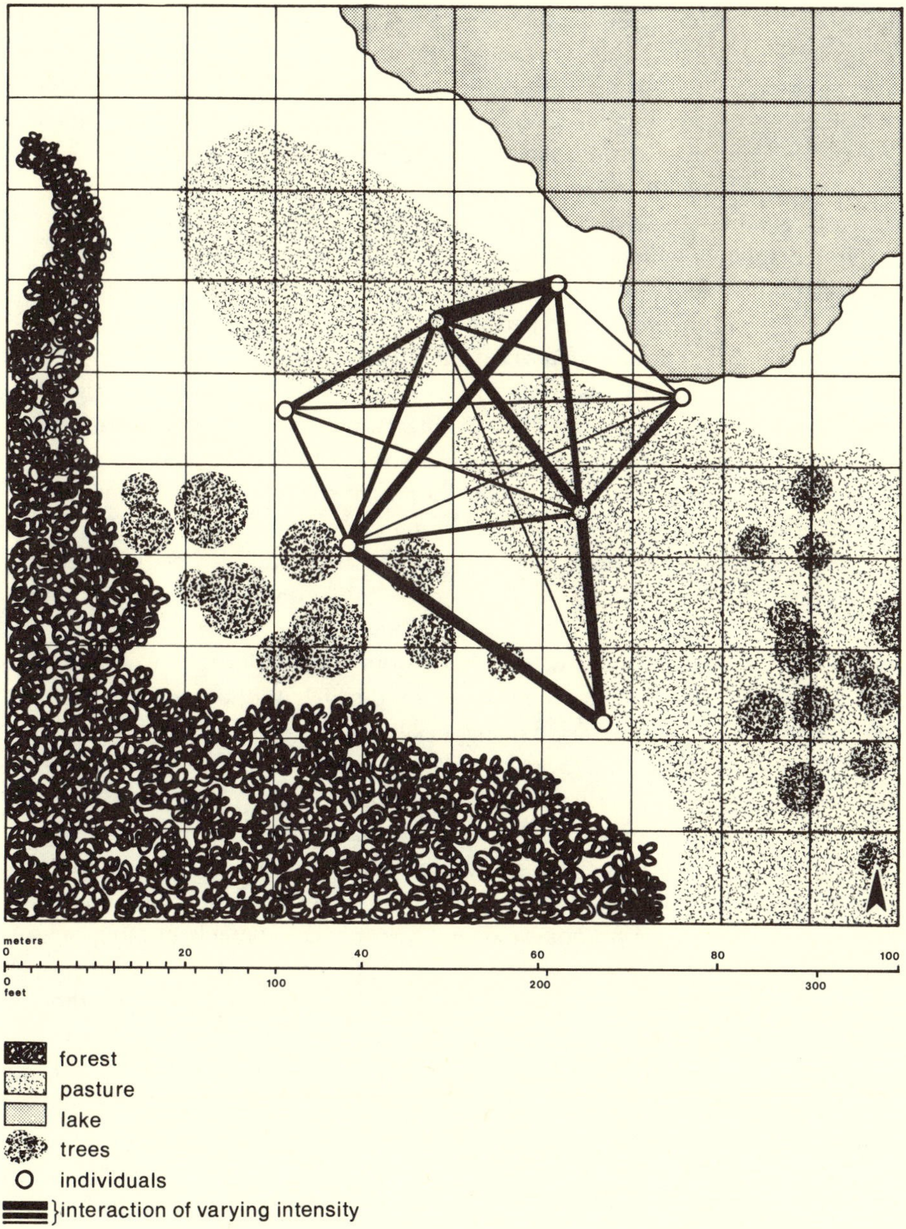

meters
0
20
40
60
80
100
0
feet
100
200
300
forest
pasture
lake
trees
individuals
interaction of varying intensity

9. Society

Society is a system of human relationships.

are so necessary for proper understanding and a proper scientific approach. For example, human aggression can be measured in such categories as aggression against Nature, against the traditional environment, or against individual human beings — which is commonly called crime. To measure human aggression properly we must understand the categories with which we are dealing and their relationships with the physical "city," that is, the total physical aspect consisting of Nature, Shells, and Networks. Then we will find, for example, that it is the poor people within urban areas who suffer most from aggression, or that the greatest dangers of aggression are caused by multi-story buildings.

15. *We have to study Society as an element of human settlements by considering it as a total network of relationships among human beings.*

We then have to face the criterion of quality of Society. To illustrate this, I select the example of human social contacts. We have said that a basic principle of human settlements is that humans want to maximize their potential contacts. For example, a woman does not want to be forced to select a boy friend or a husband only from among the ten free men of her village, but from the many people in an urban area. A big urban area, however, does not always offer contacts of quality. There need to be the proper clubs, neighborhood coffee houses, or other meeting places for there to be quality and hope. The conclusion is clear: if we are to benefit from the maximization of potential social contacts, these contacts must be of quality. Without quality the advantages of the big city are lost in many socially significant ways.

16. *We can understand Society and its operation as a system only by looking at the quality of all human contacts.*

From consideration of the quality of human contacts we move to the organization and structure of Society as a whole. Quality in human contacts requires places for proper contacts, and this means clubs, restaurants, coffee houses of a certain size. There is no hope for quality in human contacts in a big railway station or airport. To have contact places of the proper size we need proper territorial organization and structure. If the city does not have neighborhoods, there is no hope for small restaurants; if it does not have small sports grounds but only huge stadiums, there is no hope for institutions providing good opportunities for human contacts. This does not mean that we do not need big stadiums; it simply means that we need all scales of units to provide human beings with opportunities for all types of social contacts. Every individual has his own needs and it is the duty of the city to offer choices to all its citizens. Proper organization and structure of the human settlement answers a great social question.

17. *To understand the previous examples of the operation of Society we must look at all scales of human settlements.*

The question arises whether there are national or international standards for Society. The answer is both yes and no. Many social problems are directly connected with the local culture and the phase it is passing through. There are several countries in which, at least in some cases (like the cultural groups near the deserts of Morocco where men and women are separated), the club or restaurant for contacts between men and women can have no meaning at all. On the other hand, the need for certain types of organizational levels can be based on international experience.

18.   *To understand better how Society operates we must remember that as yet there are no general international standards, although some of them, such as those applying to human aggression and defense, can be accepted as such.*

4. Shells

We must use the term Shells rather than the term buildings for the same reasons that we use the term human settlements instead of cities. Humans have always used Shells of all kinds, from caves to skyscrapers. In the term Shell we include caves, tents, huts, the elaborate monuments of the past like the pyramids of Egypt or of Teotihuacan, and the greatest buildings of the present. I will name no particular buildings from our era because contemporary judgements often lack objectivity and are much more influenced by fashions than by substance. Only history can decide which buildings will have historical value.

Moreover, by the term Shell we do not mean only the area covered by the Shell, but the total space directly related to it. In the Shell of a house we include its courtyards and gardens, and in the Shell of a tent we include the much greater area outside it where the people sit, deal with their products, cook, and keep their animals. In the same way a whole sports ground is a Shell even if none or only part of it is covered by a roof. It is used as a Shell for sports and has all sorts of constructions. It is not like a city park, which may well contain some Shells but belongs to Nature because the function of the park is not to protect people, as do Shells, but to expose them to the natural environment.

Shells must be divided into categories, beginning with housing and shopping (which is second in importance although it is usually forgotten). Then follow such categories as education, health, administration, protection (police and armed forces), industrial plants, storage, etc. Air and other terminals must be considered parts of Networks because an air terminal has no meaning and cannot exist without an airport. This is analogous to the Shells (coffee houses, restaurants, storage places, etc.) inside a park which belong to Nature as does the park.

19.   *We must consider all Shells, including caves and skyscrapers, and the ground rationally belonging to them even if not actually covered by a Shell.*

Once we have arranged the Shells in categories we can estimate their numbers, but this is a difficult task. Think of references to numbers of houses that do not

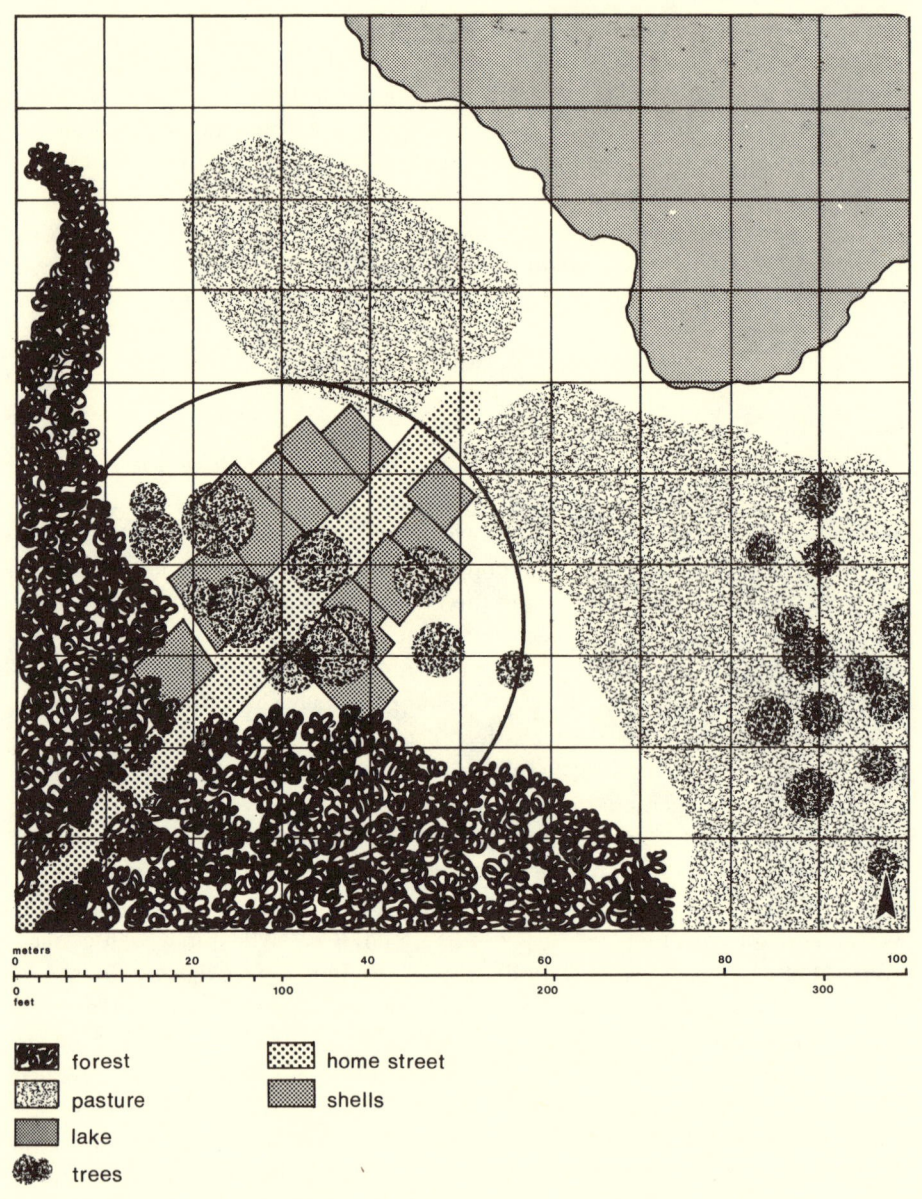

forest
home street
pasture
shells
lake
trees

10. Shells

Balanced organization of a housegroup on a home street

distinguish between one-room slum dwellings and multi-room villas. In the same way it is meaningless to speak of the numbers of shops if small traditional shops are confused with supermarkets. We would have the same problem with numbers of hospitals if we did not refer to the number of beds and other facilities they include. The conclusion is clear: We must deal with numbers of Shells in every category, but doing so requires defining the real contents of every kind of Shell and the services it provides. Numbers of Shells without such definitions are meaningless and their comparison with population figures is also meaningless.

20. *In order to determine the numbers of Shells, we must define the real contents of each Shell and its subunits, houses with rooms, schools with classrooms, etc.*

The situation is more difficult when we move from numbers, which are at least measurable, to quality, which is a vague notion varying greatly from case to case and time to time. Some people consider an old neighborhood with narrow streets and small attached houses to be of high quality, others consider a neighborhood of detached houses, low density, and big gardens to be of quality. Some people even are attracted by high-rise apartment buildings, at least until they understand, especially if they have young children, the great deficiencies these buildings have. It is my experience that a recognition of quality is most difficult for people who live in the era of explosions and changes. Almost no one realizes what this may mean for such matters as culture, habits, needs, or civilization. The conclusion is clear: When we speak of quality we must be aware that on this subject there is no international or even national agreement. The only people who can decide about the quality of Shells are the inhabitants of the Shells themselves provided, however, that they have not been confused by the explosion. It is easier to talk about quality in a traditional human settlement than in a new one.

21. *When we move from numbers to quality we must remember that there are no international standards. We must know the local situation very well in order to express an opinion.*

Then we move to the organization of Shells, because no Shell has value if it is in the wrong environment of Nature, Society, Shells, or Networks. Who would like to live in the most beautiful traditional home if it is on a major highway or in the most polluted part of the city? What is the value of high quality homes if they are built in such a low density area that no one can walk to their neighbor and safety is very low? What is the use of good houses it there are thousands of them together without any shops, schools, etc. at the proper distances? The satisfaction gained from a Shell depends not only on its quality, but on the organization of the system in which it lies. No cell can survive in an organ or organism unless it lies among other cells and is interconnected with them in an organic and healthy way (Fig 10).

22. *We can not judge the conditions of Shells unless we know how they are connected with the total environment existing around them.*

Finally, we have to deal with the question of standards. How big should a room be? What is the best shape for it? What is the best relationship between number of rooms and people? The answers are difficult to find and we deal with them when setting up goals (Part 3), but here we can speak of the existence of some standards which must be respected internationally. These are the technological standards connected with human safety. There can be no argument in favor of an electric line that does not follow international standards for complete security of people and Shells.

23. *International standards concerning Shells can be set only in terms of technological aspects dealing with safety and security.*

5. Networks

All kinds of Networks made or used by humans belong to this element of human settlements. Human-made Networks begin with paths, first created by hunters walking from caves to water sources, and end up with modern systems such as satellites providing us with all types of information. Networks used, although not made, by humans include such lines as navigable rivers and such nodal points as natural harbors. In the same way humans used caves as Shells to live in, they used and are still using parts of Nature as parts of their Networks. Such cases are complex, as no judgement about the use of a river can be formed by looking at it only as a part of a Network; it must also be studied as a part of Nature.

24. *The complete system of Networks consists of two parts, natural ones, such as rivers, and human-made ones, such as canals.*

There are many types of Networks, starting with the movement of people and ending up with the transmission of messages. I speak of the movement of people, not of transportation, because the second expression, although more commonly used, leads us to forget that people move a great deal by themselves before needing means of transportation. Such incorrect conceptions led many cities to design transportation systems without regard to the natural movement of people, thereby creating many problems for humans. The many types of Networks can be divided into the following categories:

Natural human movement (from paths to large human streets),

Human transportation on land, water, or air,

Movement of goods (liquid and solid),

Movement of energy or messages.

25. *There are many types of Networks dealing with the movement of people, goods, and messages.*

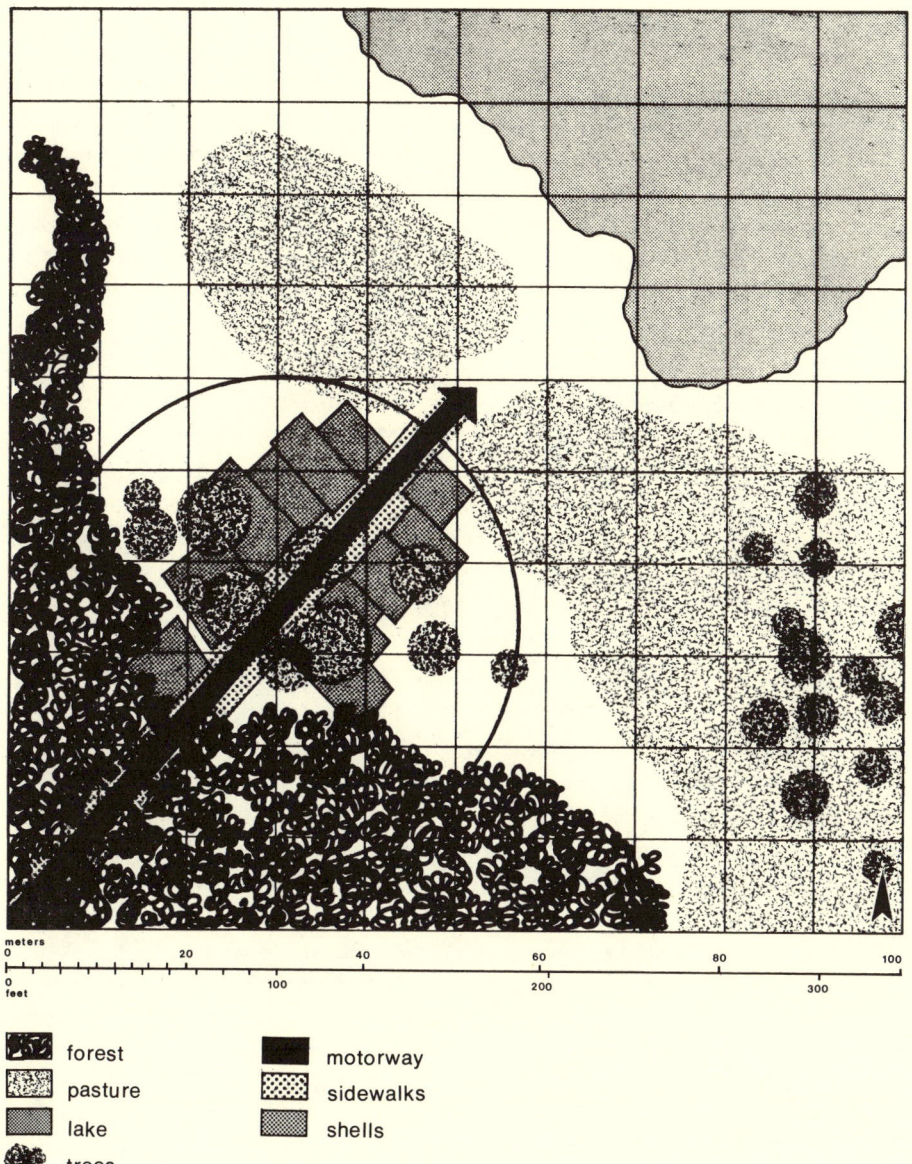

forest
pasture
lake
trees

motorway
sidewalks
shells

11. Networks

When automobiles came, they took the middle of the road, destroying the balance and pushing people onto the sidewalks.

As in the case of Shells, it is extremely difficult to determine actual numbers. To speak of a city which has a certain number of streets is meaningless unless we know their length and many other characteristics. For each type of Network we should make a list of all types of dimensions important to understanding their actual or potential role. I make the distinction because the actual role may be much smaller than the potential one, not because of dimensions but because of quality and standards. One road may be as long and as wide as another but its actual service to the city may be much less if the surface is unpaved. It also may be less because of its turns and curves, but these may not be changed easily in a built-up part of the city and thus its service is not related to quality but to structure.

26. *As the Networks are very complex, we must study every aspect of their structures, not only their numbers, before we judge them.*

Structure and quality demonstrate how very complex is the study of human settlements. When considering structure, we cannot limit ourselves to materials and the ways in which they are used; we must also look at what is called design. When considering quality, we must look at both the level of the design and the appreciation of its usefulness by non-experts.

The structure of a Network, for example, is difficult for non-experts to assess and is best judged by experts. The quality of a Network is best judged by its users.

27. *The structure of Networks must be judged technically by experts. The quality of Networks must be judged culturally by public opinion.*

As with Shells, we cannot judge Networks if we do not consider their organization in relation to each other and to all human settlements. What is the good of a city having enough roads and railways for the internal movement of people if one of its areas possesses none of them? We cannot report the satisfaction in terms of numbers, structure, and quality if organization is lacking, as is the case in many human settlements, some parts of which do not have any of the services readily available in others. Another result of organization is the effect Networks have on the other elements. What is the success of electrical Networks serving the countryside if the beautiful landscape is marred by electric lines crossing in all possible directions without any real organization? What is the quality of an excellent highway if it cuts through an existing community and separates the people from each other? We can make no reasonable judgement about Networks if we limit our attention to their existence and do not relate them to the total system of human settlements.

28. *Networks cannot be judged without relating them to the other four elements (Nature, Anthropos, Society, and Shells) and assessing the influence the other elements exert.*

Finally, we have to deal with standards. The basic criterion, as with Shells, is the safety of people and the environment. As most Networks use huge amounts of energy, their standards are imposed by technology and are increasingly related to rules which have no connection with the locality. These international rules are produced by constantly improving technology for the safety of human beings, goods, and the total environment, and for saving cost and energy. Networks are based more on international standards than Shells, which are more related to the locality and its culture. As such, Networks indicate a move from local culture and civilization to an international technology creating ecumenization.[13] This does not mean that Networks should ignore the values of the locality or, for example, the human needs for walking. It means that Networks should follow international standards while at the same time respecting all values in the areas through which they are passing. Networks must marry the international with the local.

29.   *A final judgement on Networks must be based on both international technological standards and local values.*

C. Ekistic units

1. Temporary human settlements

In most human settlements people settle permanently and their Shells and other facilities remain, usually to be used by others when the original inhabitants die or move out. Temporary human settlements, however, do not have permanent inhabitants, nor any permanent human-made Shell or Network. They are settlements erected and dismantled over short periods ranging from one night to several months. They are the oldest type of human settlements surviving. Those still inhabited by hunters, as in the case of the Lapps in northern Scandinavia, we can consider over ten thousand years old. Those inhabited by nomads who live on their own domesticated animals, as in Afghanistan or Iran and many other places, we can consider ten thousand years old. A newer type of temporary human settlement is inhabited by people who work for several different landowners and migrate from place to place in accordance with the season.

One basic aspect, of course, of temporary human settlements is their location, as they differ greatly if they are in snow covered areas or in the African savannah. We may understand them only if we understand the total territory within which they move.

Next we must consider how often they move, how long they stay in each place, how they are organized — in one group every night in all seasons, or in different smaller groups for certain periods.

In each case we must understand their relationship to all parts of Nature. The hunters, in order to survive, must have a permanent relationship with certain

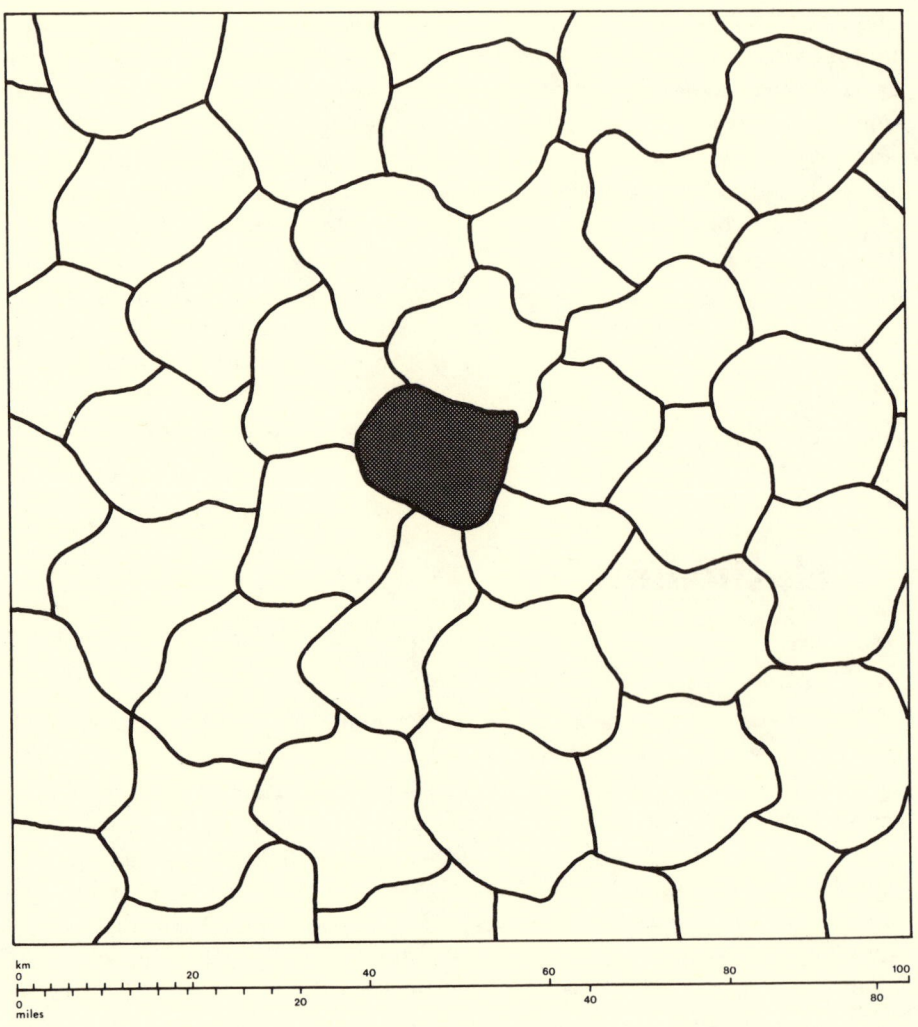

km
0   20   40   60   80   100

0   20   40   80
miles

■ territory of a band   (average radius, 8 km)

12. Temporary human settlements

The territory of hunters' human settlements

groups of animals; they attack Nature, but live in ecological balance with it. Even those who live by attacking have learned how to achieve balances which many of us have not yet understood. We need the same understanding. How long do nomads stay in any one place? Do they exhaust all food supplies before they move? Are they forced to move because of the changing climate? In studying the living conditions in temporary settlements we must be aware before all else that these people do not have a permanent environment and that this is fundamental to everything else under study. No permanent basis means changes, often daily, in everything else. The aspect of Society follows and we find that temporary human settlements always belong to very small social groups of tens of people. Temporary human settlements not only lack permanency, but also consist of very small social groups.

If we move to the study of their Shells, we find that their main characteristic is that they have to be set up and then, sometimes the next morning, moved somewhere else. This may mean very light tents or, in some cases, new huts built in every location with local materials and subsequently abandoned. In essence there are no human-made Networks, except that some groups may travel always to the same areas and this may lead to the creation of a primitive Network of paths.

30. *The most primitive human settlements are the temporary ones, which are tens of thousands of years old. We tend to ignore them in our modern approaches, studies, and programs.*

2. Villages

Villages are those human settlements mostly inhabited by people dedicated to cultivation, including agriculture and cattle breeding. In accordance with the Ekistic Population Scale (see Appendix 2, Table 7),[14] the population of a small village is 250 people (100-750) and of a village 1,500 people (750-5,000). This does not mean, however, that we do not in some extreme cases have some smaller or larger villages. They are called towns by their inhabitants and those of the neighboring small villages, but the big-city people call them villages.

31. *Villages are human settlements with populations ranging from 100 to 5,000 people, of whom the majority are farmers. Smaller or larger human settlements with the majority of their populations farmers are also classed as villages.*

There is no agreement concerning what villages really are as they play several roles. We badly need a generally accepted definition in order to make the necessary comparisons on an international scale, since we can increase our knowledge only by proper comparisons.

32. *There are 3,747,610 villages all over the world or 26.3% of all human settlements. They are inhabited by 1,569 million people or 43.6% of the global population.*

Villages were first created ten thousand years ago in many parts of our globe in places where, mostly, they still exist. We must understand where they are and how old they are because only by doing so can we become aware of all their problems. We also must understand why they were created, because they often were created in remote and unsatisfactory areas in difficult times such as during foreign occupation or feudal control by more successful areas; in such cases we may expect their decline and death.

33. *Villages must be understood in terms of age, location, and the reasons for their creation.*

13. Villages

The next step is to learn about the territory of the village. A village does not consist only of its built-up area or its cultivated area, but of its total territory, including mountains, rocks, and deserts or lakes with which the inhabitants have created an ecological balance, without which they would not have survived. After determining the total territory we must learn the use to which it has been put, where it has remained free of human intervention, where people only hunt or collect timber or other resources, where they cultivate, and where they build. In the same spirit, we also can learn where the situation is stable without any changes in territorial use and where changes have occurred either because of the expansion or curtailment of human activity. Such changes explain the settlement's dynamics and make it possible to understand its negative or positive prospects.

Following this analysis, we must understand how the built-up and cultivated areas are arranged within the total territory. Sometimes they are one built-up and one cultivated area, as we usually imagine villages to be. In many cases, however, this is not the case and the village is divided into many housegroups or even single farms with wildlife between them. We must understand the causes of this structure, which may be coincidental or may have been imposed by Nature, because of such factors as the kind of soil and the existence of water.

34. *The territorial use and organization of the built-up parts of the village must be understood.*

We then turn to Shells and try to understand their numbers, structure, quality, and the satisfaction people gain from them. No matter how good the Shells may be, nevertheless the village may be suffering from other problems great enough to cause its abandonment. We have many examples around the globe where villages with houses of great value were abandoned by their inhabitants. I point this out to remind those who look at villages only from an esthetic point of view that Shells are only one out of five elements and that for any system to be healthy all its elements must be in good condition and in balance with the others. It is far better for a village to cultivate successfully and have poor Shells than the other way around.

Networks play a major role in the condition of the village. If not properly connected with other human settlements the village will find itself in critical condition. Even if the yield in produce is high there would be no hope for economic success and survival without suitable Networks. This case reminds us that the Networks in human settlements are not only those within them which can be seen, but many more and of different categories. In villages we must take into account all types of Networks in three territories: in the built-up area itself, in the total territory of the village, and in the broader territory connecting the village with other villages and at least one polis. Without normal Networks in these three territories the village system is deficient.

35. *The human artifacts of Shells and Networks, which define the physical*

living conditions within the village, as well as all Network connections, must be understood.

We can then study the structure and operation of the village Society. Is the village's Society in normal contact with the communities of nearby villages? Does it have equal privileges with the nearby polises or not? Is it composed of people with equal rights or is it a feudal Society? Are the village people divided by race, religion, etc? Only by understanding how the Society operates in terms of political, administrative, and social aspects can we understand the frame within which humans live.

Finally, after carefully looking at all the other elements, we turn to Anthropos, the individual human being, and examine his satisfaction with village life. We begin with equality, which has long been forgotten in many villages in which women are the slaves of men, or children are deprived of all their rights, or those who do not own land are really the slaves of those who do. We look at working conditions in the fields, at living conditions inside the houses, at streets and squares, and at the methods by which the individual is able to visit the town or to communicate with it. Finally, we should not forget that a judgement of the village depends upon each individual, the freedom he has and the services he receives in terms of such things as his education, health, and welfare.

36. *We must understand all social and humanistic aspects of village Society and the individual inhabitants.*

3. Polises

Towns or polises are human settlements of which the majority of the inhabitants are occupied in urban services, from personal services to modern industry and technology. I say the majority of the inhabitants because gradually there may be larger human settlements in which a significant part of the population may cultivate outlying fields. Such human settlements may be a new and different type. According to the Ekistic Population Scale, the size of the typical small polis is 10,000 people (5,000-30,000) and of the typical polis 75,000 (30,000-200,000).

37. *A polis is a human settlement with 5,000 to 200,000 inhabitants, the majority of whom are occupied in urban services. Until a different term is created for those human settlements of equal size which may have a majority of farmers in the future, each human settlement within these population limits will be called a polis.*

As there is no international agreement on what the polis is and how it differs from the city, these very specific figures have been proposed in Appendix 2, Table 7.

38. *There are 40,692 polises all over the world or 0.3% of all human settlements. They are inhabited by 807 million people or 22.4% of the global population.*

Polises were created 8,000 years ago and since have spread out to or been created afresh in most parts of our globe where villages formerly existed. They now exist almost everywhere, and usually are the nodal points of systems of villages, or of other systems spreading out from larger centers of human settlements, such as industrial or administrative centers. In this second case the

14. Polis. Kafue, Zambia

polises are no longer centers of systems, as they usually were in the past, but satellites of broader systems of which they now form a part. It is, therefore, important to understand the reasons for their creation and the extent of the territory depending on them or related to them. This is especially important in the first and more traditional case, in which a polis is the nodal point of a system of villages, because before we can understand its real role and function we must understand what is happening in its total, not only its restricted, territory. If the wider territory has problems of decline, the impact on the polis may be disastrous as it no longer will have a region to serve. There are cases, however, in which a polis may be constantly developing in spite of a declining region. This may be caused either by farmers moving to it but continuing to work on their farms, or because completely new functions have developed.

A polis is the center of a Daily Urban System (DUS), which is changing enormously with the increasing mobility of its people. In the past, farmers who could spend one hour travelling in each direction to supply the polis and be supplied by it lived in villages at an average of 5 km away from the polis. Now the same farmers can commute 30 km in each direction per day if they can afford to use a car or a tractor. In such cases the territory depending directly on the polis has increased tens of times. The Daily Urban System has been changed radically. In the same way a broader region depending on this polis is influenced enormously and the distribution of the population may be changed completely. Remote villages may be abandoned or changed into resort areas for inhabitants of their own polis or of more remote ones.

39. *Polises must be understood as centers of changing Daily Urban Systems (DUS) and of their broader regions.*

To do this we must clearly understand the total territory of the polis and how it is used. The polis was created as the center of its area. If today its agricultural area is abandoned because of a decline in incomes or, on the contrary, is more developed because of new methods of irrigation, the polis will be immensely influenced. In the same spirit not only agriculture but all other uses of the total territory must be understood, from wildlife and its development (negative or positive) to the built-up areas of the whole region.

Even this achievement is not enough; we also must understand the physical formation of the total territory. Cultivation may increase, but a new irrigation system may require new centers to control the canals and so many people to serve them that the polis may change but not grow. The physical formation of the total region related to the polis must be analyzed. The polis depends on the life and evolution of the total system related to it. In most cases private initiative is responsible for the organization within the polis, although sometimes, especially under a socialist system, government initiative is responsible. The forces are so great that, unless we analyze each aspect of the total situation, we are likely to commit grave errors.

40. *The territorial formation and organization of the total region related to the polis must be analyzed and understood.*

The study requires a detailed analysis of every characteristic of all the Shells, whose requirements are much greater than those in villages. A village house without a water supply, for example, is bearable because tradition has taught that it is natural to fetch water from the village fountain, but this would be considered impossible for a polis. The criteria change completely. In a village the houses may have big gardens, but in a polis that badly needs economy in space and energy this is completely unreasonable. With the change of dimensions of human settlements, all solutions, criteria, and standards must change in many ways. Of course, this statement does not include all technological criteria, but only those criteria related to the use of urban space, which is different from village space.

The differences between village Networks and polis Networks is even greater. In a village we can accept roads with many irregular turnings in a form imposed by chance, but we cannot accept them in a polis except in small, old neighborhoods. The larger a human settlement, the more its Networks need careful design. They need to become straight lines and conform to an orthogonal grid, which alone provides maximum economy in structure and function.

41. *The Shells and Networks of the polises must be analyzed and judged according to different criteria than those applied to villages.*

After understanding the physical structure and its efficiency we must study Society to understand its organization in space. The old polises in many cultures and civilizations were well organized into communities, which had many advantages for their inhabitants who could feel "at home," but today human settlements are not socially organized in space in accordance with our present needs. This creates many disadvantages and an increasing inability to solve many social problems. We must try to relate all social aspects to the territory that has been analyzed. Only the interrelationship between social aspects and territorial problems can help us to full understanding.

We can now try to understand the satisfaction each Anthropos derives from the overall situation. This study should proceed by ekistic units, starting with room and house, progressing to housegroup (it may be too noisy), to neighborhood (it may have disappeared), to large neighborhood (it may have a supermarket but no social services such as schools and first aid stations), to the small polis (it may be disappearing), to the large polis which may have all the characteristics of an explosion. In this way we can understand why many people may say they were much happier before the explosion, although they have contributed to it by their insistence on greater economic activity.

42. *A full social and humanistic analysis is necessary to help us understand the relationship of humans to their polis.*

4. Metropolises

Metropolises are human settlements with a minimum of 200,000 and a maximum of 10 million inhabitants. These people work at almost all types of professions. A typical small metropolis has 500,000 and a typical metropolis has 4 million people. There is no international agreement on the size or any other characteristic of the metropolis.

43. *A metropolis is a human settlement with a minimum of 200,000 and a maximum of 10 million inhabitants. There are 560 metropolises on earth, inhabited by a total of 455 million people, 12.6% of the global population.*

15. Metropolis. New York City, U.S.A.

The human settlements we have examined so far have been known for thousands of years and the human experience gained from them is vast even though we do not use it properly. Only the big empires of the past, however, created small metropolises with up to a million inhabitants in their major centers, such as Rome, Teotihuacan, Constantinople, Peking, London, and Tokyo. No other metropolis reached one million inhabitants before 1825. The existence of these few small metropolises over a period of 2,000 years in different parts of our globe and at different periods has not allowed much human experience to be acquired. We could have learned from them. We could have studied the huge problems created by traffic in ancient Rome, but we have not done so. Neither have we studied nor learned from the perfect organization of ancient Peking. It is because we know nothing about metropolises that none of the present ones are successful.

What is the territory of the metropolis? This is a very difficult question to answer and sometimes, because there are many metropolises playing so many roles that their territories overlap with many others, there is no answer to it at all. That all roads lead to Rome was true throughout the Roman Empire, which was clearly the territory of Rome. Now, however, there are metropolises like Detroit, Michigan, which in one way is the capital of the whole globe, if we think only of the automobile industry, but is not even the administrative capital of its own state. The capital of Michigan is Lansing, about 80 miles from Detroit. A metropolis like Lusaka in a relatively isolated country like Zambia has the whole country as its own clear territory. The situation was comparable before World War II for many European metropolises, especially on the borders of France and Germany; this is so no longer. The European Common Market is gradually drawing together many metropolises into overlapping systems. We can no longer be sure in many cases of the broader metropolitan territory. We can, however, understand the metropolis as a Daily Urban System. By using data from the United States, where a systematic study has been carried out, we can see how big the Daily Urban Systems of eleven cities were in 1960 (Fig. 16) and how big was their average area (Fig. 17).

44. *Metropolises must be understood as centers of changing Daily Urban Systems and as poles of many other areas differing greatly in type and territory.*

Metropolises attract visitors from the whole globe, but we cannot study the globe as their territory. We must understand their broader roles, but the territory we should study is that directly belonging to them. If we are interested only in the present, the Daily Urban System is enough, but since we study the present in order to assist the future, the study territory should be larger. In defining it we need to understand how far the influence of a given metropolis extends in relation to the metropolises closest to it. Where do people of the region go for shopping, entertainment, and other services? The answers indicate

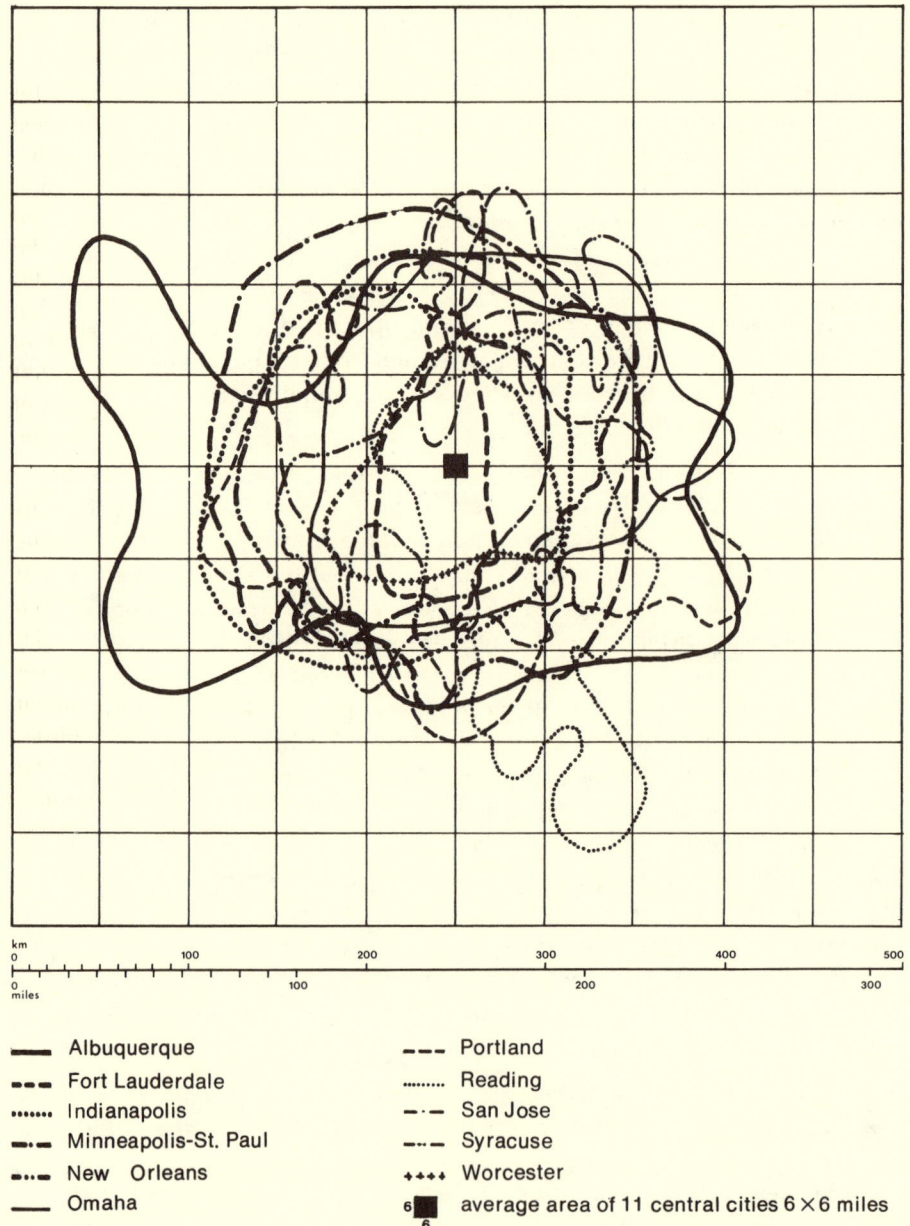

— Albuquerque			- - - Portland		
- - - Fort Lauderdale			.... Reading		
.... Indianapolis			— · — San Jose		
—·— Minneapolis-St. Paul			— ·· — Syracuse		
—··— New Orleans			+ + + + Worcester		
— Omaha			6 ■ average area of 11 central cities 6 × 6 miles		

16. Daily urban systems of eleven United States cities in 1960

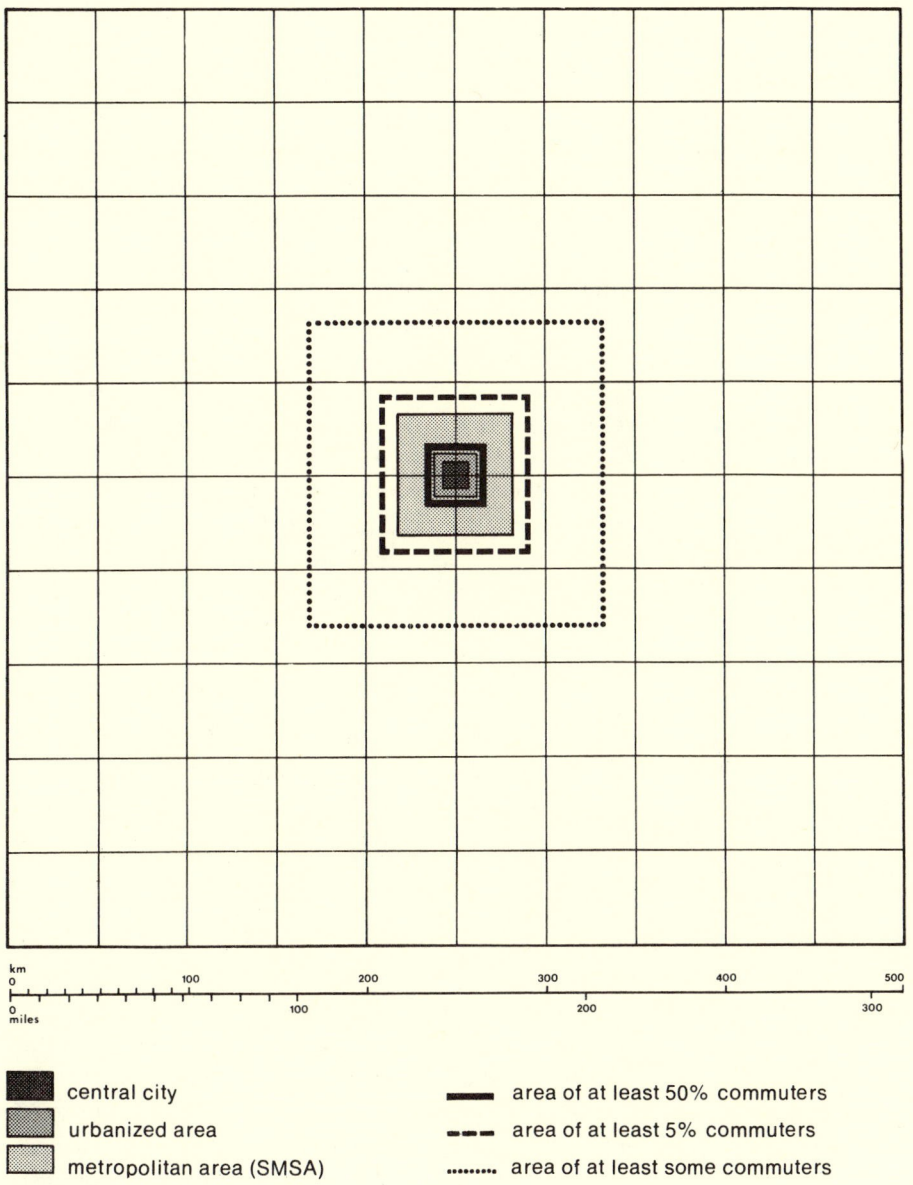

central city
urbanized area
metropolitan area (SMSA)

area of at least 50% commuters
area of at least 5% commuters
area of at least some commuters

17. The average area of the daily urban systems of twelve United States cities in 1960

how far the influence of the metropolis extends and how far some day the Daily Urban System will extend. An example is Cleveland, Ohio, which made a study showing how far its Northern Ohio Urban System (NOUS) reaches (Fig. 18). We need a full and detailed analysis of Nature within this territory. After this analysis of Nature we must study the evolution of human inspired activities, because such activities include human aggression against Nature. It is here that in most cases we witness the change, usually without any guidance, from a static metropolis to a dynametropolis. In this process Nature is really attacked and there is no hope of controlling the situation if we do not understand the system as a whole and its dynamic changes. The metropolis does not simply grow from its center outwards. If the center is overloaded and if there are some other attractive centers, for example, of transportation or economics and administration, we may witness an explosion somewhere else which will influence the whole metropolitan system. We must understand the whole Daily Urban System and its future in order to understand the actual metropolis and its future.

45. *The territorial formation and organization of the urban region of the metropolis must be analyzed and understood in detail. Its existing and possible future relationships need only be understood in broad outline.*

When we move to the element of Shells in a metropolis we can no longer go into detail, as it is impossible on this scale of ekistic units 9 and 10 to give details concerning ekistic unit 3. Many metropolitan studies fail because of the attempt to cover too many details. What they should do is recognize the conditions of housing and other buildings down to the definition of general neighborhoods in which, for instance, there are low densities that make the area uneconomic or in which there are high densities that make it a problem area even though incomes may be high. The overall view of the metropolis must give us the general image of the situation created by Shells, but no details concerning them.

What increase enormously in importance at the metropolitan scale are the Networks. Many of the developments at this scale are, almost exclusively, the results of Networks. The opening of a new major highway to the south of a metropolis may create completely new conditions and attract many developments where nothing had been built before. Similar or even major changes may occur if a new airport or port is created in an area where no activity existed earlier. In such a case there is an even greater need than in a polis for a rational approach to the whole system of Networks. The larger the scale, the greater is the importance of Networks. On the small scale of the neighborhood the Network must respect the individual and his safety, especially the safety of the child. On the big scales the standards guarantee this automatically; what really matters is the overall concept of the system of transportation and related Networks.

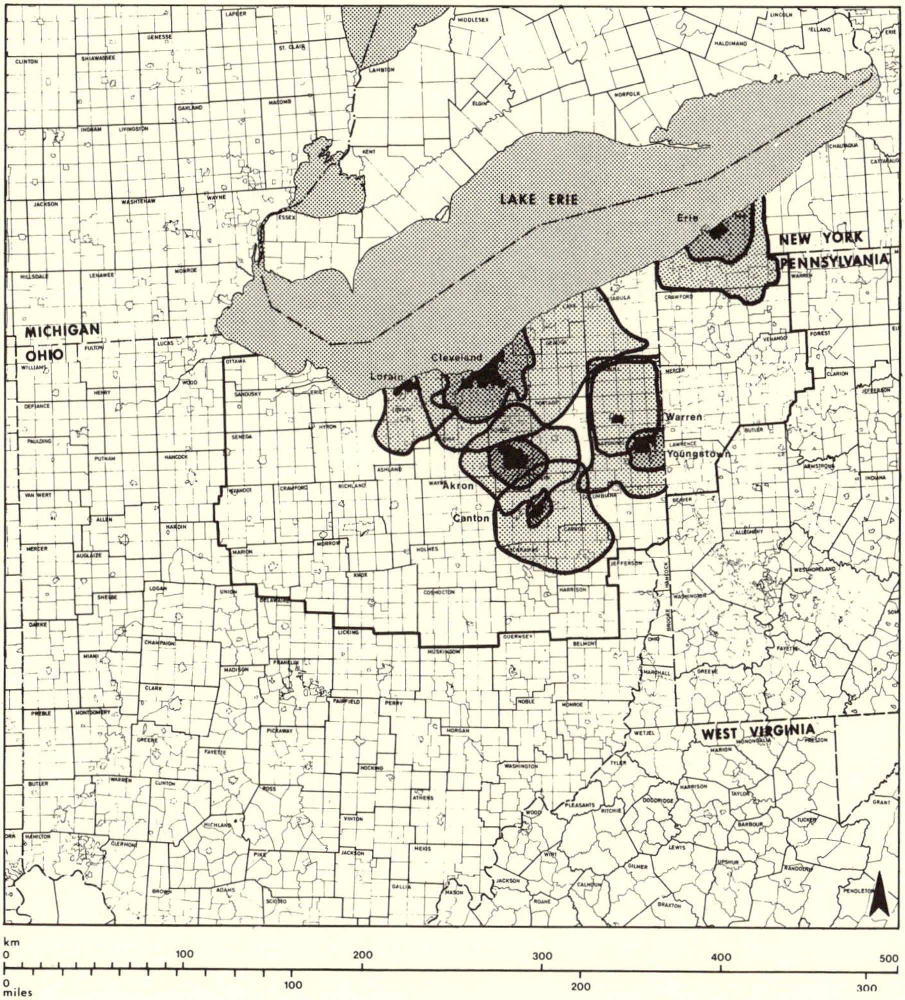

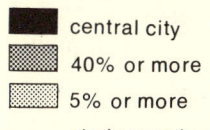

Percentage of residents commuting to central city:

- ⬛ central city
- ▨ 40% or more
- ▦ 5% or more
- — study area boundary

18. Northern Ohio Urban System (NOUS)

46. *The general conditions created by Shells must be well understood. Networks must be judged with increasing attention because of the major role they play in metropolises.*

What is lacking more in a metropolis than in a polis is social organization. The reasons are simple. As we have seen when speaking about polises, the explosion of cities did not give us the opportunity to organize the new metropolises socially. The administrative organization inside the metropolis corresponds more to the past than to the present and future since the administrative boundaries usually do not change, although the human settlements change from outlying villages and polises into organic urban parts of the metropolis. This makes many problems of great social importance, such as crimes in the city, very difficult to understand and to solve. There is a great difference between recognizing the existence of social problems and of finding solutions, especially in the larger human settlements as we do not relate Society to the total environment. Only recently, for example, has it been understood that violent crimes occur more frequently among the lower income groups regardless of race or any other factor.

An individual's reaction to life in a metropolis cannot be understood unless we consider it by ekistic units analyzed in the ways already explained. A poor urban dweller may prefer to live without his family, which he left in the village, or with his whole family in one room in a slum area instead of in the beautiful house in the country in order to have the job with sufficient income, which is not available in the countryside. In this case quality of life is not as important a consideration as the income and the services to be gained.

47. *To understand the relationship of humans to the metropolis, we must analyze all aspects of social importance and their relationships to the other elements of human settlements like Nature, Shells, and Networks.*

5. Megalopolises

Megalopolises are human settlements with a minimum of 10 million and a maximum of 500 million inhabitants. A typical small megalopolis has 25 million and a typical megalopolis has 150 million people. There is no international agreement on the characteristics and size of the megalopolis.

48. *A megalopolis is a human settlement with a minimum of 10 million and a maximum of 500 million inhabitants. There are 19 megalopolises on earth, inhabited by a total of 490 million people, 13.6% of the global population.*

The formation of the megalopolises became apparent after World War II, so 1945 may be taken as the year the process began. No megalopolis was ever created in the past so we have no idea of what they are and where they are going. We simply are seeing the beginning of the process. Our eyes are opened by such studies as J. Gottmann's *Megalopolis: the Urbanized Northeastern Seaboard of the United States*[15] and several others, and we end up with predictions about their future.[16] We can learn about all the types of human settlements we have discussed so far by studying the past and the present, but we do not have enough data on the megalopolises because no completely formed megalopolis, even one formed in the wrong way, yet exists. They are all still being formed, and this is why they have not really been recognized. Only the study in depth of all human settlements will make us aware of the principles

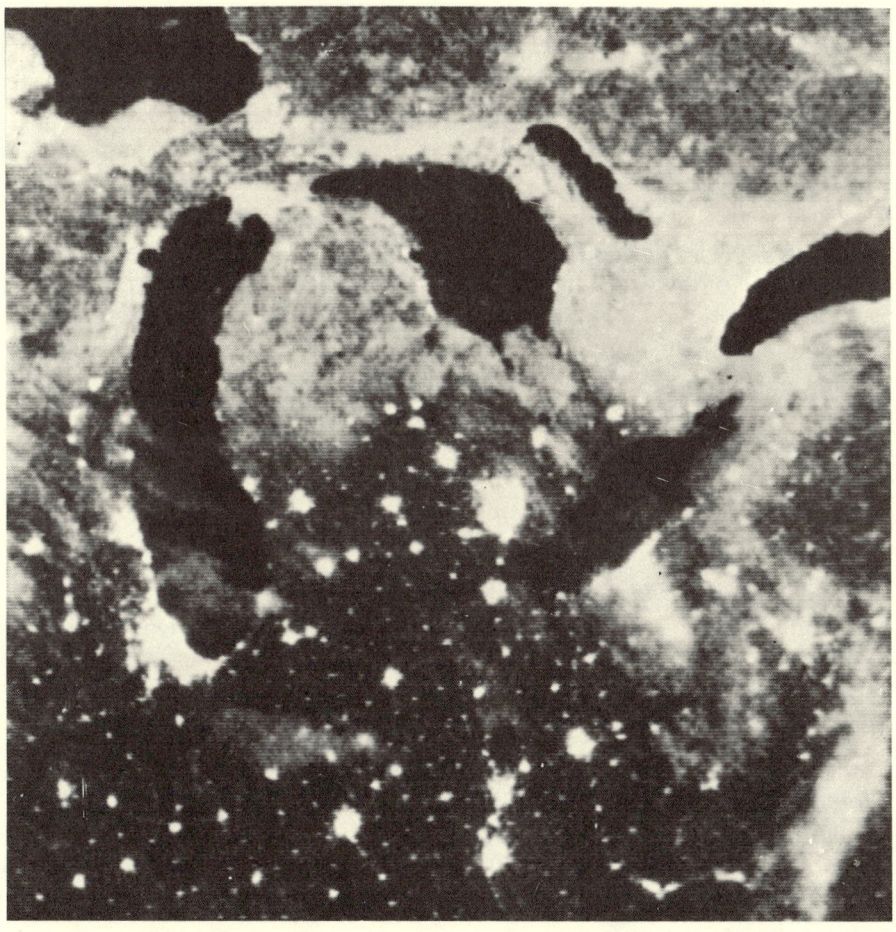

19.   Megalopolis. The Great Lakes Megalopolis photographed from a satellite

governing human action in forming human settlements and only with this awareness can we understand how natural is the formation of megalopolitan human settlements. This is one more reason why we need ekistics, the science of human settlements. We cannot hope to understand settlements now being formed for the first time and we cannot act on their behalf unless we learn through ekistics the principles that guide them.

One basic question concerns the territory belonging to the megalopolis. As we have seen, the territory of metropolises can be considered to include the entire globe. This, of course, also is true for megalopolises. They cannot really exist unless they play many roles, including a global one.

When we use the term megalopolis we are not referring only to the better known megalopolises such as the Northeastern Megalopolis in the United States, the Great Lakes Megalopolis, the Northwest European Megalopolis, the Eastern Chinese Megalopolis, or the Japanese megalopolis, Tokaido. There are megalopolises which are just forming, hardly suspected, as in the Nile and Suez area and in southern Nigeria. Their importance is increasing as transportation centers, in terms of resources, natural or industrial, in terms of population, etc. We can discern the megalopolises which already exist and those which will be born in the near or distant future. They all start with a global territorial importance because of their role and end up with the relatively minor territory which they physically occupy. We can define megalopolitan territory in the same way we define metropolitan territory. What is important is the kind of Daily Urban System under formation, how far it goes today and what possible boundaries exist for the future, which we can determine by examining the neighboring megalopolises and defining the probable dividing lines between them. In this way we can see the outer boundaries of the megalopolis of the future.

49. *Megalopolises must be understood as major urban systems connecting several metropolises into a much larger urban system with greater complexities and greater potential.*

To understand the growing megalopolis we must be sure we understand its relations with Nature. For example, if we do not recognize that the potential future of the Northeastern Megalopolis of the United States is defined by the Atlantic on the east and by the Appalachian Mountains on the west, we cannot understand first, why it connects the entire coastal area including Boston, New York, Philadelphia, and Washington, and may in the future extend further south and perhaps north and, second, that its western boundary line divides it from the Great Lakes Megalopolis. By following the same process in greater detail we can study where its future ports will lie when the present ones will be overloaded, and so on.

The study of Nature also will show how the major metropolises of the megalopolis tend to be united into a system, where this system can be expected to grow, and where the new nodal points will be. The greater the ekistic unit with which we are dealing, the greater is the influence of natural formations. If, for example, we were to open a tunnel through the Appalachian Mountains and vastly improve connections between both sides of the mountains, this would change the fate of the polises on both sides of the mountains. It would not, however, change the fate of the megalopolis as a whole; it would simply facilitate its development.

50. *The natural territory of the megalopolis must be understood. It must be studied in terms both of its international role and its internal delineation.*

We must study the question of Shells in the megalopolis in the same spirit in which we studied Shells in the metropolis, and this means that we cannot enter into details. The scale of the megalopolis is such that we cannot study even the unit of neighborhoods. In terms of Shells what we can study is the general situation down to the unit of the small polis. We must find the general characteristics of polises in terms of Shells and the conditions created by them for the whole unit. A polis with good housing but without the proper connections between Shells or without service buildings must be understood as a polis with hope for good living conditions in Shells but in need of action. This is the spirit in which we have to look at Shells in a megalopolis.

The element of Networks has to be seen in two ways. First as global connections in terms of land, water, and air and second as an internal system of the megalopolis. The first view can change the future of the international role played by the megalopolis because there is as yet no global concept of the international transportation system. Many areas with potential natural megalopolises have not yet realized this, which retards their development. The lack of badly needed transafrican highways impedes the formation of the African megalopolises. They are lacking because Africa was colonial territory when the era of major change began in 1825, and the colonizing forces were interested in developing nodal points only on the coasts, that is, on the way out of Africa. Only if we begin our study of Networks in this way can we proceed to the internal system of the megalopolis. Then we can be sure that we have not conceived the megalopolis only in terms of its past but also in terms of its future.

51. *The Shells of the megalopolis have to be seen as systems polis by polis, but the Networks have to be seen as forces connecting the global role of the megalopolis with its internal structure.*

No megalopolis on our globe has yet been recognized as an administrative unit. This is a simple demonstration of the fact that there is no social, administrative, or political recognition of the megalopolis. Political recognition is the most difficult, because parts of several megalopolises belong to different nations. Although the Eastern Chinese and the Japanese megalopolises have no direct problems of national connections, because they are and will remain inside only one country, such megalopolises as the Northwest European and the Great Lakes

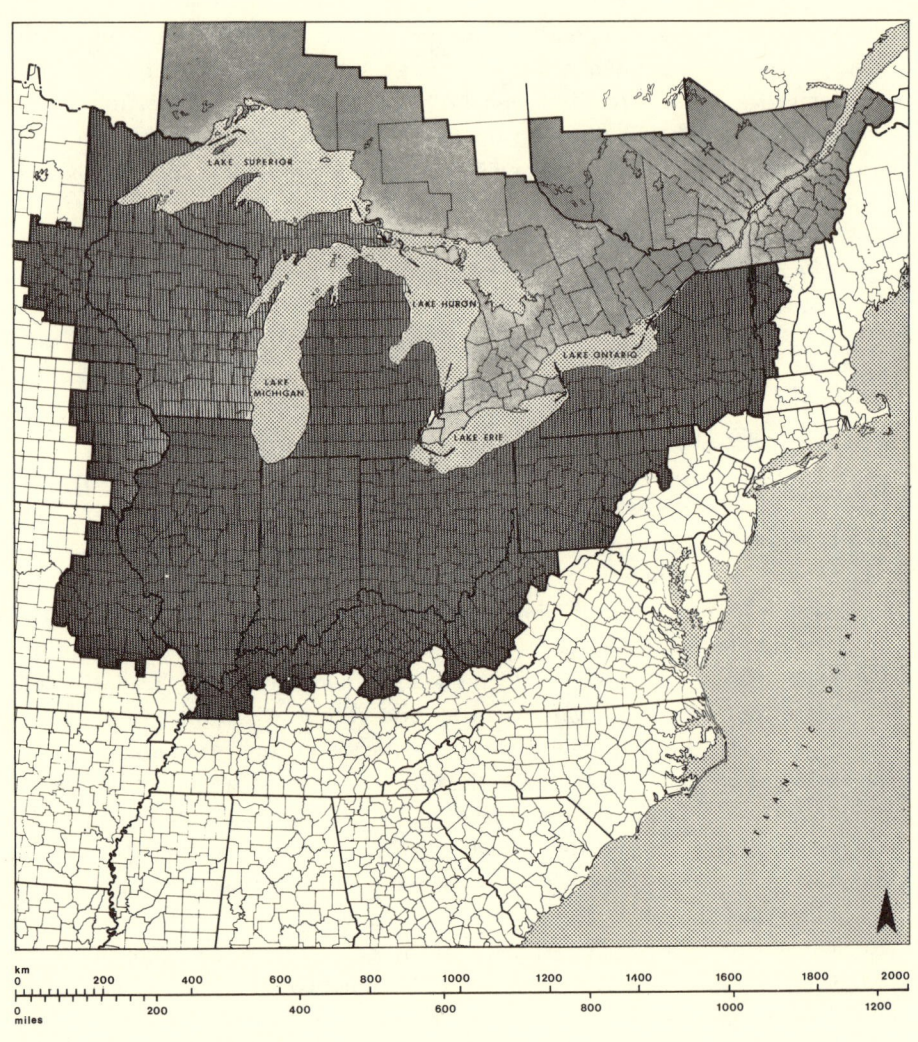

■ Great Lakes Megalopolis Region — Canada
■ Great Lakes Megalopolis Region — U.S.A.

20.   The Great Lakes Megalopolis

46

megalopolises cover territories belonging to several countries. The Great Lakes Megalopolis covers 754 American and 112 Canadian counties (Fig. 20). The studies about it were carried out only by private initiative. We badly need governmental action to recognize the changing and developing new systems of human settlements. Individuals have not yet understood that the megalopolis exists, but they well know the major advantages a megalopolitan area offers them. Otherwise why do they increasingly tend to live inside it? Megalopolises are growing in population more than other areas, and this is because the megalopolis offers many more choices for employment and services. Would an individual interested in his own progress, health, and welfare not prefer some corner of the megalopolis over an outlying human settlement? Isn't such a choice more reasonable for a family whose members have so many varied needs?

52. *We badly need to recognize the existence of the megalopolis and what it means both for the individual and for Society.*

6. National systems

The contemporary administrative systems of our globe locate almost all major authorities for action in human settlements at the national government level, and our major concern for action should lie at this level. Our first obligation is to understand the national systems of human settlements. The concept of the nation state is not a new one; but in the past, although the government occupied the capital city, the power for action for human settlements really lay in the hands of various local authorities, especially in times of war. Only in our era, through modern systems of transportation and communications, have the central authorities acquired real power. Even those national governments which administer many states with quite independent local authorities retain control of legislation and major budgets.

Our real task, therefore, is to study the national systems of human settlements and try to work through them for action on all possible levels. Action should be undertaken at all levels, starting from the smallest and private level of the individual's room, and progressing through larger units until we reach the national level.

When dealing with a national system the difficult questions concerning the limits of human settlements do not arise, because national boundaries are clearly set and much stronger than local boundaries. After studying everything inside the national boundaries, however, we should see how the national human settlement system is influenced by forces beyond the national boundaries. This is not easy. To do so we must study all types of human settlements and their possible connections beyond the national boundaries. There are nomads who move annually through more than one national territory. There are farmers who own land on both sides of a border and cultivate it every day. There are

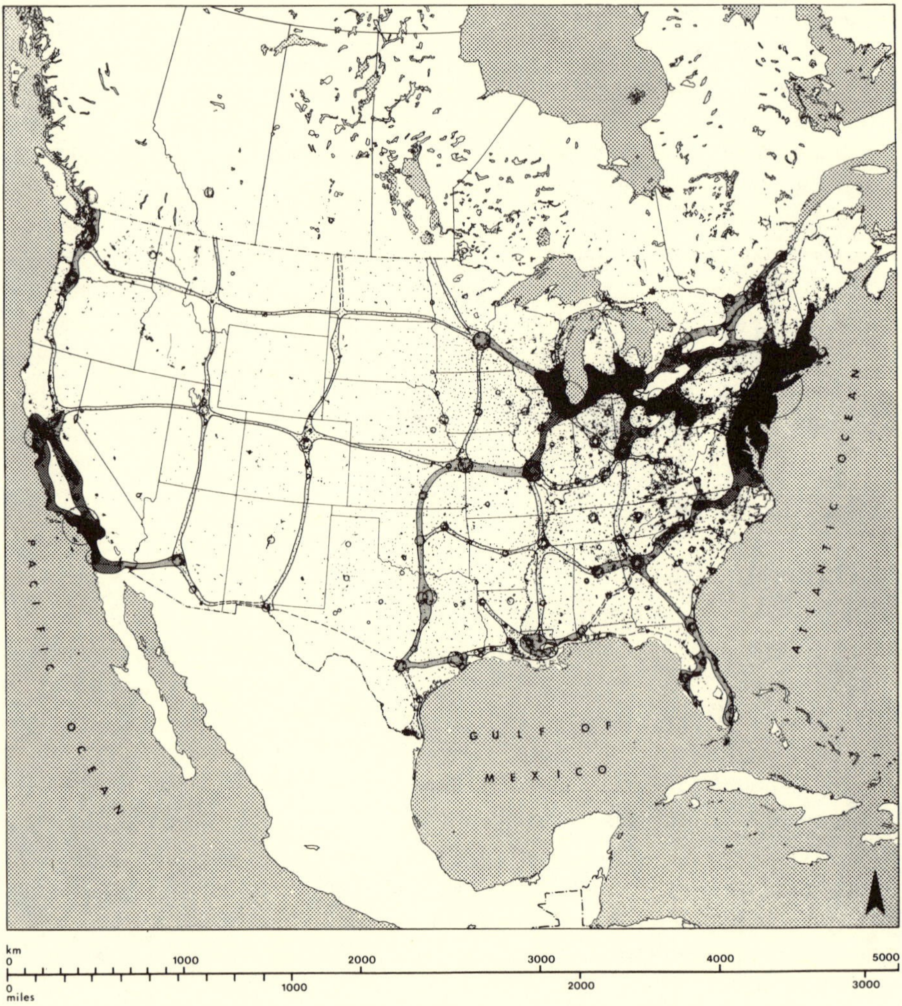

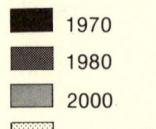

Date of formation:

- ⬛ 1970
- ⬛ 1980
- ◼ 2000
- ▨ connective branches

21. National megalopolitan system, U.S.A., 2000 A.D.

towns, metropolises, and megalopolises which exist on both sides of national boundaries. Such cases cannot be overlooked. Moreover, some national centers depend on their connections with the human settlements of other national states because of the existing international Networks and their nodal points.

53. *National systems of human settlements must be studied in great detail and understood in terms of their connections with broader systems of human settlements beyond national boundaries.*

There is no hope of carrying out the previous task unless we analyze the total natural environment in the best possible way. The fate of all settlements depends first on geography and topography. There will be no village if the land cannot be cultivated or animals cannot be fed and there will be no urban and particularly no industrial development without a plain. As we have already said, we need a detailed study of the topography and all characteristics from soil to climate.

Then we must look at all human settlements and how they are connected with the total natural environment. These relationships will not surprise any real experts, because the relationships are rational and can be well understood. But all people concerned with this subject will be greatly helped if they understand the system that has developed, almost by itself, in some instances over thousands of years.

54. *Basic for an understanding of national systems of human settlements is a detailed analysis of the element of Nature and the interrelationships between it and all human settlements.*

Shells can be investigated and understood only within the frame of the previous task. At the national level the study of Shells cannot go into detail but it can discover general characteristics indicating where the problem areas are. The scale of the study depends upon the dimensions of the national state. Some nations, like the USSR, are so large that they contain many megalopolises, while others, like Cyprus (500,000 people), are as small as a small metropolis. Andorra, with approximately 20,000 people, is an even smaller nation. The "national scale" means many very different scales. In the large nation states we should start our analysis by region and megalopolitan formation, while in the small ones we can start by learning immediately about the units of neighborhood.

Networks must be approached in the same spirit. Only the large Networks can be investigated at the national level. What is a small and what is a large national Network depends on the territorial extent of the nation. Nevertheless, when dealing with Networks we must understand how they develop beyond the nation's borders. Many Networks reaching the borders can be of major importance for the nation. If, for example, electricity or other power lines reach the borders, they may connect with the adjacent country's power lines to supply the energy the nation may lack.

55. *The system of Networks must be understood in the broadest possible frame, beyond national boundaries, in order to reveal the real prospects for the future.*

Within the framework established by the above territorial analyses, we can proceed to the social and individual concerns of Anthropos. An example is the relationship between a particular aspect of Shells or Networks, let us say a water supply system, to a decreasing population. If all physical aspects are satisfactory, we can assume that the population decline is caused by social reasons. If a lack of water frequently coincides with the population decline, then we can assume that the causes of such a major social phenomenon as population decline are not entirely social. If the decline in population is the same for all age groups, it may be caused by the increasing productivity of farmers using new technology, thus causing fewer familes to be needed in the same rural area. If the decline only affects the younger adults, it is probably because the attraction of the metropolis has induced them, individual by individual, to leave. Different phenomena cannot be understood and classified if we do not manage to connect each of them with both physical and social concerns.

56. *Analysis of national systems of human settlements can be successful only when we relate the physical with the social phenomena.*

7. International systems

There is no international system of human settlements. We must learn why there is none, whether or not there will be one in the future, and how we can approach our human settlements internationally. The first human settlements were temporary, independent settlements. But the day came when they began to cooperate, at least during certain seasons, for economic, social, or cultural reasons through the creating of centers of common interest, such as some of the caves of Paleolithic France which served a whole group of bands living in temporary human settlements.

Later there were villages, which probably were independent of each other until their inhabitants learned the advantages of cooperation and the first town was born. Gradually this approach was imitated by many neighbors, and areas like the Middle East or Greece, covered by hundreds of city-states, developed. The next step was the unification of city-states within an empire. Empires, at first very small, gradually grew into huge systems. The last empire was the British one which was representative of the principle of "all roads lead to Rome" — all sea routes led to London.

During the thousands of years of city-states and empires the organizational principle was one central city as a basic pole radiating its influence over the whole territory. This was both a strength of civilizations created by city-states

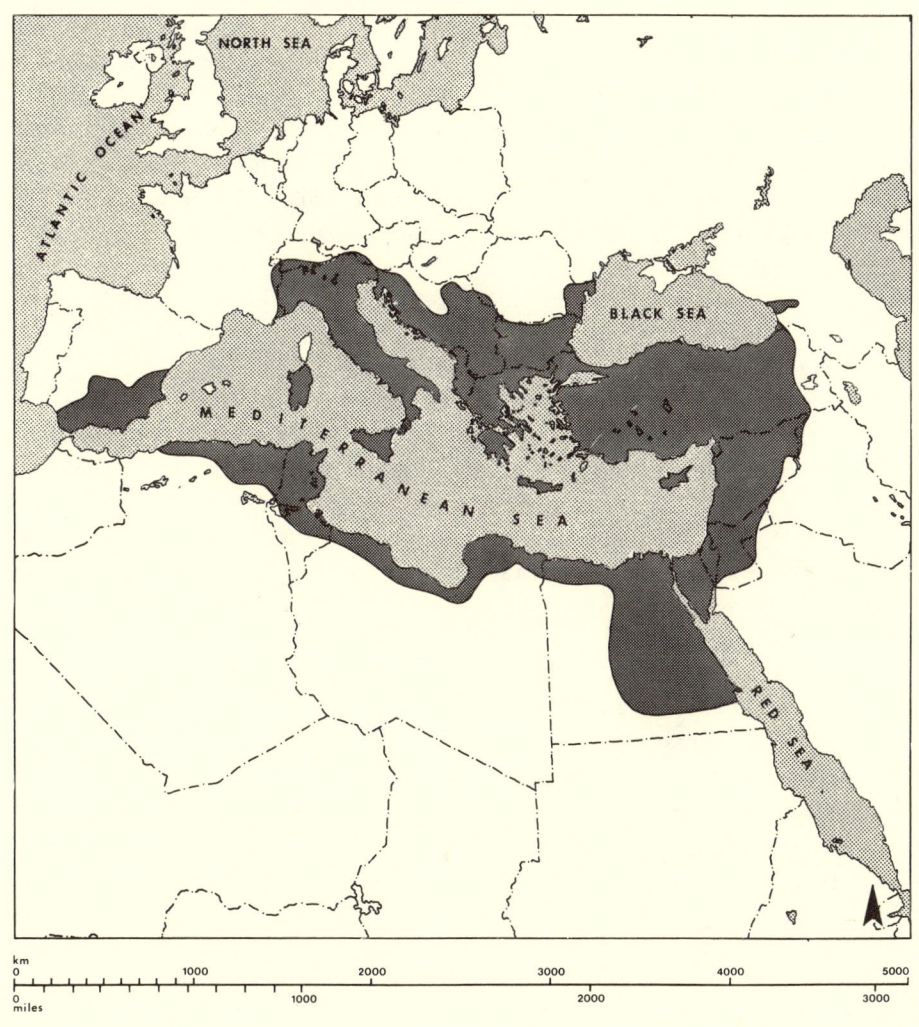

22. The Byzantine Empire at its maximum extent,
6th century A.D.

and empires and a weakness, for every other human settlement was dependent on the capital city. Civilization was connected with the notion of the unique advantages of a central city and the subordination of everything else.

Now we have entered a new era. Although there still are a few colonies, which are in their last phase, there is no state so powerful that it can impose its views in general or system of human settlements in particular throughout the globe. This is why we cannot speak of an international system of human settlements. It does not exist.

Some countries try, and correctly so, to preserve their own cultures, but they can do so only to a certain degree. Isolated civilization do not exist in our era, for wherever a science or technology first develops, it gradually spreads everywhere. Neither, on the other hand, is there a global civilization. We live in a transitional period moving from separate civilizations to a unified ecumenization. This ecumenization will not depend upon one center but will depend instead upon a system of centers around the globe. This is also why we are so confused. For the first time, after thousands of years, we have lost the approach of the ancient isolated civilizations, which were based on one center. We are progressing towards a globe of equal people who will not be controlled by any single center but who will live in many centers in a unified system.

This transitional phase of civilizations intensively affects human settlements on the international scale for several reasons:

1. As there are great differences in the levels of human settlements among all nations, the changes cover a greater spectrum.
2. As some countries are being invaded by the forces of new technology at much higher speeds than those countries in which modern technology is developed, the changes are more radical.
3. As there are new international air connections, some human settlements are developing as poles of international Networks at unprecedented speeds.
4. As the new defense, or war, systems require new types of international Networks, new developments appear in areas which previously did not have any such installations.

The conclusion is clear: At the international scale we have radical changes taking place at high speeds. In a few generations we will not simply have the many megalopolises, but also a global system of human settlements which we call Ecumenopolis. It will cover a very small percentage of the earth's surface, no more than 2.5%, but it will be an international system connecting the many national systems into one. We can understand how this will come about if we remember the historical process: temporary human settlement, village, polis, metropolis, megalopolis, continental systems of human settlements or eperopolis (continental city), and, finally, Ecumenopolis (global city). As a megalopolis is formed not by eliminating the metropolises but by absorbing them into a broader system, so the Ecumenopolis will be formed by absorbing several eperopolises into a global system.

The structure of Ecumenopolis can be understood if we follow the plans giving tentative ideas of Greece's future small megalopolis (Fig. 23); Europe's eperopolis, which can be called Europolis (Fig. 24); and the Ecumenopolis (Fig. 25). We can now see why, in addition to the national systems of human settlements which may be called Brazilopolis, Indiapolis, or Zambiapolis, we should keep in mind the need to develop broader systems around important nodal points on our globe, to develop multi-national systems of human settlements like Panamapolis or Arabopolis around the Panama or Suez canals connecting many nation states for both national and international benefit.

We must now turn to the urgent question of how we can approach the immediate problems of human settlements in an international way. The task is very complex and difficult for several reasons, such as:

1. Whereas with food we can calculate the total needs in calories, etc. for every nation, this is not at all easy for human settlements.
2. Whereas we can clearly define the ultimate goal of health, it is not easy to define for human settlements.

In dealing with human settlements we cannot send houses for millions of people, nor even just roofs. Human settlement problems must be solved locally. The major difficulty is solving in an international way local problems of a very special character which really require local solutions. To overcome it we must carry out the following tasks:

57. *We need to understand the subject in a systematic way. This requires international acceptance of a system including many facets, ranging from the proper terminology to the taxonomy of human settlements as an international evolutionary phenomenon (like flora and fauna for which there is a useful precedent).*
58. *We need to develop a science of human settlements in order to agree on problems, goals, policies, and programs. Without such a science we will continue to lose our time in long and meaningless discussions without hope for an international agreement.*
59. *In this spirit we must become aware of the definition of problems of human settlements.*
60. *Similarly, we must be able to define the goals in dealing with human settlements.*
61. *This effort must conclude with concrete policies and programs.*

The first two of these five statements are covered by Part One of the present book in a way which can be understood by any type of reader, and are dealt with in more detail in the appendices and other publications.[17] The other three statements on problems, goals, and policies and programs are dealt with in parts two, three and four.

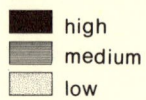

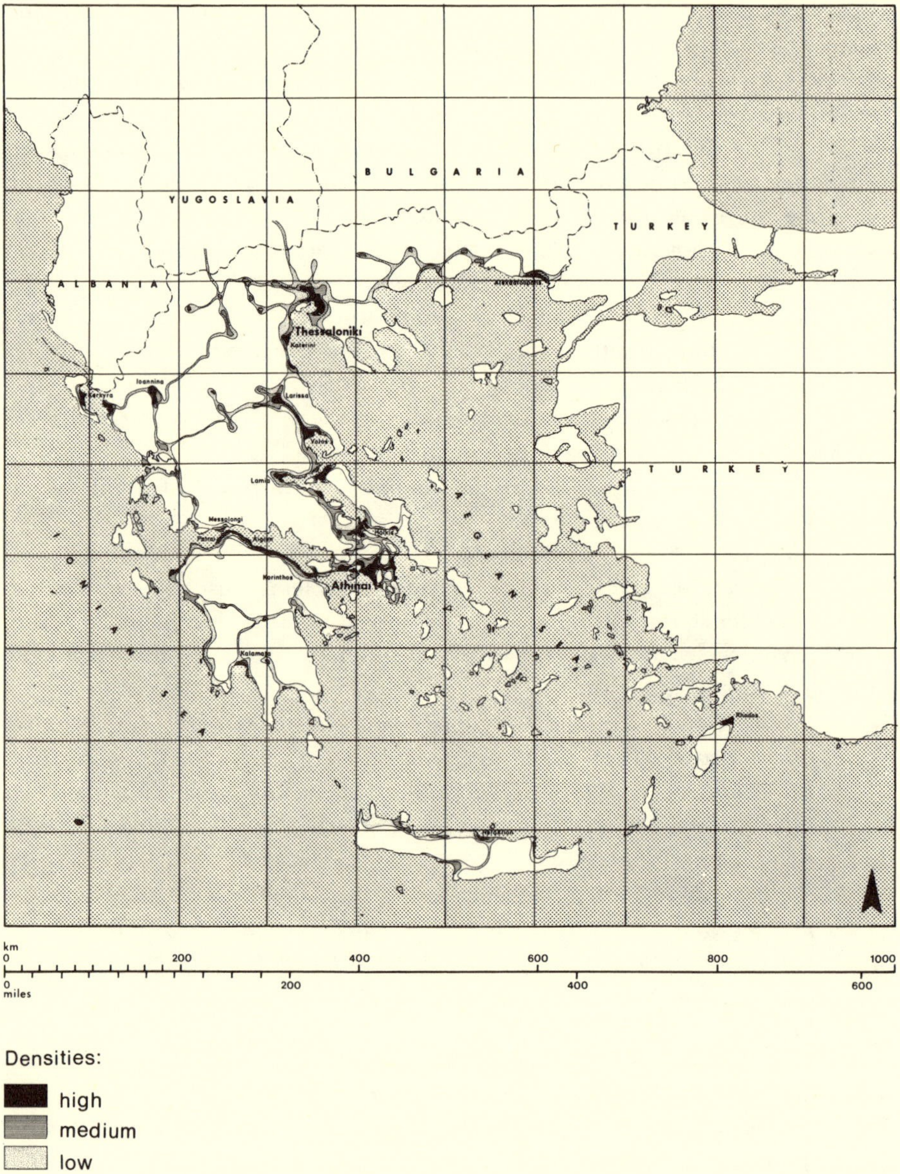

Densities:

- high
- medium
- low

23. Megalopolis in Greece

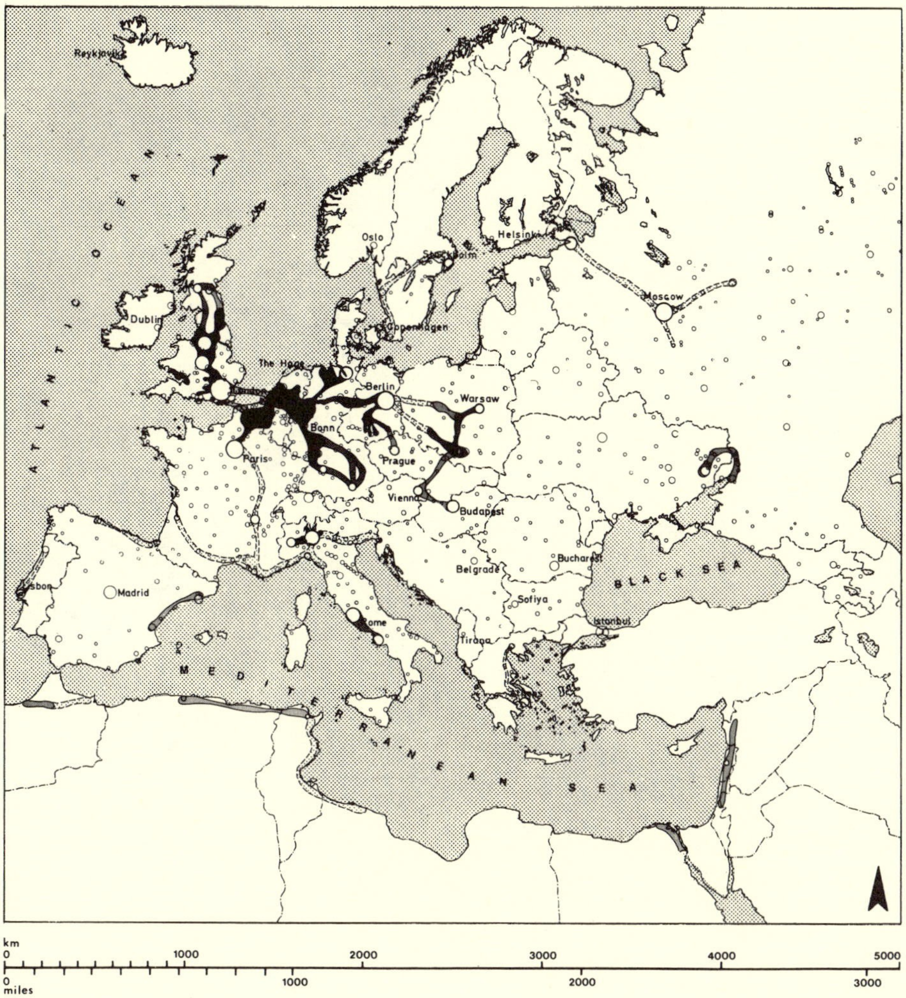

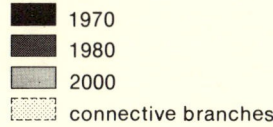

Date of formation:

- ■ 1970
- ▨ 1980
- ▦ 2000
- ⬚ connective branches

24. Europolis, 2000 A.D.

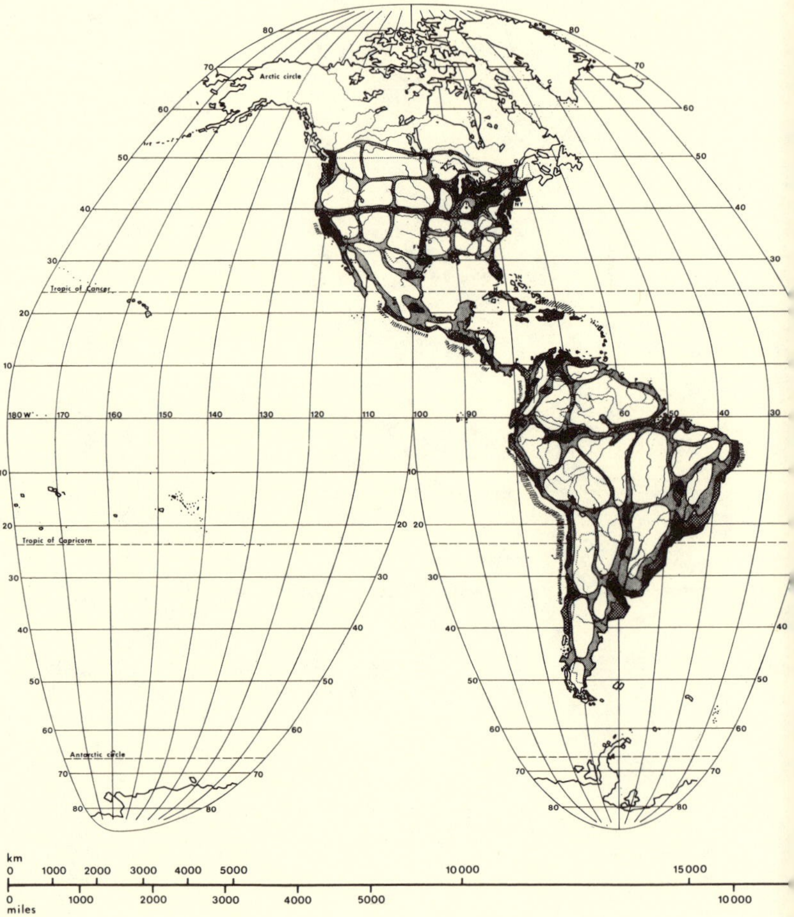

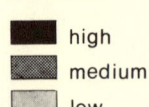

km
0   1000 2000 3000 4000 5000   10 000   15 000
0   1000 2000 3000 4000 5000   10 000
miles

Densities:

■ high
▨ medium
▢ low

25. Ecumenopolis, 2100 A.D.

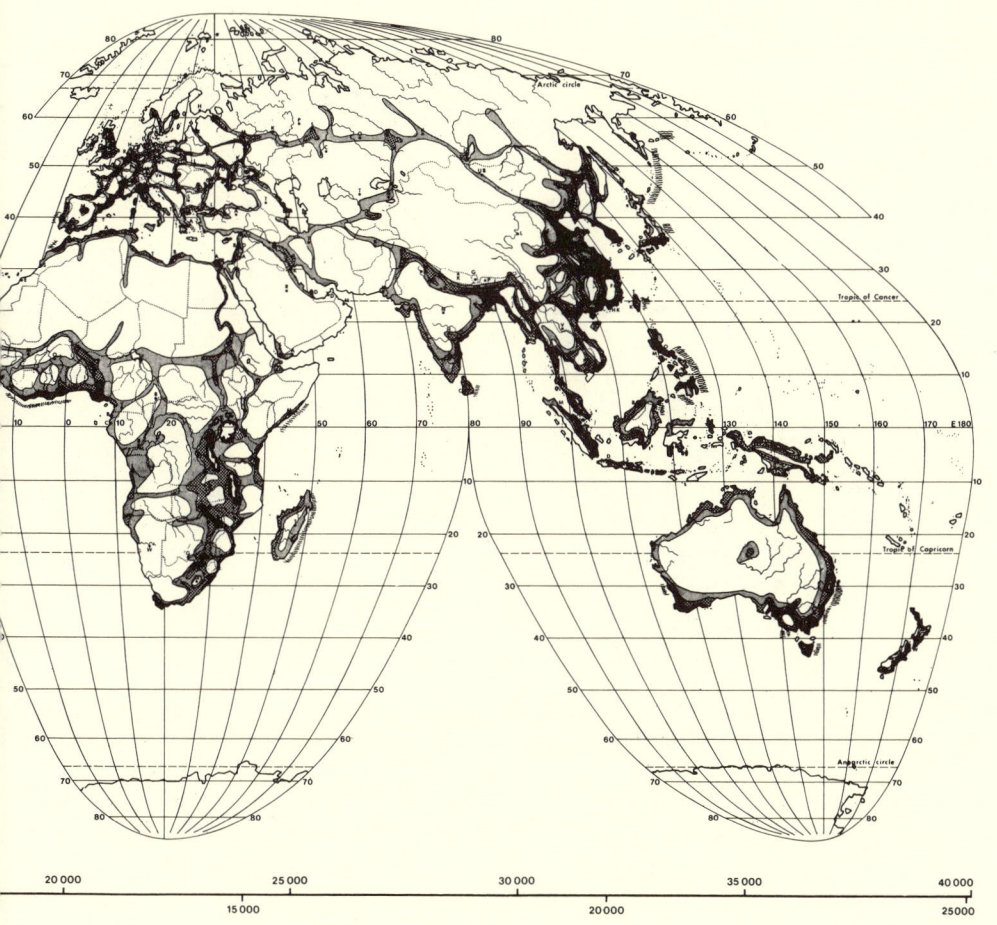

20 000   25 000   30 000   35 000   40 000

15 000   20 000   25 000

ie total image

After examining the different types, elements, and aspects of human settlements it becomes clear that we need a way to classify each aspect and present an overall image of every aspect of human settlements. For this we must use the Anthropocosmos model, the only model capable of giving us the total image of human settlements.

62. *We need to proceed with a model, which we call the Anthropocosmos model, of the complex system of human settlements.*[18]

The purpose of this chapter is to help us clarify the term Anthropocosmos and to understand how we can be more successful in dealing with human settlements. Anthropocosmos is our system of life and the human settlement is our goal. The purpose of the Anthropocosmos model must always be to serve Anthropos and not any special interest working against the broader human goal.

Its basic tasks are:

1. the overall concept of *Anthropocosmos,*
2. the notion of *human settlements,*
3. the *language* we should use,
4. the *taxonomic frame,*
5-8. *basic classifications,*
9. a working *model of Anthropocosmos,*
10. the *selection and evaluation of data.*

We need to create a model which can help us understand how to conceive and build the whole Anthropocosmos properly. To do this, we must:

1. Define our total system of life — Anthropocosmos — and create a systematic framework so that any part of it can be clearly located within it.
2. Define all relationships (causal and non-causal) that may exist between any parts of the system so that we can understand their functions and changes.
3. Define a method to evaluate all parts of the system and their interrelationships (including those that cannot now be scientifically measured), so we can recognize the relative importance of each situation and each problem.

Each human settlement contains so many individuals, organs, cells, and elements that there is no hope of progress unless we develop a comprehensive model, the Anthropocosmos model (see Fig. 33), to include each element, aspect, and relationship within each settlement. Into this comprehensive model we can insert data from all the disciplines concerned. The model can also help develop a strategy for breaking down mental barriers and connecting disciplines. Thus we may avoid inter-disciplinary anarchy and build up the concept that settlements are a total system.

The only way to mobilize the many disciplines for the benefit of human settlements is to guide them towards making the needed interconnections, and to create a framework which can contain all the contributions they want to and can make.

One of the negative comments made about the possibility of a scientific approach to human settlements is that they are so different from each other that a systematic study of them is impossible. It is fortunate that Carolus Linnaeus was not impressed by such comments because there are much greater differences among the different kinds of plants and animals; yet in spite of this we have both botany and zoology. There is no question that we need to find a systematic and scientific approach to human settlements.

One of the difficulties of developing a classification system for human settlements is that we have to deal with much smaller total numbers than when dealing with animals or plants. Altogether there are no more than a few tens of millions of settlements (if we do not consider house units but only entire settlements), whereas there are more than 300,000 species of plants and more than one million species of animals; and new discoveries increase these numbers by 10,000 to 20,000 a year.

A basic need is to develop an accepted vocabulary, so that all people dealing with human settlements can understand one another. One of the main reasons we are so confused today is that we have no accepted vocabulary. A shared vocabulary, furthermore, is needed to make possible the necessary comparative studies which can lead to a systematic taxonomy. For example, we can regard the total human settlement as consisting of four types of areas: the Natureareas (where Anthropos is only a visitor and hunter), Cultivareas (where Anthropos cultivates Nature), Anthropareas (where Anthropos lives, using Nature's territory for his houses, work places, entertainment, sports, etc.), and Industrareas (where Anthropos transforms natural resources, as in mining and industry).

The next task is the creation of a taxonomic frame for a systematic understanding and classification of Anthropocosmos and human settlements. Taxonomy is the basis of "the theoretical study of classification, including its bases, principles, procedures and rules,"[19] and numerical taxonomy uses taxonomy as the proper term.[20] The following classification system uses both Aristotelian logic, as Linnaeus did, and taxonomy which provides a means "to arrive at judgements of affinity based on multiple and unweighted characters without the time and controversy which seem necessary at present for the maturation of taxonomy judgements."[21]

The first problem is how to proceed to classify human settlements. At present we have only very general categories, such as villages, polises, and metropolises. Among several efforts at more specific classification there is a tendency (especially since photography is the main method of visual presentation of human settlements) to attempt a classification on the basis of their appearance and to speak of a morphogenesis. But a "purely morphological definition must be subordinated to the concept that the species is composed of populations in which variability is inherent."[22] We have to find a way to measure all possible characters.

I propose a taxonomy of human settlements similar in structure and terminology to that of animals and plants (Fig. 26). A proper classification requires the consideration of a very great number of characteristics, but I am only using a few here to demonstrate the process that we need to achieve this goal.

There are some basic differences between the taxonomy of plants and animals and the taxonomy of human settlements. While it is clear that the taxa of plants and animals are mainly based on their genetic inheritance, this can be disputed for human settlements. Another difference is that most human settlements are still alive, although they may have undergone positive and negative changes. This means that two small towns very similar in structure and form, may not be able to be classified in the same taxon if one is losing people and the other is not. In other words, our classification cannot be limited to identifying species but must also include the phases and conditions of life inside human settlements. It is necessary to bring in the notion of developmental phases (like an applied science of medicine for human settlements), since a classification referring only to a static situation may confuse the situation instead of clarifying it.

By starting with measurements we can follow a process step by step, each based on one or a few characters because if we use too many characters we can get

	Rank	Characters and Views
1.	division	basic dimensions and economic functions
2.	class	Ekistic Population Units
3.	order	central and peripheral
4.	genus	structure and function (compact or dispersed, etc.)
5.	section	structure and function (natural, planned, both natural and planned, static, dynamic, etc.)
6.	series	structure and function (radical, orthogonal, etc.)
7.	species	satisfaction of five principles
8.	variety	satisfaction of five aspects

26. Taxonomy of human settlements

confused. I next present measurements in two dimensions: population and territory. This is not a new approach; experts like Berry and Garrison have stated that "city-size relationships are a base on which to build or to relate city-size relationships to other relationships."[23] But they are only a base. We need a total approach.

The Ekistic Population Scale (EPS) (Fig. 27) starts with unit 1 (Anthropos or a single individual). The next unit is two individuals. The third unit is the nuclear family (estimated as five members). After the family unit we proceed by multiplying each successive ekistic unit by a standard figure of seven.

Ekistic Population Scale		Persons
15	Ecumenopolis	69,206,436,005
14	eperopolis	9,886,633,715
13	small eperopolis	1,412,376,245
12	megalopolis	201,768,035
11	small megalopolis	28,824,005
10	metropolis	4,117,715
9	small metropolis	558,245
8	polis	84,035
7	small polis	12,005
6	village	1,715
5	small village	245
4	housegroup	35
3	family	5
2	couple	2
1	Anthropos	1

27. Ekistic Population Scale

The Ekistic Territorial Scale (ETS) (Fig. 28) starts from the total habitable land of the globe which I have taken to be 135,750,000 sq km (excluding the Antarctic). I then proceed on the basis of the theory of spatial organization developed by Christaller.[24] The Ekistic Territorial Scale moves from the total habitable land down to unit 1, corresponding to the human bubble of 4 sq m, to unit -1 for standing persons, and to unit -2 for persons tightly squeezed together.

Ekistic Territorial Scale		Square Meters
18	biosphere	
17	all habitable land	135,750,000,000,000.000
16		19,392,857,000,000.000
15		2,770,408,000,000.000
14		395,772,000,000.000
13		56,538,000,000.000
12		8,077,000,000.000
11		1,153,850,000.000
10		164,836,000.000
9		23,548,000.000
8		3,364,000.000
7		480,570.000
6		68,650.000
5		9,800.000
4		1,400.000
3	house	200.000
2	room	28.059
1	human bubble	4.084
— 1	standing person	.583
— 2	squeezed person	.083

28. Ekistic Territorial Scale

Figure 29 shows the three hundred possible interrelationships of population and territory. We must also consider a third characteristic of the human settlement; its main economic function.

The order under which any settlement should be classified depends upon whether it has one level (like an isolated village) or many levels (its own territory plus that of other settlements which depend on it or serve it). For example, as megalopolises may range from 10 to 500 million people, we can classify the Roman or Chinese empires and the U.S. Northeast Megalopolis as megalopolises on the population scale, but there are enormous differences in the territory each covers. Furthermore, imperial Peking (with one million people) must be distinguished from a modern small metropolis (also with one million or more people) because imperial Peking served a much greater area and population than the modern small metropolis.

Structure and function depend, in terms of their interrelationships, dimensions, and location, on the four areas (Naturarea, Cultivarea, Anthroparea and Industrarea). The human settlement is then examined in terms of the five elements (Nature, Anthropos, Society, Shells, Networks). For example, general population density in any of the four areas is a relation of Nature and Anthropos in the total area, whereas housing density is measured by Anthropos and Shells, in relation to a specific part of the Anthroparea.

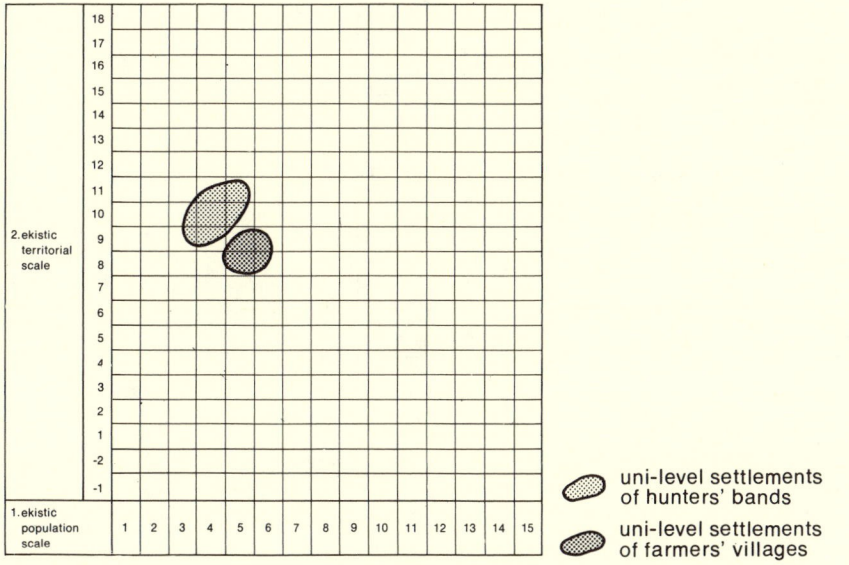

29. The model of basic dimensions

Models of structure and function are the basis for taxonomy of genus, section, and series (See Fig. 26).

Without time dimensions, interaction and function do not exist in any living system. Thus Figure 30 demonstrates the interactions between the five elements and the human settlement in terms of time. The divisions on the ordinate record the forces that have created the human settlement. The divisions along the abscissa record when the various events or actions took place and how long they lasted. It is here that the distinction can be made between static and dynamic settlements (dynapolis).

Basic dimensions are some of the criteria for identity, taxonomy, and classification. An elephant and a rat are different in many other ways than size. We must distinguish criteria not only in terms of dimensions, structure, function, and time, but also by quality and the satisfaction created.

To deal with the very difficult question of happiness or satisfaction, I turn to the five principles which have guided Anthropos throughout history (Fig. 31). These can help us evaluate many dimensional and non-dimensional problems. For example, the density inside the Anthroparea in relation to Shells can provide an answer to the satisfaction of the third principle of protective space. This answer is not complete, however, unless we clarify the aspect from which we evaluate the situation: economic, social, political, administrative, technological,

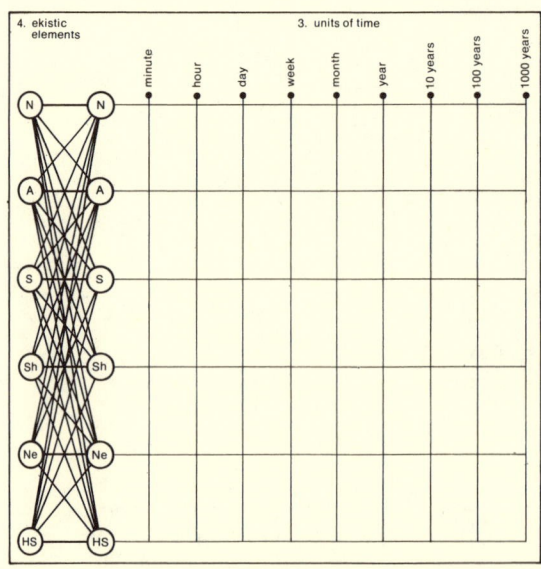

30. The model of structure and function

or cultural. Our judgement here also depends on whether we are considering desirability or feasibility.

This model enables us to clear up some of the confusion concerning the meaning of satisfaction. If some inhabitants of a small and beautiful "ideal" polis say that they do not like it because it does not have a university, a big hospital, or enough jobs, this means that they do not like this species of settlement, and would prefer a metropolis or larger human settlement. A cat can be the most beautiful cat in the world, but a person may hate it because he likes only horses or dogs. Through this type of approach we can also learn whether an "ideal" town which is beginning to be abandoned (because the first and second principles are not being satisfied) could change its situation by developing better connections through high speed routes and also whether such action would or would not be feasible.

Through continuous classification we have reached the point where the Anthropocosmos model (incorporating dimensions, parts, elements, structure, functions, and criteria) can help us conceive the ideal yet feasible human settlements we need. After completing this model (Fig. 33), we can see that the structure and function model (Fig. 30) represents a very small part of the basic dimensions model (Fig. 29) and the satisfaction model (Fig. 31) a very small part of the structure and function model (see Fig. 32). The image incorporating every-

5. aspects / 6. principles	desirability					feasibility				
	E	S	P	T	C	E	S	P	T	C
1. maximum of contacts										
2. minimum of effort										
3. optimum of protective space										
4. optimum of quality of the total environment										
5. optimum in the synthesis of all principles										

Aspects:

E   economic
S   social
P   political
T   technological
C   cultural

31. The model of satisfaction

The model of basic dimensions

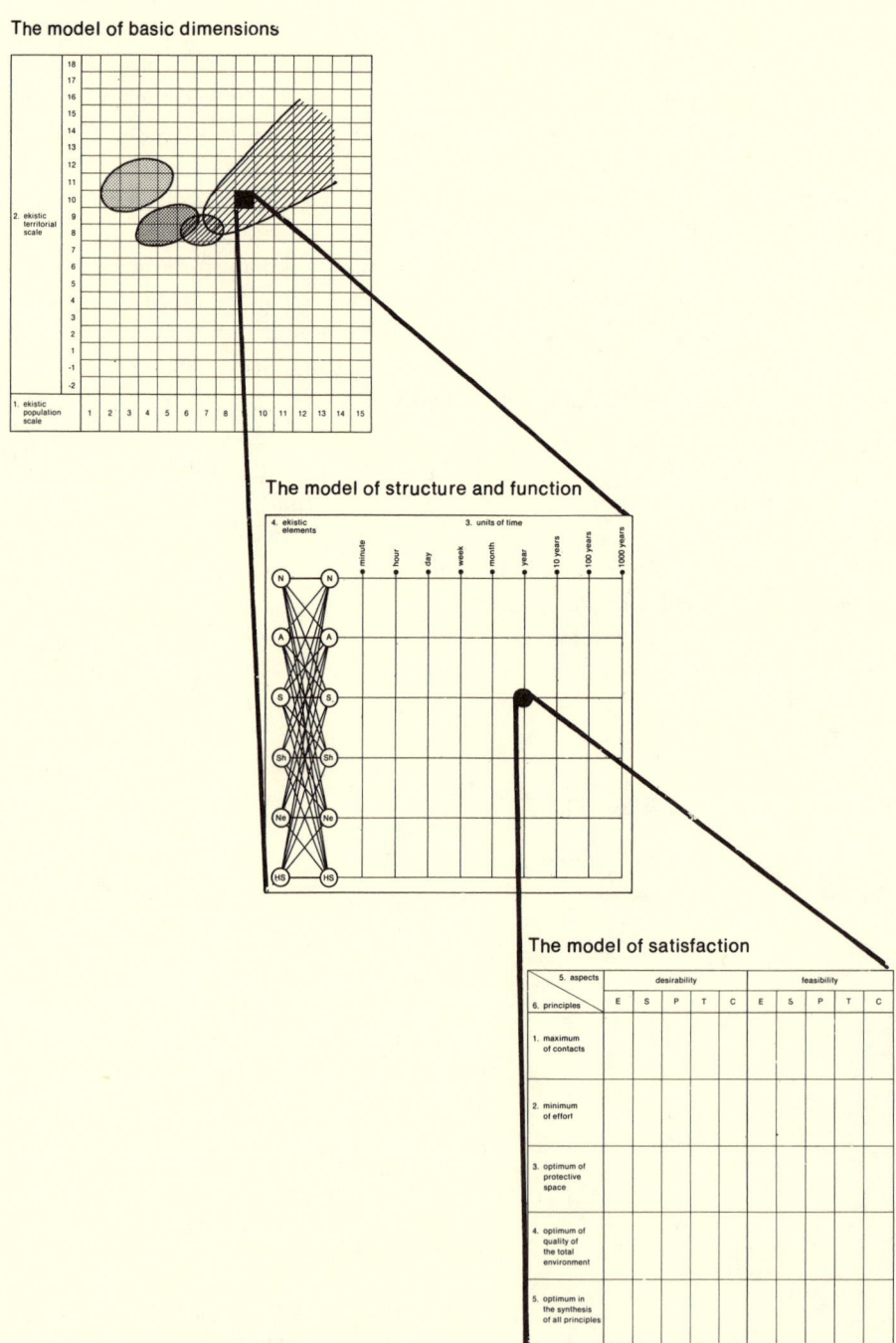

The model of structure and function

The model of satisfaction

32.   Combination of three models

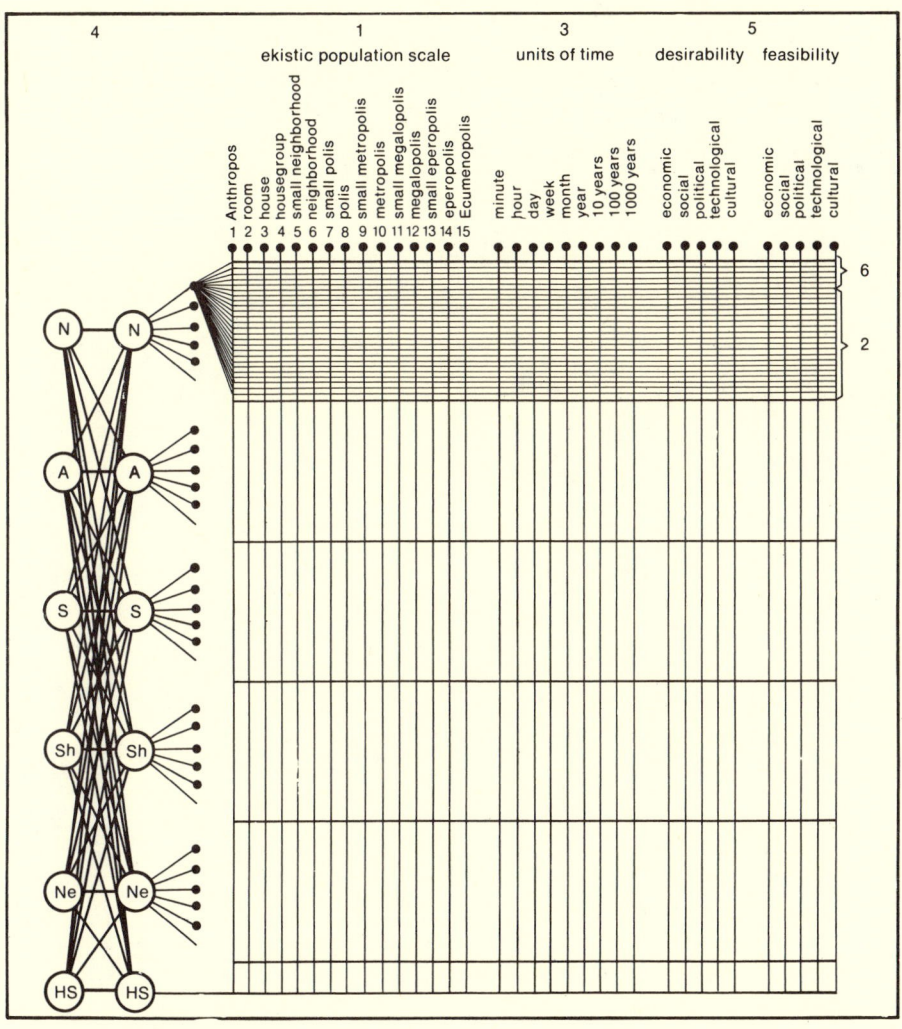

1. ekistic population scale
2. ekistic territorial scale
3. ekistic time scale — part of 1
4. ekistic elements — part of 2
5. aspects — part of 3
6. principles — part of 5

33.   The Anthropocosmos model

thing in the same grid (Fig. 33) provides a framework which can explain all the dimensional relationships. Obviously, in the simplified way the total is presented here, the Anthropocosmos model cannot incorporate all aspects.

What such a model does is provide a frame for systematic organization of the material, the preparation of algorithms; operations research; exact calculations by computers (for which reason it has to lead to code numbering).

Once we agree, even tentatively, on the Anthropocosmos and the Anthropocosmos model, we have to collect and evaluate data on enough human settlements to represent the global situation.

Part Two

The Problems of Human Settlements

A. The problems

After examining human settlements in general in order to understand them, we must examine their problems in particular in the same way doctors examine their patients in order to make the proper diagnosis and prescribe the proper cure. There is no hope for a cure without a precise diagnosis, which requires full knowledge of the patient. A detailed handling of this subject is dealt with in *Ekistics; an Introduction to the Science of Human Settlements.*[1] Here I will describe the situation only in general terms.

The problems of human settlements are so many that it is impossible even to name them. Every human problem can be called a problem of human settlements since it occurs in them. If someone dies in his home or even in a national park, the problem can be termed a human settlement problem since it occurs in a human settlement. This definition can be justified theoretically, but is probably misleading. Nonetheless, in some cases it may be the best, for if the death was caused by falling down steps in the park then the problem is directly related to human settlements and the safety conditions within them.

We can, in the same way, become confused by broader social problems. If we visit a human settlement and find that its leaders are the wrong people we, correctly, can call this situation a human settlement problem. We cannot, however, connect this problem directly with the human settlement in order to find the solution. This problem makes the human settlement suffer, but the solution lies not in the ways we handle the human settlement but in the ways the settlement's inhabitants choose their leaders. If we try to include such situations in our survey we will end up in confusion. I have seen this situation in many cities around the globe and it is distressing.

63. *To understand the problems of human settlements we must have the courage to include only problems directly connected with human settlements as systems of life.*

As the problems of human settlements raise the issue of to which territory they belong, we must remember the Ekistic Territorial Scale presented in Part One. When we find a polis supplied with water from a river which has become polluted, this is a situation which must be clarified in territorial terms. The problem certainly belongs to the polis, but if the pollution is caused by metropolitan industrial plants up river we cannot limit the problem to the polis. Before attempting to solve it, we must place the problem within its broader territorial frame. A systematic approach to the matter of problems in territorial terms is essential.

64. *To clarify the problems of human settlements we must define the extent of their influence on the human settlement territory itself, and whether and how they are related to any broader territory.*

To make this view clearer I refer to the many technological problems of Networks. It is true, for example, that automobiles require many measures for greater safety and it is true that they belong to the road Networks, but it is completely unrealistic to say that the people dealing with human settlements ought to improve automobiles. The maximum that they can do is discuss this

34.   The problems of human settlements. Liari, Pakistan

problem with the people who deal with automobiles, both in government and private industry. This is the only solution, and it is also valid for millions of other problems and situations. It is a matter both of knowledge and intellectual courage to select the real problems of human settlements out of the chaos of a multitude of problems.

After doing so, we will find that the number of problems selected is still very large and that the only way to proceed is by classifying them systematically. They should be classified by beginning with the elements concerned and then proceeding in a systematic way.

65. *We must classify the problems of human settlements in a systematic way.*

It is necessary also to evaluate the problems in terms of their importance. In having to deal with 100 problems for a human settlement, there is a great difference if all are of equal importance and if three of them are considered as being the most urgent, ten second in importance, and so on. We need guidance in order to proceed to the study and diagnosis and to action. I have seen many instances around the globe in which the lack of an evaluation of problems led to endless discussions and no action, or to action on too many programs so that no real results were achieved and the people in charge of the various programs accused each of wasting funds.

66. *To classify the problems properly, we must evaluate them clearly so they can be seen in terms of their priority.*

We must implement the above statements in terms of which problems are directly connected with human settlements as a system, and then classify and evaluate them. The present book cannot do this for every case, but it can demonstrate the method by which practical results can be obtained.

B. Ekistic elements

There are two reasons why it is important to determine to which element any problem of human settlements belongs. First, because only in this way can we be certain what we are talking about. If we speak of environmental problems we need to clarify whether we mean all of them or whether we are referring mainly to social problems or to those belonging to Nature, Anthropos, Shells, or Networks. The second reason is that only if we do so can we turn to the real experts in each field of knowledge and receive the necessary advice. It is also in this phase of our work that we can determine whether or not the problem we are dealing with really belongs to human settlements. I can mention three examples of this case.

In one city I heard the members of the municipal council protest about the public demonstrations which were blocking two public squares and thus disturbing the operation of the city's center. The demonstrators in the first square were students who had no open space inside their campus nearby where they could gather in large numbers. The campus was not designed properly, and thus this was a social problem of human settlements belonging to the element of Shells. The lack of a big conference hall or square inside the campus was the real problem, even if the demonstration was concerned with a social issue.

The demonstrators in the second square were workers from the city's factories, gathered to hear their leaders speak from the union's offices on this square. This was a problem of human settlements, but it could be called coincidental. Unless we believe that the use of every single building must be planned in advance, we can not know who will rent space in the buildings surrounding public squares, nor what new needs may be caused by various occupants. The problem in the second square, then, is a social one influencing the traffic Networks, but we cannot face it as a normal problem of human settlements. In fact, it is a social and political problem.

The police in a certain city were worried about the large number of accidents involving children being hit by cars in the streets. They thought the problem

35. The problems of the elements of human settlements

could be solved only by imposing greater punishments, but there was also another solution. This was to change the streets from two-way automobile traffic to one-way streets, in which accidents are less frequent, and to purely human streets without any motor vehicles.[2] This problem starts with human beings, that is with the element of Anthropos, but also involves the elements of Society and Networks. We start with a human problem, consider it in terms of administration (Society), and then consider it in terms of Networks, which provides the real solution. Thus the human problem has to be seen as how to turn Networks into human Networks.

67.   *To be certain that we understand to which elements a problem belongs we must review all elements and the relationship they might have with the problem at hand. This is where the Anthropocosmos model is helpful because it reminds us of all the factors we must check.*

1. Nature

There are far too many problems of Nature as a part of human settlements because we are in the middle of the era of human aggression against Nature. We do not know how to deal with Nature when it comes into contact with our exploding human settlements and we commit many crimes. It is impossible to describe all these crimes; our only possible contribution is their systematic classification. This, in our overall effort, is our real obligation, not to describe or solve every problem but to lay the foundation for a systematic approach to the problems of Nature and human settlements.

The problems of Nature can be classified first by the parts of Nature (water, air, climate, flora, fauna) and, second, by their character. This "character" is often overlooked as we usually stress only pollution, for example, especially those aspects of pollution on which some experts have done much work, such as air and water pollution. To be realistic, we must classify all problems of Nature in relation to their permanency. In this way we can recognize four categories as follows:

1. Complete elimination of natural resources. Here we must include the resources, such as metals, oil, and gas, that we take from Nature and that cannot be renewed. We must be aware that for a particular human settlement someday, and we must specify the date, the resources which probably created it are going to disappear. Land resources are in the same category — they are eliminated because we permit human action in them, such as the construction of skyscrapers. There is no hope of ever reclaiming this land for wildlife or cultivation unless we consider the new jungle which will grow when, eventually, the area is abandoned. The same problems exist in those coastal areas damaged by the construction of such things as artificial harbors and docks. In these and in many more cases, natural values are permanently lost.

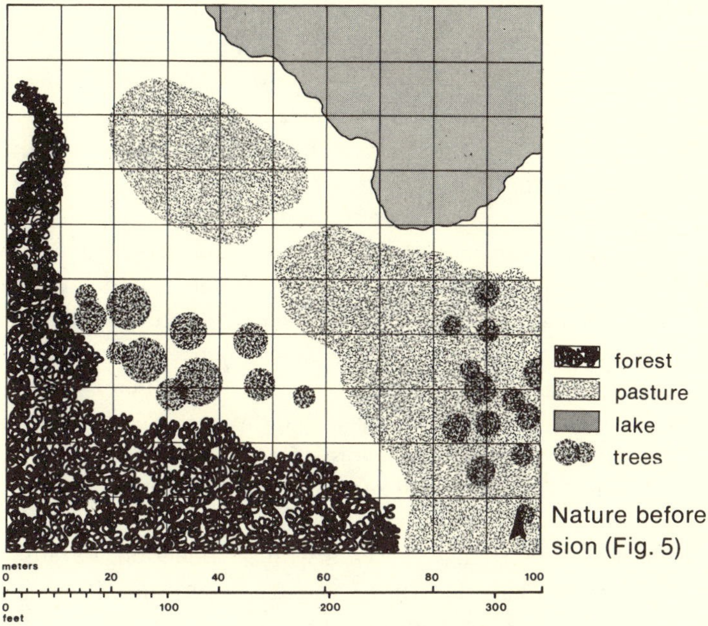

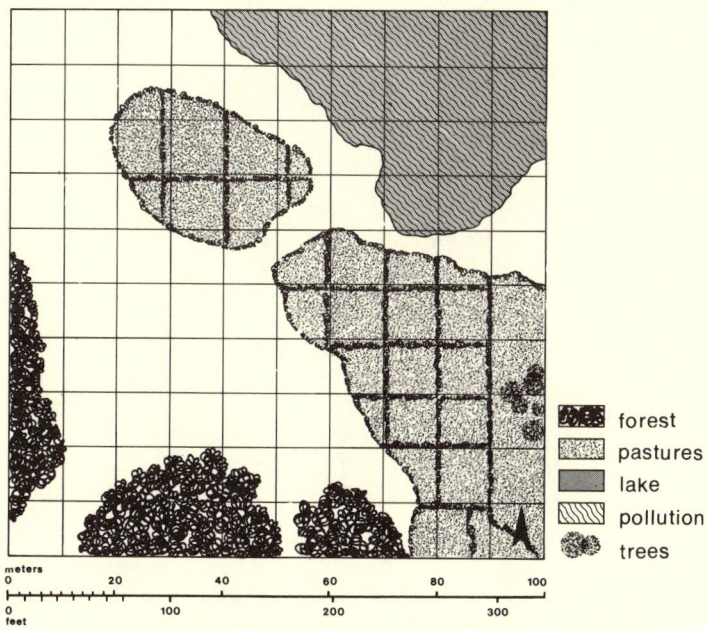

forest
pasture
lake
trees

Nature before human aggression (Fig. 5)

meters
0   20   40   60   80   100

0
feet   100   200   300

forest
pastures
lake
pollution
trees

meters
0   20   40   60   80   100

0
feet   100   200   300

36. Problems of Nature

Human aggression eliminates and pollutes parts of Nature.

2. Temporary elimination of natural resources. This category includes problems that can be overcome. Cutting down a forest, for example, to create a golf course is a problem, but it is temporary in that the forest can be reestablished in a few decades. If we allow the construction of only a few houses at low densities then we can hope to reestablish the pre-existing natural environment or a related one. The same is true for a coastal area or a river if our technological intervention is on a small scale. We must prevent the people who actually steal resources from using this approach and eliminating the natural environment forever under the pretext of temporary action. This strategy often is used.

3. Permanent pollution of natural resources. In such cases we pollute the land or the water in such a way that cannot be rectified by natural evolution. If we put many old cars in a certain land area, we have in fact polluted it permanently, because not only is the surface occupied, but the soil is also polluted for decades at the least and its quality changes forever. Another example is the depositing of chemicals into a lake that will remain there for long periods or even forever.

4. Temporary pollution. This is usually the case with air pollution, because any wind can carry away the pollutants. This, however, can cause misunderstandings, for the pollutants may be blown away from one human settlement but may remain forever on our global scale. Also, as we are not yet certain about the endurance of a polluting force, it may remain indefinitely on the earth's surface. A pollutant must be considered permanent until science can prove that in the long run the biosphere can eliminate it. Similar cases exist for water resources and occasionally for land, flora, and fauna. We must be very slow to describe a pollutant as temporary; to do so we need an expert opinion.

Considering all four categories of the problems strengthens our awareness of the need to define the impact these problems have both on the territory of the human settlement under study and on the broader territory they may affect.

68. *To be certain about the problems of Nature we must classify them by their parts as well as by the four categories of complete elimination, temporary elimination, permanent pollution, and temporary pollution of natural resources.*

2. Anthropos

As already discussed in Part One, human beings should be studied here as single individuals apart from the problems of the operation of Society. This study can be based on many systematic approaches, but in terms of human settlements we must proceed on the basis of two frameworks which can help us understand and classify the innumerable aspects presented by an element as complex as Anthropos. One framework, the twelve phases of human development, already has been presented (see Fig. 8). The other is the four parts of

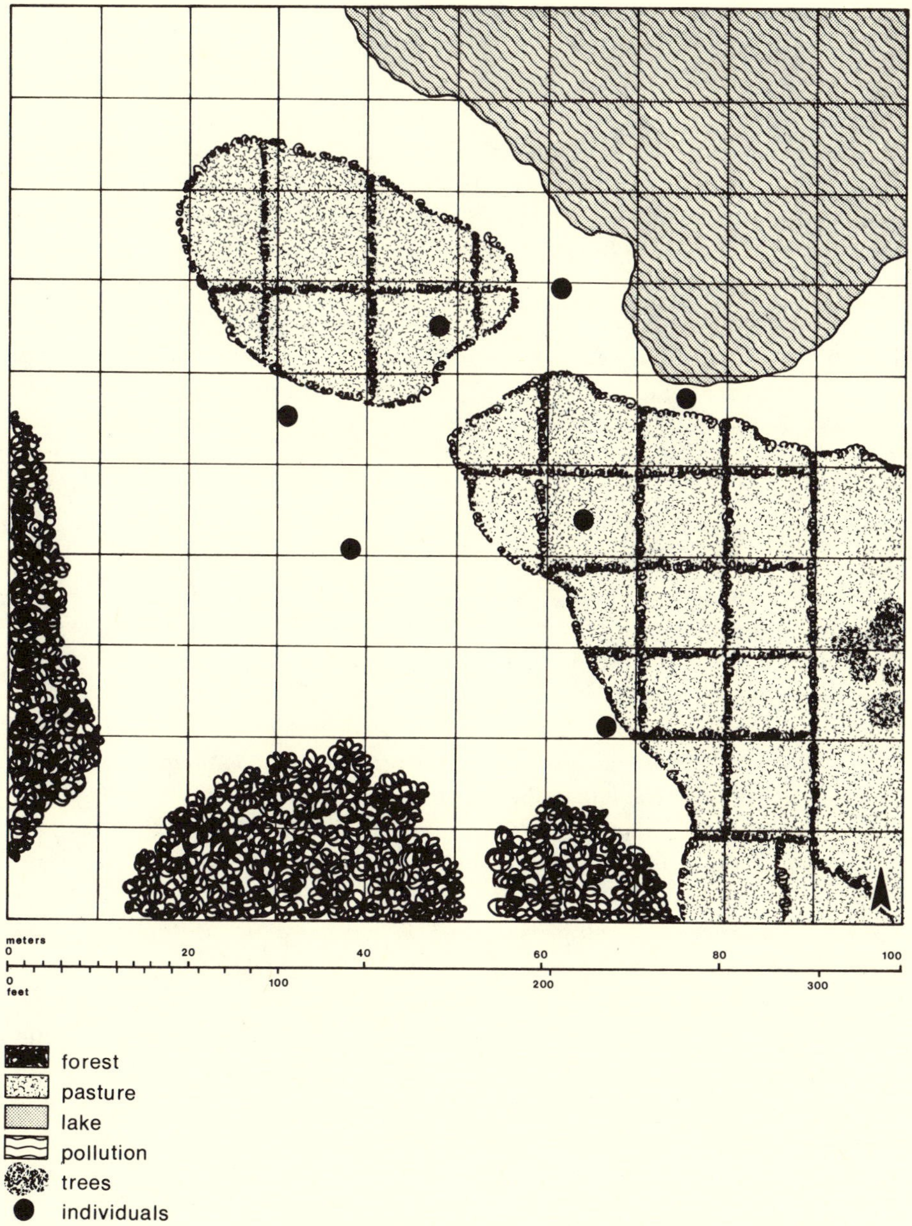

forest
pasture
lake
pollution
trees
● individuals

37. Problems of Anthropos

Anthropos in Nature which he has partly eliminated and polluted

the human system (body, senses, mind, and soul or psyche). We will proceed here with an analysis of the problems of the four parts of the human system. It is impossible to deal with all such problems; we simply will lay the foundations to enable the process to begin.

When we examine the problems of the human body we should start with the most important ones and then move to the less important ones. The most important problem for human survival is the existence of the proper quantity of oxygen, without which no life can exist even temporarily. This is a problem of Nature as well as of Anthropos, so we must use the Anthropocosmos model of human settlements which includes the interaction among the different elements. The complexity of the human system requires this problem to be presented at two points: the interaction of Nature on Nature (decline of quantity) and of Nature on Anthropos (threat to his survival).

In the same way we can understand the problems created by the lack of the proper quantity or quality of food. The question then arises whether or not the problem of food is a problem of human settlements. If there is not enough food in a big metropolis, a simple decision of the administration can solve the problem without there being any impact on the human settlement. So we do not have to consider it as a human settlement problem of metropolises. On the other hand, if a village does not have enough food for several years running (not just for one year which may be accidental), the problem is definitely a human settlement problem because there is no longer any balance between humans and Nature. Either the humans will die, as sometimes still happens, or they will abandon the village. The fate of the human settlement changes. From this simple example we can see that there is frequent confusion as to whether or not a problem belongs to the human settlement. But we can put an end to this confusion.

69.   *We must consider all problems of the existence of Anthropos to be human settlement problems until we have investigated each specific case.*

After considering the problems related to the existence of the human body we must turn to the physiological aspects related to its dimensions. We know from long experience that no one likes to live in a room smaller than 3.50 by 3.50 m (11.5 by 11.5 ft), which can contain four human bubbles.[3] We stay in smaller units, such as a train compartment, but only for a limited time. Research carried out for spaceships has shown that a comparable unit of at least 3 by 3 m (10 by 10 ft) is a reasonable living space for a few days. Long human experience teaches us that humans need to be surrounded by a certain dimension of space. For example, when we work at a desk we cannot stand the wall so close in front of us that we can not stretch our arms.

70.   *Although there are no international standards, we have enough experience to determine the proper human dimensions of the space needed by humans for physiological reasons.*

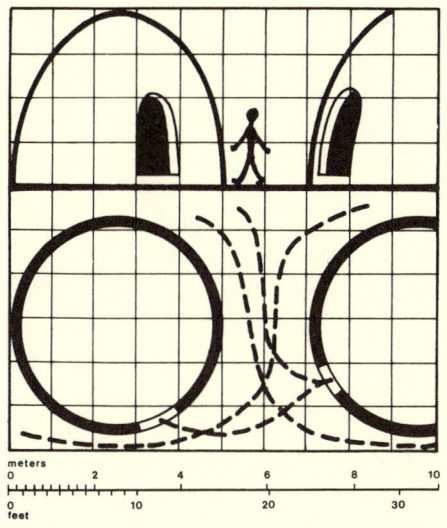

Two separate, unconnected rooms can remain independent units, but people tend to bring them together to save energy.

Two separate, connected rooms cannot remain independent units. They create many problem surfaces and are very expensive.

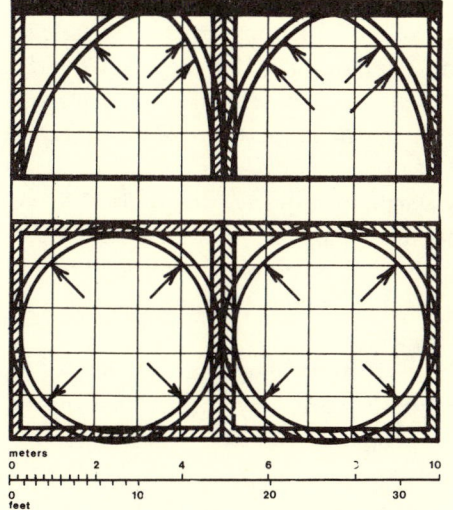

Two connected rooms tend to eliminate the problem surfaces. They tend to a minimum total area and a maximum economy.

Two connected rooms are united into one structure.

38. Formation of the room

The next part of the human system we have to examine is the senses. Through 10,000 years of experimentation by a very great number of cultures and a large number of civilizations we have learned much about how humans tried several solutions and finally reached some conclusions. I will mention one example: the formation of the room. Humans first built all kinds of rooms from different materials and in different forms, shapes, and dimensions. This evolution of the room took more than 10,000 years — rooms were built in the Paleolithic period — led to one conclusion: every culture and civilization adopted the orthogonal room with one flat roof as soon as it could. There are still people who build huts of all sorts, including dome-like huts, but this is because they do not have the experience or the materials to build the orthogonal room. This common evolutionary trend is caused by the physiological needs of Anthropos, who does not like his eyes to see curved walls or roofs (Fig. 38). This conclusion is the result of a detailed study which did not find one case for which this evolutionary trend was not valid.[4]

The experience leading to those solutions reached because of the desire not to be bothered by noise, smell, or touch is similar. As soon as humans could change shapes and use different materials to serve their corresponding senses they did so. Although we have not necessarily come to the same solutions, the trends are uniform. They are leading towards similar solutions which some day may become international standards.

71. *To understand the problems of human settlements in terms of the human body and senses we must understand international evolutionary trends. We must then compare the particular case we are studying with the evolutionary phase the people in this particular case could be expected to have reached or should be helped to reach.*

If we are dealing with nomadic bands which are expected to continue living in the same way for, let us say, one generation, the fact that they do not have orthogonal rooms cannot be called a problem. Their problem is to build better tents, and this only if there are no other far more important problems, such as food supplies, requiring much greater assistance.

72. *When dealing with problems of human settlements, we should try to understand not only whether or not they are human settlement problems, but whether or not they are problems of a normal evolutionary phase through which human settlements pass.*

Then we come to a judgement of the human settlement in relation to its satisfaction of the other two parts of the human system, the mind and the soul. No real research has been carried out in this field, but we know from experience that different kinds of people in different cultures and even within the same culture, have completely different opinions on the quality of a given human settlement and its parts. Some cultures still prefer low density suburbs and much vegetation, whereas others prefer higher densities without vegetation. There is no way of knowing which preference represents a more developed phase of a neighborhood. It is difficult to decide how to locate those problems connected with satisfaction of mind and soul. Perhaps this can be done for the first phases of human development, that is for those phases in which children have not yet learned about their culture and thus may not be influenced by it, but only by the international standards of human needs.

73. *More than in any other case, the problems of human settlements in terms of mind and soul must be judged by the inhabitants of the human settlements themselves.*

3. Society

We must study the problems of Society in the same spirit we have studied the problems of Nature and Anthropos. There are so many problems of Society that we should not make the mistake of connecting them all with human settlements. Let us take, for example, the political system in a certain country. I have seen many countries change their political systems completely without influencing in any direct way their human settlements. If, however, the ownership of land and the problems related to it are greatly influenced, the human settlements and their problems will be affected. In general terms we must be aware, however, that many different political systems make the same mistakes in handling human settlements. As yet little is known about human settlements and there are no political systems which can pride themselves on being particularly knowledgeable. Some countries simply are more successful than others and this is so because of many reasons. We can learn that a problem of Society is a human settlement problem only by examining each case.

74. *To be certain about problems of Society we have to classify them by their parts.*

To achieve this goal we must, as in the case of other elements, classify the different phenomena of Society in such a way that we can insert all cases. The best way is to start with the size of the social unit. Just as we cannot succeed in facing human settlements without first clarifying the size of the settlement with which we are dealing so we must clarify the size of the social unit with which we are dealing. The lack of proper social contacts has a different impact in a neighborhood than in a metropolis. Let us take the problems of security. There may be major avenues in a metropolis on which one can walk safely at night because they attract many people, whereas at the same time one cannot walk safely in one's own neighborhood. In another metropolis the situation may be the reverse, with no safety in the central area at night, if it is abandoned by its people, but relative safety in its outlying neighborhoods. There are also cases in which the situation changes within a few years. In some cities many personal crimes are committed in densely inhabited centers and the low density areas consider

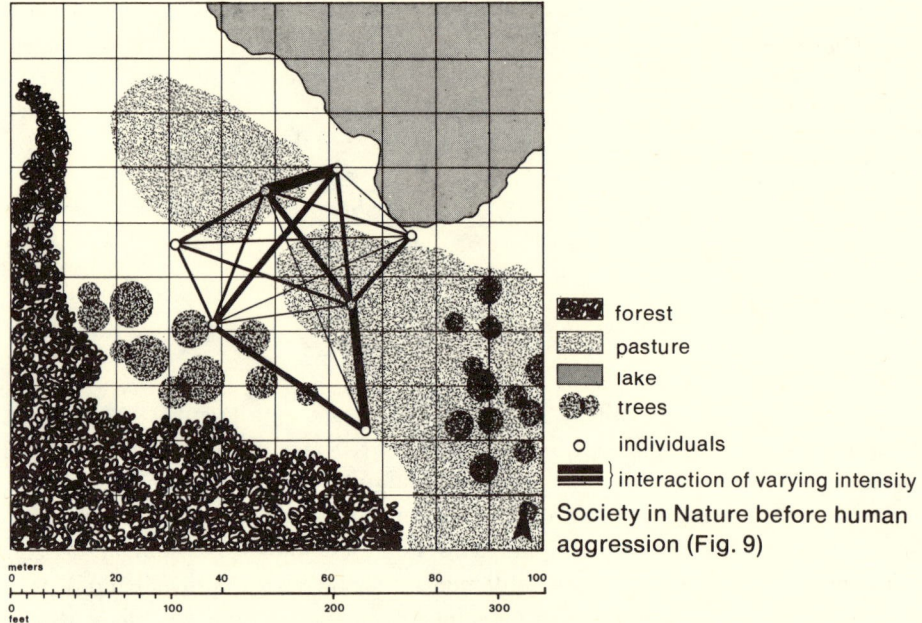

forest
pasture
lake
trees
o   individuals
} interaction of varying intensity

Society in Nature before human aggression (Fig. 9)

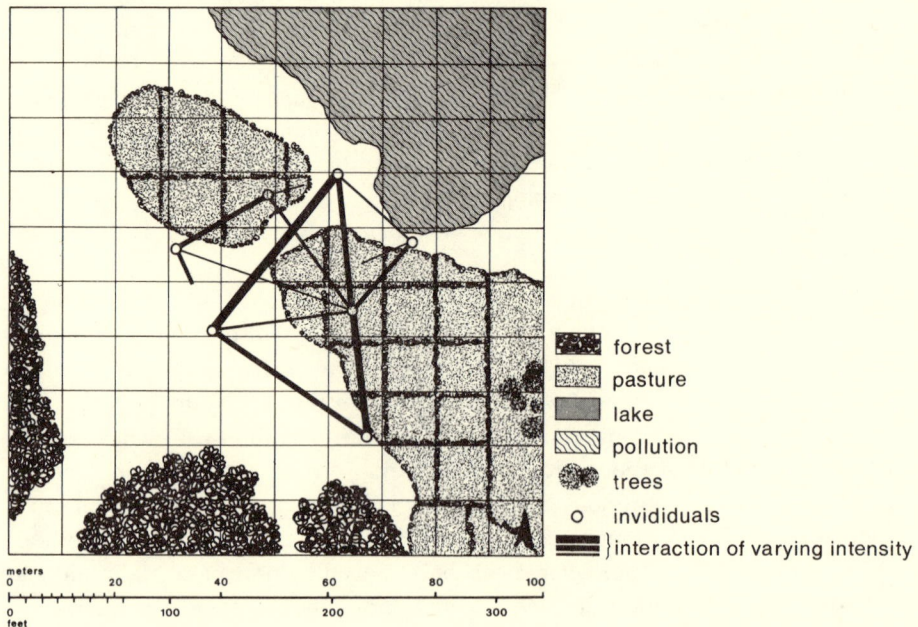

forest
pasture
lake
pollution
trees
o   invividuals
} interaction of varying intensity

39.   Problems of Society

Society in Nature, partly eliminated and polluted by human aggression.
The system of relationships is damaged.

themselves safe. But when stringent measures are taken in the center of the city, personal crimes start occurring in the so-called safe areas. Only a detailed study can really prove how the total system works.

75. *To understand social problems we must locate them by units defined by population size and territory.*

Figure 40 illustrates the relationship between the two types of scales. The territorial units occupy the vertical line and the population units occupy the horizontal line so we can immediately recognize the difference between a population unit of 2,000 people (let us say a well formed neighborhood unit) in a village from a comparable population unit in a metropolis. The sizes are the same and many other aspects, such as the houses, may appear to be the same, but the social problems may be different. There may be happiness because of real cohesion in the village neighborhood, and much unrest because of the breakdown of social units in the metropolis neighborhood.

After correctly locating the unit size we must turn to the different categories of social groups forming this unit. They cannot all be the same. Even in isolated bands and villages, where there may be many uniformities, there are great differences between age groups. In the larger units there are many other dif-

social units		units of human settlements → name of unit / population
Anthropos		Anthropos — 1
room		room — 2
house		house — 5
housegroup		housegroup — 40
small neighborhood		small neighborhood — 250
neighborhood		neighborhood — 1,500
small polis		small polis — 10,000
polis		polis — 75,000
small metropolis		small metropolis — 500,000
metropolis		metropolis — 4M
small megalopolis		small megalopolis — 25M
megalopolis		megalopolis — 150M
small eperopolis		small eperopolis — 1,000M
eperopolis		eperopolis — 7,000M
Ecumenopolis		Ecumenopolis — 50,000M

40. The model of basic dimensions: the relationship between social units and ekistic units

ferences, such as racial, national, income, and religious, differences. All these form many categories of people inside the one social unit we are studying.

76. *We must recognize the different categories, such as national, racial, economic, religious, and age group categories inside every social unit. Only when we recognize them as separate categories can we hope to properly locate social problems.*

One way to help us understand these problems is to use colors for the different categories. For example, I have experimented with the story of the "blue people." My experience in my own country is that in almost every village people speak of at least one "crazy" person in their village. I have met many of these "crazy" people. I realized that sometimes the so-called crazy person really was crazy, but sometimes he was a normal but very different person — different from the average village inhabitant in that he was an artist, a political leftist, or a genius. I decided when speaking of villages to call these people the "blue people." This was successful because blue, finally, did not mean anything other than different. Categorization by colors can demonstrate the social categories with which we are dealing.

77. *It can be very helpful if we use colors to represent the many different social categories, such as red for political aspects and green for different income groups ranging from dark green for high incomes to light green for the low incomes.*

After defining the social unit and the social categories we can begin to locate the differences between the different groups belonging to each category. These are such problems as equality, social contacts, aggression, security, and organization. On the aspect of organization we should not forget that many groups are stronger inside a broader social group or major human settlement because of their great internal organization and self-support. This can happen either through being imposed from the top, as in colonial empires or secret services or, more frequently, from inside the social group as is the case with many nationalities infiltrating other areas.

78. *We must define all social problems on the basis of social units and categories, always remembering that social problems are the problems of interaction between people, the centers in the network of relationships.*

4. Shells

Although Shells first attract our attention as they are the most symbolic element of human settlements, all their problems never are analyzed simultaneously. The main reason is because the accepted systems of administration leave each different kind of Shell to special agencies or ministries. One report speaks of houses, another of schools, and there are occasional reports about Shells for commerce, for entertainment, or for such symbolic buildings as churches, temples,

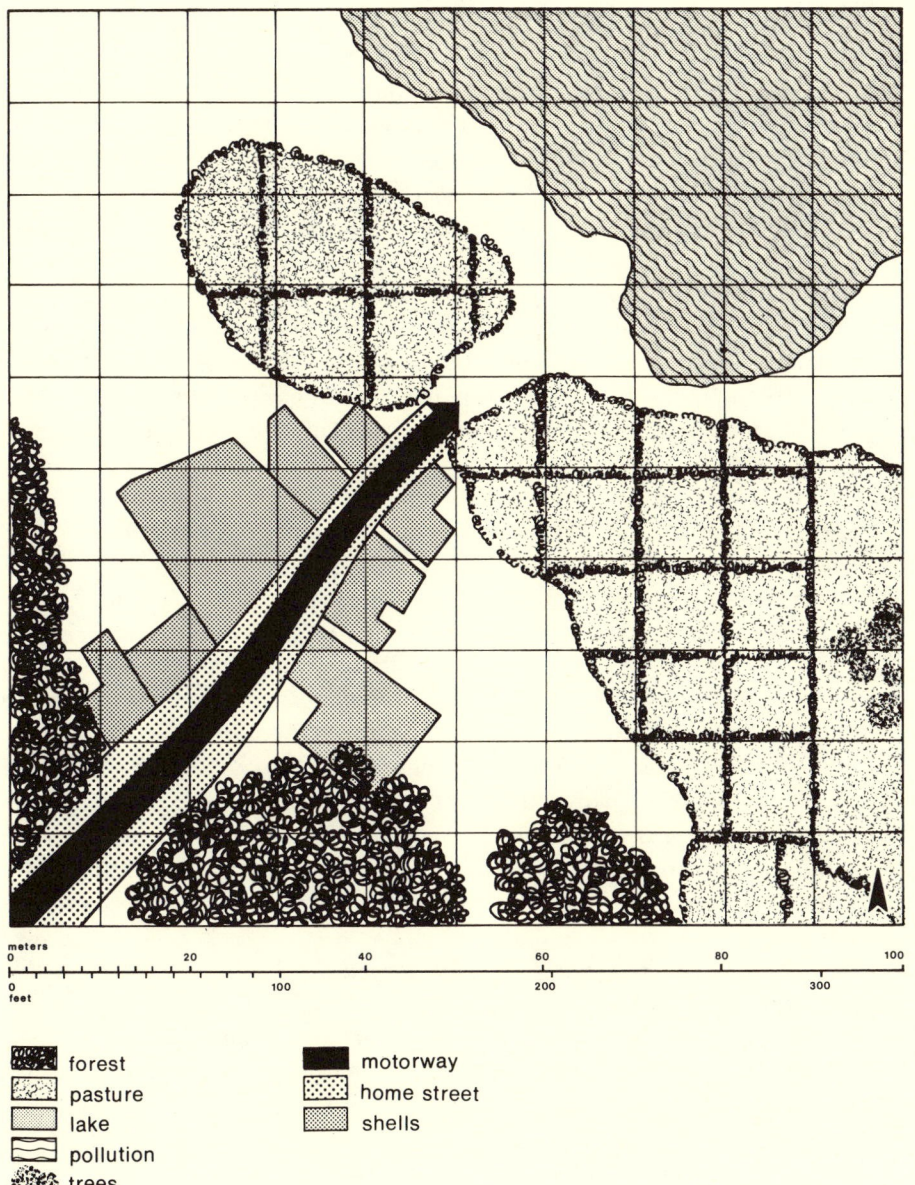

meters 0	20		40	60	80	100
0 feet		100		200		300

forest

pasture

lake

pollution

trees

motorway

home street

shells

41. Problems of Shells

Some Shells have been changed and are now much larger multi-story buildings. A balance no longer exists between the old and the new Shells. The quality of life has been changed because of the changing Shells.

and mosques. We need to have, however, an idea of all the different kinds of Shells, as we have seen in statements numbers 19 and 20. Once we have done this we must relate these figures to the numbers of people living in and being served by the human settlement we are studying. We must proceed with these proposals first in order to evaluate the problems.

79. *When we know the number of Shells which exist we can compare them with the number of people and acquire the first idea of the real relationships.*

Then we approach the real problem. There are so many houses, but how many more actually are needed? We cannot answer this question in any reasonable way if we have not determined our goals. But this is very difficult, as we will see in Part Three. To say that every family must have a house is simple, but if we are in the phase of transfer from patriarchal families to nuclear families the unit we have to supply with houses is unknown. Equally unknown are the numbers of rooms per house, and many other factors. The only way to face this problem is to set up a standard as a working assumption for immediate needs and measurements.

80. *We must estimate the size and volume of needed Shells on the basis of a certain standard, without forgetting that this standard is only tentative.*

This whole effort starts with houses and their rooms. Some of the types of Shells, such as schools which can be classified by the number of their classrooms can be measured, while others, such as buildings for entertainment or cultural needs, may not be measurable. These types of problems can only be answered properly if we make certain assumptions in a systematic way as we will see in Part Three when we discuss goals. The standard already mentioned is related to numbers and dimensions; but what about the quality of the Shells? To this very difficult question we can only anwer in the same way we have in the above statement.

81. *We must estimate the quality of needed Shells on the basis of a tentative standard.*

We then move to the organization of the Shells into housegroups, neighborhoods, etc. Again there are no international values and no standards. Thus we must again make assumptions based on the experience already gained, as there is no other solution.

82. *We must estimate the grouping of the needed Shells on the basis of a tentative standard.*

Related to the problem of quality is the need to save those Shells of the past which represent certain historical and cultural values. This does not mean that their standards should be accepted today, but it does mean that we should respect the old standards as they were in the era when these Shells were created. Major buildings and monuments of the past are now not only in great danger of being demolished, but also of decay from many causes, including air pollution. Such important monuments as ancient Greek temples, even the Parthenon on the Acropolis in Athens, are suffering from air pollution. For such cases we need another approach.

83. *Many Shells of the past have major problems caused by a decline in their initial quality. The best of these Shells must be saved.*

At this stage we must remember that all these problems have two facets, for we must consider both the needed and the existing Shells. When we decide that a certain standard of house requires plumbing facilities, we cannot leave already existing houses without water. Thus the problems always have a double expression.

84. *In defining the problems we must refer both to the existing and to the missing Shells.*

5. Networks

The problems of Networks are much more complicated than those of Shells for many reasons, two of which are as follows. We can see the Shells but we do not see many Networks. Thus we often forget the existence of those Networks which are underground, or some very simple ones like the pedestrian paths. Another reason is that modern technology has created a far greater revolution in Networks than in Shells. Many of today's Networks, such as electricity and telecommunications, did not exist a few generations ago. When dealing with human settlements we do not always remember all Networks, some of which may have to be added later, thereby creating all sorts of problems.

85. *We must understand that all types of Networks form part of the total system.*

Unless we relate all Networks to the people they serve we cannot judge the real problems. An example is the small town which in the past had an ideal road network, but now that it has become part of a metropolis it must serve ten times more people and its road network is inadequate.

86. *Once we have an image of all existing Networks we can measure the Networks against the number of people they serve to receive the first image of the real relationship.*

We then can start the analysis which leads to the definition of the real problems. When we know about roads and people in every area of our human settlements we can calculate how many cars should come to each area on each road and thus we can define the real traffic problem. We will misunderstand the traffic problem if we consider only what we see, because the existing facilities do not indicate the real needs. To do this we must make some assumptions about needs, and this requires standards based on a realistic assumption of the needs to be served.

87. *To calculate the dimensions of the problem of Networks we must assume certain standards and then estimate the needed Networks, keep-*

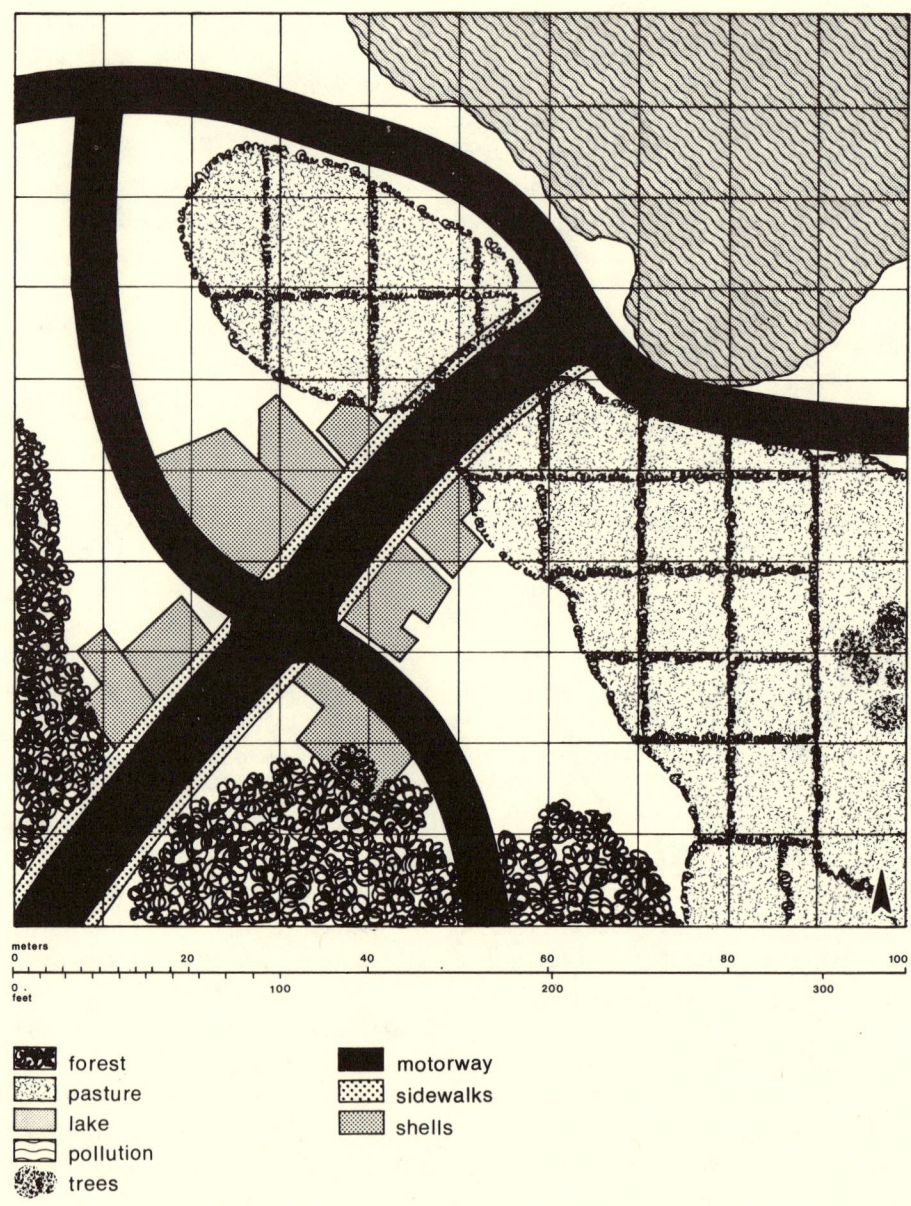

| | meters | | | | |
| 0 | 20 | 40 | 60 | 80 | 100 |

| | 0 | | | | |
| feet | 100 | 200 | 300 | |

forest
pasture
lake
pollution
trees

motorway
sidewalks
shells

42. Problems of Networks

When big buildings replace the earlier small ones, sidewalks are eliminated because of the wide space required for the increased number of automobiles. The whole system of Networks is uncoordinated.

ing in mind that these estimates are valid only on the assumption of tentative standards.

With this process we can make calculations for many types of Networks. These calculations are relatively easy for roads or water supplies, but are much more difficult for other Networks, such as telephone lines, because if there are no telephones in the area and incomes are low it is very difficult to calculate the dimensions of the problem. In such a case it is accurate to say that no one has a telephone at home; but we need to know how many people can afford to have a telephone, and when. The basic assumptions regarding reasonable standards are even more necessary when we turn to quality.

88. *We should calculate the problems of the quality of Networks, both those Networks now in existance and those which are missing, on the basis of assumed standards, always keeping in mind the hypothetical nature of our calculations.*

The problems do not apply only to single Networks, but also to all the Networks taken together as a system. We necessarily come to the same conclusion: Our calculations must be based on assumptions.

89. *To define the problems of the total organization of Networks as a system, we must make assumptions about the system that is lacking, always remembering the hypothetical nature of our calculations.*

We do not need only to create new Networks but also to save several existing Networks which are in danger. For example, many pedestrian paths have been lost because of the expansion of motorways, although they are badly needed both to preserve past culture and, simply, because humans need to walk.[5]

90. *Several Networks of the past, necessary for many human needs, are being gradually eliminated.*

This review of the problems of Networks leads to a similar conclusion to that reached for Shells (Statement No. 84). The real problem is a double one. It is a problem both of the missing Networks and of the deficiencies of the existing ones. Once we have made the assumptions about standards which must be the criteria for what we are lacking, we should calculate both how many Networks are lacking and what are the deficiencies of the existing Networks. I have seen many efforts which concentrated only on one aspect of this double problem, but without both aspects we can not be sure about the real situation. Many cities, for example, have applied urban renewal programs concentrating on new Networks and Shells. Unfortunately, in the process they have damaged many of the existing values.

91. *In any effort to define the problems of Networks we must work on both the existing and on the missing Networks.*

C. Ekistic units

1. Temporary human settlements

The first problem is simply that there still are temporary human settlements in existence at the end of the twentieth century, ten thousand years after humans started changing their human settlements. If we remember that civilization is related to permanent human settlements after they become ripe enough to create systems of polises and villages, we must recognize that we learn from temporary human settlements. Their existence helps anthropology, ecology, and other fields of knowledge to understand human evolution and the evolution of the balances humans have achieved with the total system of Nature.

92.   *The greatest problem for temporary human settlements is the fact that they force their inhabitants to live in a most primitive way.*

43.   Temporary human settlements in Iraq

There are more urgent problems, such as a crisis in the permanent ecological balance which had permitted hunters and nomads to survive. An example is a major drought, which makes the animals on which the humans depend (either as hunters or as nomads moving with their own flocks) begin to disappear, causing famine. We should not forget that drought is not the only cause of such a crisis in the ecological balance. In many cases problems are created by human action which changes the development of a certain area and eliminates some natural resources.

93. *The most dangerous problems for temporary human settlements are changes of climate and human actions which threaten the resources and conditions of their existence.*

The other problems of temporary human settlements are minor, but they certainly exist. Nomads are so exposed to Nature that they have no protection from natural catastrophes. They also lack all sorts of services, such as education, medical services, welfare, and entertainment. From the point of view of Society the inhabitants of temporary human settlements have no real hope of rational and useful broader contacts since their method of survival imposes a small band as the only social unit. In terms of Shells there are all kinds of problems, such as the type of tent a nomad uses, but there is no reason to describe them, as they are unimportant in relation to the major problems we have already seen. The situation is comparable when we turn to Networks, for in temporary human settlements there are only rudimentary Networks.

94. *Not one of the elements Anthropos, Society, Shells, or Networks exists in a satisfactory way in temporary human settlements. Each of them creates problems which, together with the problems created by the other elements, convince us of the unacceptable situation created by temporary human settlements.*

2. Villages

For the first time in human history, villages are being abandoned on a global scale. Villages have been abandoned many times in the past but on a smaller and local scale. The causes were foreign invasions or new opportunities for better jobs in other areas. As soon as these causes ceased to exist, the people returned to their villages and rebuilt them if they had been destroyed or built new ones in the same abandoned areas. The present-day phenomenon is not only global in its extent but also threatens to be permanent because industrialization and new modes of life have now offered people many more opportunities in other more central places. These places can be nearby or distant or even in different countries and continents. Many villages have been abandoned because of international shifts of populations to the Americas, to Australia and New Zealand, as well as now lately to western Europe.

95.	*The greatest global problem of villages is that they are often abandoned by their people moving to other higher income areas.*

This happens to lower income villages because their inhabitants are the first to be attracted by higher incomes and new opportunities. The problem is so great that some countries, especially socialist ones, react to it by not allowing the movement of people to other nations or even to their own urban areas or by sending students or civil servants back to the villages to revive them and help their inhabitants. Despite these efforts the difficulties continue and the trends remain internationally the same.

96.	*The greatest problem of villages, the tendency of their inhabitants to abandon them, remains despite many attempts to overcome it.*

There are, however, villages in areas of small incomes which are abandoned, not for another nation or to another very distant place, but for the nearby polis. This is completely different from the previous examples. In this case what is being abandoned is not the villages as complete systems of life, but only their built-up areas. The villagers have discovered that by using machines they can move their families to the polis where they can enjoy all the town facilities and

44.	A village near Benghazi, Libya

then use the machines to travel to and cultivate their fields. This does not really create difficulties; it simply means a restructuring of the human settlement in the countryside and it may well mean a better economy and a better social life. Even the houses of the village are not lost because they are kept as traditional homes and used on certain occasions, inspired by culture or economy.

97. *The problem of the transition of village inhabitants to nearby towns often helps new systems of agricultural life develop. It is only a temporary problem for each area.*

A similar though not identical problem occurs when villagers move to a metropolis which is the center of their whole region. In such cases village production may be slowed down or stopped, causing an economic problem for the region or the country. By moving, however, the villagers gain a higher income and better services; otherwise they would not have moved. The village and its agricultural activities are abandoned and a change begins to occur in Nature which slowly changes from cultivation back to wildlife. Because of this change, particularly if the village houses have historical or cultural value, the abandoned village may become an area for second homes for inhabitants of the metropolis. In this way it may become a new type of human settlement, perhaps called a village, but really a suburban human settlement for relaxation or entertainment.

98. *The moving of villagers to a nearby metropolis transforms the village into a suburb. This is an easy and temporary problem.*

In addition to the problems of changing villages, there are problems of villages which do not change. For each of them we must ask: Will they remain the same villages forever, or will they follow the trends of the problem villages we already have discussed? The answer is not an easy one, especially for those low-income areas where no changes are under way or foreseen. Generally speaking, in this period of global change through which we are passing, most villages will be affected; they either will be abandoned or their role will change. If we are optimistic we would say that this will happen to all villages within two centuries. This idea will not easily be accepted in the immediate future because a realistic view of an earth with equal nations and people has not yet been accepted.

Since even the most optimistic projection will require five or six generations,[6] we must look at the whole situation in the following way:

1. The trends for changing the fate of villages will spread to more regions and countries because of rising incomes.
2. It will take many generations to be sufficiently widespread for us to know whether all villages are going to be affected.
3. In the meantime we must learn when we may expect the fate of a village to change.

This last point poses our problem realistically.

99. *Most, perhaps all, villages will change their character, even if their land is retained for cultivation or is expanded, and become parts of urban systems.*

We must examine every village that shows no signs of change, because we cannot recommend any program for ameliorating life in a village if within ten years the village will be abandoned by its inhabitants because it has no economic future. Instead of building a school which will be useless in ten years, wouldn't it be better to spend the same money educating the villagers about the changing world and helping them to decide when and where they will move? We should not think that change will occur only haphazardly because of economic progress. Often it will come through the application of programs reforming rural areas, some of which are beginning to be applied.

100. *Any definition of a problem concerning a village must begin by recognizing whether and when the general conditions which led to the village's existence may be changed.*

When we know this we can turn to the detailed problems of the particular village we are studying and decide on what has to be done. If complete abandonment is to be its fate, we cannot invest in it except for the period it will be inhabited, and this length of time defines the type and degree of investment. If, however, we know that the village will play a different role, such as being inhabited as a suburban area, then long term investment is far more justified. For example, we can provide it with a water Network that will continue to be used.

Once we know how long the present situation is going to last, then all problems can be recognized and classified in the spirit of the five elements in their order of difficulty: Nature, Shells, Networks, Society, Anthropos.

101. *Analysis of the problems of villages must be made on the basis of the five elements in the following order: Nature, Shells, Networks, Society, Anthropos.*

3. Polises

The polises are changing, as we have seen, and they face many problems. This is most obvious in those polises operating as centers of regions in which the villages have been abandoned because their land does not yield sufficient income. Villagers from such regions do not move to their central polis but to quite different regions, causing a major decline of the total population served by this polis and a great decline in its morale and economy. The future of such a polis is very dark unless it has some monument attracting many visitors or a new highway or airport introducing new functions into the area. But these are exceptional and coincidental cases. In fact, such a polis is usually doomed.

102. *The greatest problems for polises are in areas of agricultural decline. Most of these polises are doomed.*

If, however, villages are abandoned because, for example, their economy allows them to use machines for their cultivation, the fate of their central polis

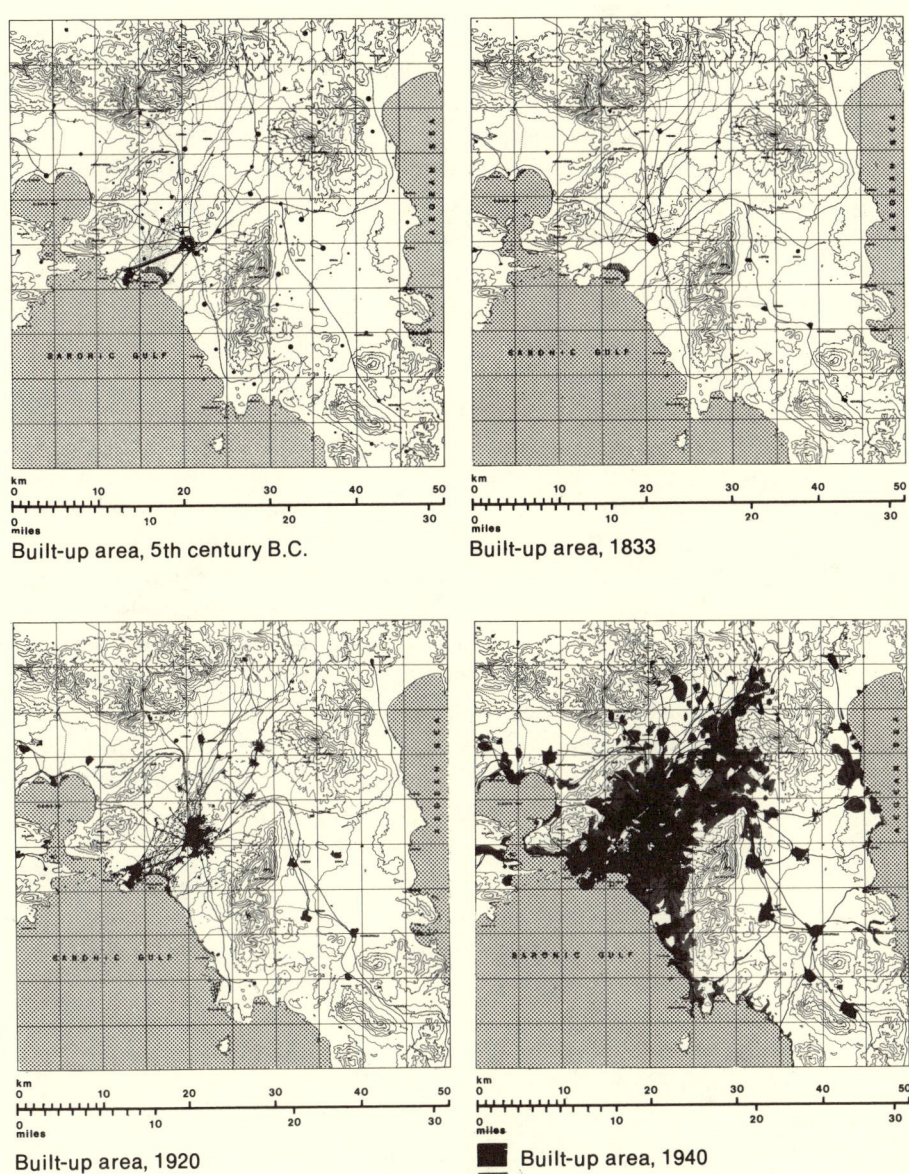

Built-up area, 5th century B.C.

Built-up area, 1833

Built-up area, 1920

■ Built-up area, 1940
■ Built-up area, 1970

45. Evolution of Athens, Greece

is very different. More and more villagers settle in it, although they continue to cultivate their land. Their income increases and they bring merchants and technicians to the polis who serve their new needs. This means an increase in population, incomes, new functions, etc. Instead of problems of abandonment and death, all problems are now related to the population and economy explosion. Mobility increases, with people moving with their machines tens of kilometers each day instead of walking only a few kilometers. This creates a need, which did not exist before, for a road Network. The result is that a much greater area is inhabited by more people at lower densities, and the needs for the area in terms of Shells and Networks of all sorts are many.

103. *Another great problem is the explosion of the polis in terms of population, economy, mobility, and area, creating many new demands.*

The problems for the polis increase if it is influenced by an expanding metropolis or megalopolis. When we discussed the Daily Urban Systems we saw that the real city extends as far as its inhabitants can move in one hour with the means of transportation at their disposal. If a polis, therefore, is within 50 km from a metropolis, it becomes a suburb of this metropolis, changing from a small regional center to become one of the many centers forming the complex system of the metropolis and the much more complex one of the megalopolis. Its problems, then, are many, and can be classified in two categories: the reduction of Nature and the new demands caused by the explosion.

The problems of Nature can be major, because the agricultural land is reduced. The main danger here comes from housing at the very low densities which are now fashionable in polises and are sometimes imposed by regulations. This creates great problems for many of the polis inhabitants who cannot afford a big plot and are obliged to stay in trailers in special camps where they live in higher densities. The arable land invaded by the expanding town cannot easily be replaced by the less fertile fields on the hills. The same danger threatens wildlife which always exists near a town, but cannot easily be saved from attack by expanding needs and interests.

The problems of the new demands raised by the explosion can be classified in the usual way by the five elements.

104. *The polises which become parts of metropolises and megalopolises cause major problems, threatening Nature and creating many new demands.*

This view of several cases demonstrates how polises are really parts of much broader systems, and must be viewed as such. In the past a polis operated as the center of its system, and once we had understood the system properly we could know the polis's problems, as we could in antiquity for city-states. This is no longer possible. The changes are so great that only a full understanding of the whole system of human settlements and all its problems can help us properly to locate the polis and understand its problems.

105. *The problems of polises are so many and so varied, ranging from threatened extinction to explosive growth, that they must be considered as parts of the whole system of human settlements.*

4. Metropolises

Unlike the human settlements we have considered so far, metropolises have no problems of decline and possible death. As far as we know there are no dying metropolises. They are centers of major regions or focal points of broader Networks whose roles may change but whose whole systems cannot decline; they are always dynametropolises. Constantly growing, their problems are related to growth rarely foreseen or planned for.

Their problems of growth can be classified in two categories: inadequate facilities, from houses to all types of services, and harmful growth in terms of speed, direction, structure, etc. The first category of problems directly affects everyone, particularly the poor. Housing for the lower income groups is always in short supply, whereas there is always enough private initiative in the private sector, in the capitalist countries at least, for the higher income groups to take care of their needs. As sufficient action is never taken early enough for the poor many slums are created either in older neighborhoods where larger houses are divided into smaller flats or in new areas where elementary attempts are made to create some, initially temporary, Shells which end up as permanent, low quality housing. This is what happens in the metropolis in terms of quality. There are extreme solutions, from very expensive to very poor ones. I have not mentioned high quality because it hardly exists. Expensive housing exists, but it either is not free from pollution or dangers from machines or is high up in skyscrapers where we cannot allow children to grow.[7] We cannot speak of high quality, only of high income solutions.

In the same way, we can study all other types of buildings where we will notice the same weaknesses. There are enough buildings for the high income classes and not enough for everyone else, with the exception perhaps of some socialist countries, though we do not have sufficient data to make the necessary comparisons. We can select schools as an example. If we study them carefully we will find no country, at least as far as we can tell from official data, where there is always a school within walking distance of all the children who attend it.

106. *In the metropolis we never have enough housing for all classes of people, nor enough of any other type of building to satisfy all citizens in terms of quality in every reasonable aspect of this demand. The problem of a lack of Shells is worsened by the differences between classes, which often do not exist in polises.*

What we have noticed about Shells is also valid for Networks, with one great difference: while poor Shells only directly affect their inhabitants and their im-

Wide World Photos

46. We all suffer today in our large and growing cities.

mediate neighborhood, bad Networks can affect a much broader area. If, for example, the wrong types of highways enter a metropolis, the whole system of roads throughout the metropolis will be greatly influenced. If the sewage system is badly planned, then the whole metropolis or parts of it may be dangerously flooded. On the other hand, some parts of the metropolis may have very bad Networks without influencing the total system. In such cases (no water, no electricity) the problem is the same as with Shells; it can be localized and can increase the inequality between parts of the metropolis.

107. *The problems of Networks within the metropolises belong to two categories: those which, as in the cases of Shells, increase the inequality between areas and those which menace the entire metropolis.*

We now move to the category of harmful growth. Because the urban explosion is happening for the first time in history, we are unable to foresee or prepare ourselves for its next stage. This is aggravated by the fact that administrative units everywhere belong to the past and are much smaller than the contemporary real metropolis. When a central city explodes into a metropolis, this influences many outlying polises and even villages which are certainly not prepared for it. The Networks remain as they were in the past or their details are only altered, and the whole system does not work effectively because there is a complete lack of coordination (See Figs. 47, 48).

108. *Most metropolitan Networks belong to the past and are incapable of serving the new needs.*

The consequences of this incapability are many. We will give one example of how inefficient Networks do not only affect the metropolis, but may decide its fate. The growing metropolis needs a new concept for its road Network to save its center from too many pressures. If the city is old and its center has many economic and cultural institutions, then the center will not be abandoned but its traffic will become congested, damaging its function in terms of time, economy, and quality of life. There are many such cases, such as the metropolises of Rome and London, in Europe, and of course many on other continents.

On the other hand, those cities which have not made sufficient investment to attract people to their centers begin to show signs of abandonment as soon as the pressures mount. First the high income families move to suburban housing, and then various institutions and corporations move to the outskirts. In such cases the centers decline in many ways, attracting only the poorest inhabitants and finally losing their central functions. This is particularly true in the United States, where mobility is high because of the large numbers of automobiles. It is not coincidental that a metropolis with such problems of abandonment in its center is Detroit, Michigan, the global capital of the automobile industry.

109. *A major problem of road Networks in the metropolises is that their centers suffer so much from pressures that in some cases they tend to be abandoned.*

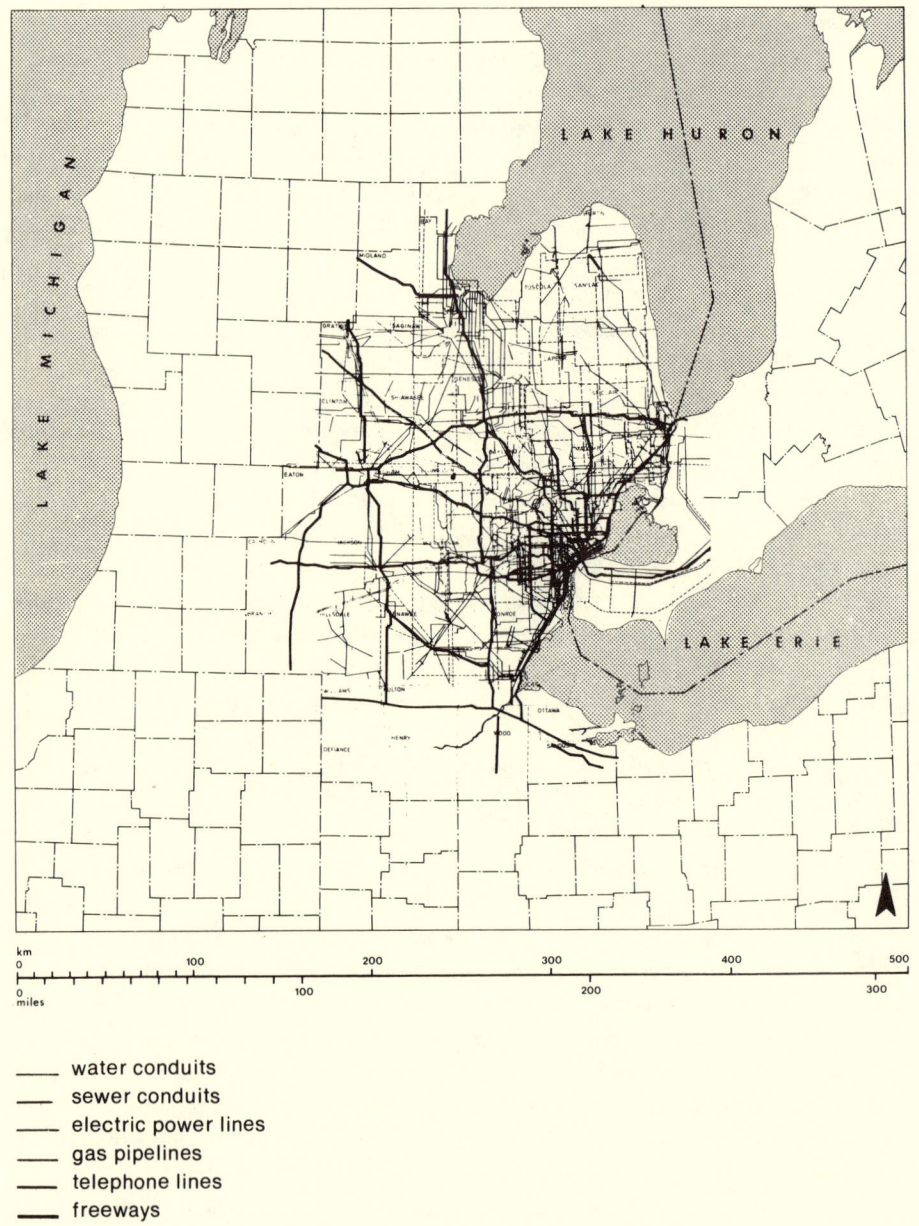

___ water conduits
___ sewer conduits
___ electric power lines
___ gas pipelines
___ telephone lines
▬▬ freeways

47.   The uncoordinated system of Networks in the urban
      Detroit area

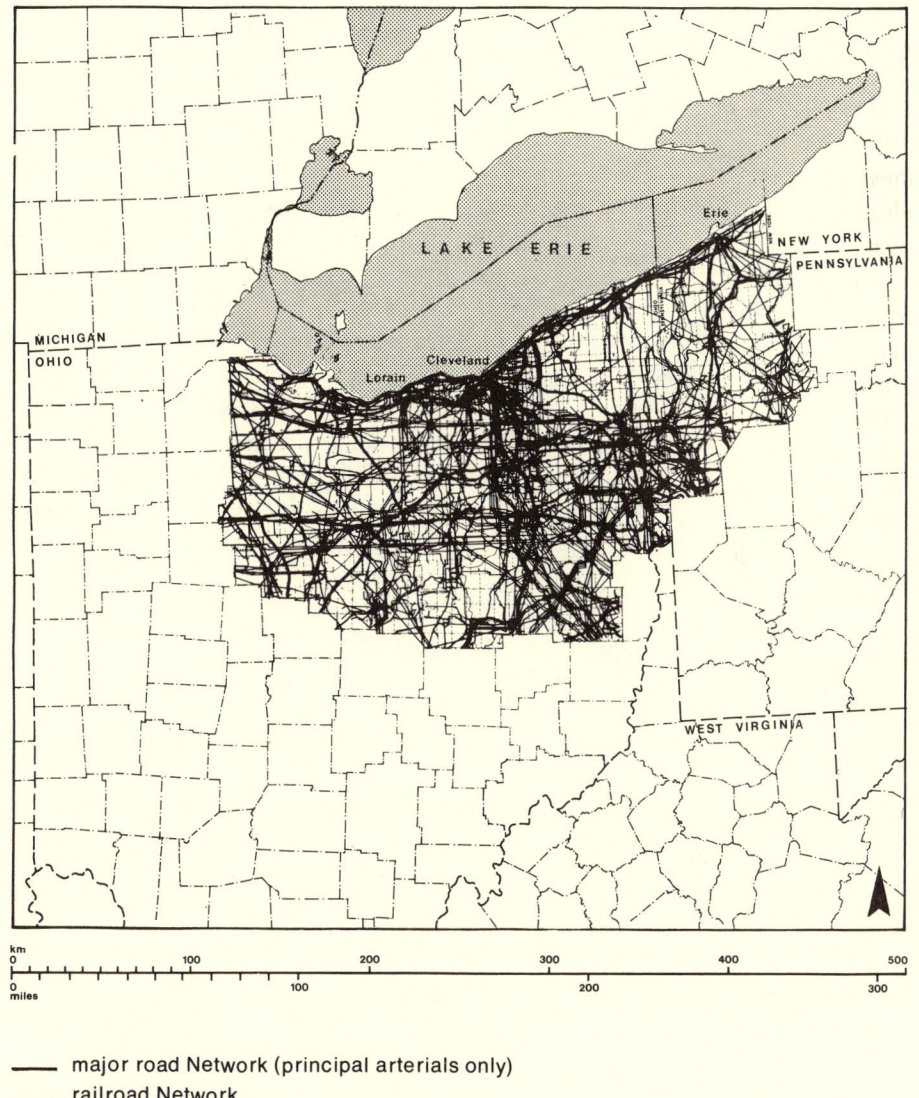

- —— major road Network (principal arterials only)
- —— railroad Network
- —— gas pipelines
- —— oil pipelines
- —— electricity transmission Network
- —— telephone toll Network

48. The uncoordinated system of Networks in the Northern Ohio Urban System

5. Megalopolises

The greatest problem of today's megalopolises is that we do not really recognize their existence. Very few studies have been made about them and even these are still in the hands of a few experts who approve or disapprove of the idea of their existence. The broader public, although recognizing their existence in practice (as shown by the fact that more and more people tend to live in them), has not yet officially recognized the megalopolis. This is why no government has recognized any megalopolis as a special administrative unit. The result is that there are not enough studies to prove their problems and no study whatsoever which goes into detail.

We can, therefore, only use our general experience and what we have learned from ekistics, the science of human settlements, to draw general conclusions about the problems and the dangers related to them. As megalopolises have just been born, there is not yet any megalopolis old enough to allow any detailed conclusions.

110. *We face today's megalopolises, which have just been born, without a sound understanding of their problems but with a general concept based on the scientific understanding of human settlements.*

We cannot enter into any details about the problems of the megalopolis because of its very large scale. When speaking of systems from 200 to 1,000 km long we should not deal even with neighborhoods, which are only up to 1,000 meters long, much less with their Shells. We also cannot deal with problems of human scale, that is with single individuals: how the child fits into the city or how people make their contacts. We have already considered these problems in the smaller scales. What we can study about megalopolises are the elements of Nature, Networks, and Society.

We start with Nature, which is in very great danger in the megalopolis, because the megalopolis must contain all types of functions. A polis and a metropolis can say "no" to a polluting industry or to a disturbing airport, but a megalopolis cannot. It cannot operate without one or more airports and it must contain all sorts of industries. How can it refuse oil refineries or other major industries which define the existence of many more industries inside its area? A megalopolis must encompass all functions, including the most disturbing ones. This means that many of its areas, and particularly Naturareas, are in great danger from all kinds of pollution. The high densities of people in the megalopolis in relation to other areas of the same country also threaten Nature. The threat to Nature is greater in a megalopolis than anywhere else (Fig. 49).

111. *Nature is in greater danger in a megalopolis than anywhere else.*

Networks are the key element to the successful operation of a megalopolis. This is not yet understood, and as yet there are no coordinated Networks any-

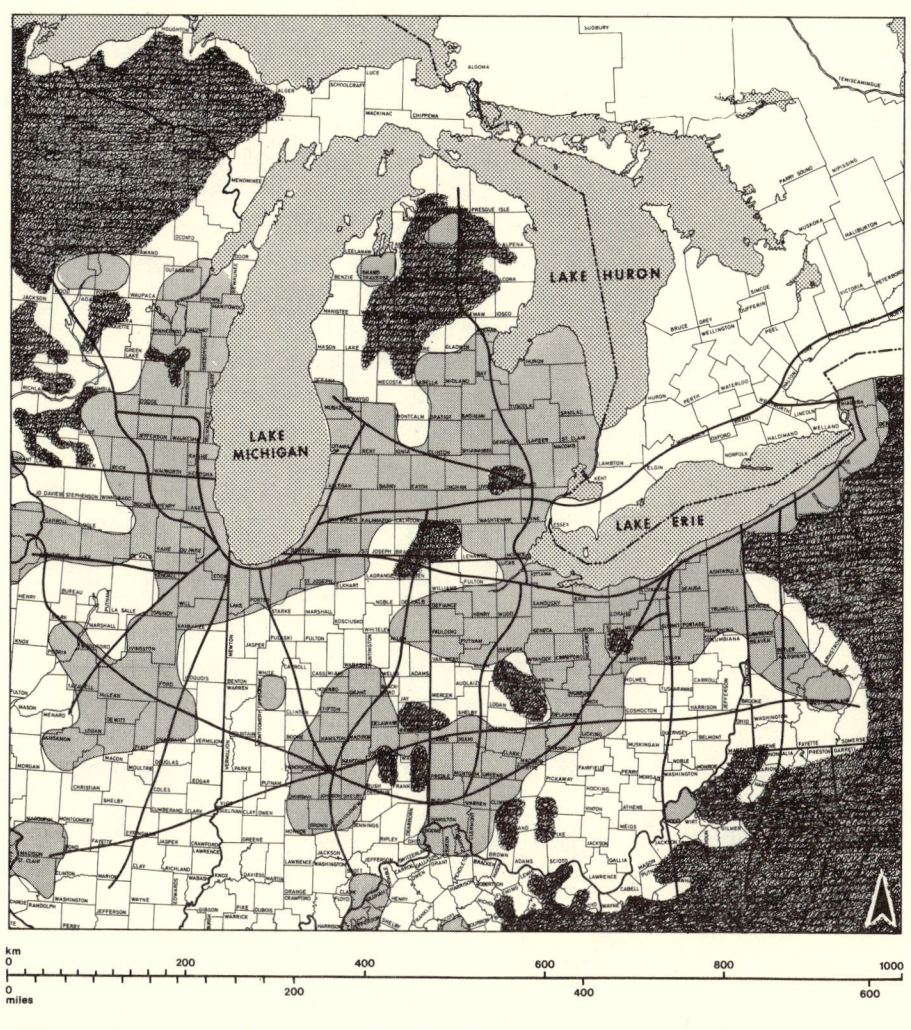

Anthroparea
Naturarea

49. Existing Naturareas and Anthropareas in the Great Lakes
    Megalopolis

where. For example, there are more airports inside a megalopolis than needed because smaller distances could be served very well by high-speed trains, which could form the backbone of the megalopolis. This has occurred in the Japanese megalopolis, which has taken the first step in the proper direction, but it has to take many more. A greater problem arises from the lack of any coordination of different types of Networks, as in the case of the metropolis. This lack of coordination leads to solutions which waste land as well as money.

112. *The greatest problem of Networks is their complete lack of coordination into a unified system in terms of operation and physical structure. Both Networks and Nature suffer from this enormously.*

The third problem element is Society. It suffers because humans as individuals form the megalopolis by their innumerable actions, but do not recognize its existence as an organized Society. When a corporation decides where to place its new warehouses it selects the location that best serves as many of its concerns as possible. This means a location strengthening the axis between the most important metropolises. In this way a new axis of the megalopolis gradually is formed. Many private actions will strengthen the development of the new axis, but there is no official recognition of this fact. Official recognition that a megalopolis is being formed must be made in order to assist and co-ordinate action. A megalopolis is a human settlement consisting of several metropolises, each in turn consisting of several polises. This is a fact. But because Society does not recognize it officially there is no territorial organization. The system remains without coordination, which alone could help its rational development.

113. *The failure officially to recognize the birth and growth of megalopolises means that many necessary measures, especially the organization of territory, are not taken.*

6. National systems

The problems at a national level are the most difficult, because at this level almost all types of human settlements can be found, enormously increasing the complexity. In Part One we have seen how carefully the analysis of the national systems of human settlements must be made in order to understand the confusing situation. Although several countries have national housing programs, no national program or authority deals with the problems of all human settlements and all their elements.

114. *Our most difficult problem at the national level is that we are not yet prepared to deal with the national situations of human settlements.*

We must proceed with a full analysis of the overall situation, beginning with geography and finishing with the human aspect, as we have seen in Part One. By using a grid having on the horizontal scale types of human settlements and

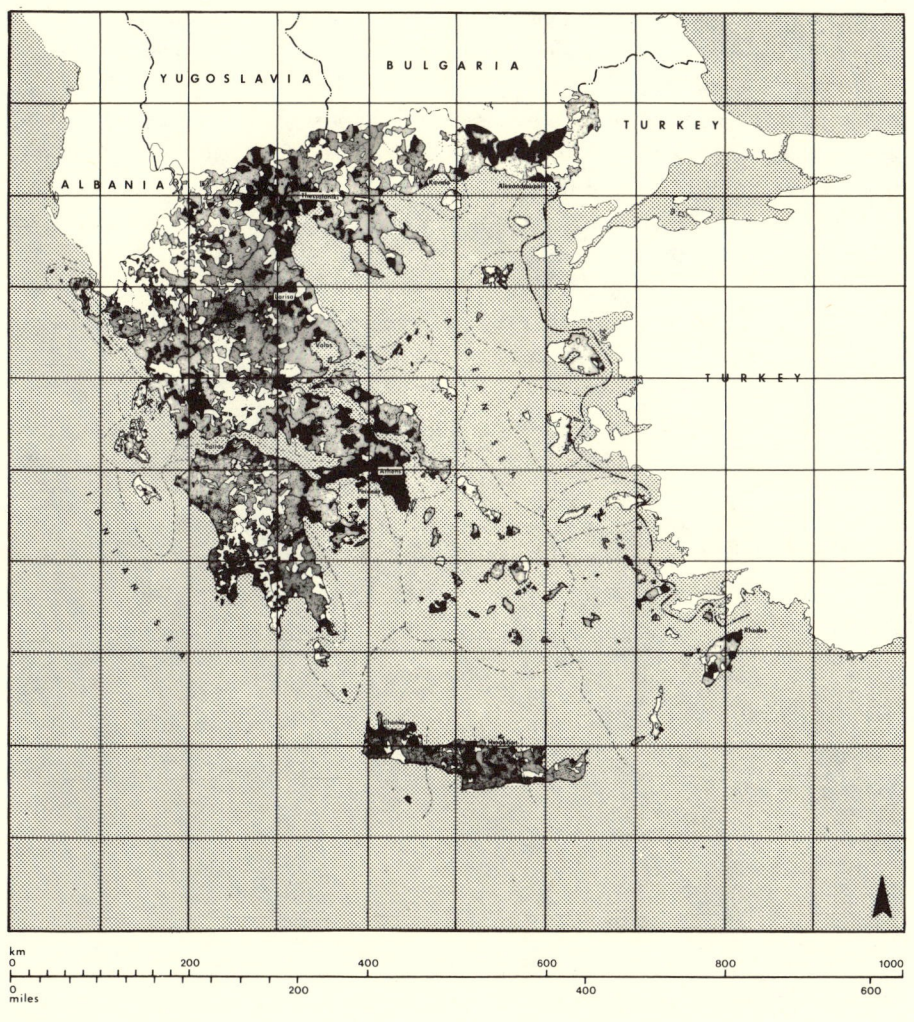

Percentage increase

■ 0 - 30

Percentage decrease

☐ 0 - 30

☐ 30 and above

50. Changing patterns of human settlements in Greece 1961-1971

on the vertical scale the five ekistic elements we can classify the major problems (Fig. 51). We can, for example, state that the greatest problem in villages is that they are abandoned because of very poor soil without irrigation, or that the greatest problem in metropolises is the poor housing for newcomers. In fact, both problems are results of the same cause: the poor soil expels villagers who move to metropolises where there is inadequate housing for them because the metropolises are also suffering. We need to understand the interconnection of problems to classify them properly.

115.   *In order to understand and classify national human settlement problems, we must analyze them in a manner which combines their different types with the five elements.*

After doing this analysis we can deal with the problems in the following way:

1. We must form an opinion about their national order of priority. If, for example, we first solve the problem of inadequate housing for the poor in the metropolises, we may increase the speed at which the villages are abandoned, thereby creating more problems for the nation as a whole.

2. When their order of priority has been determined, we can measure the numbers of people affected by the problems. This is not easy to do. It is not, for example, only the people who leave a village who suffer; those who remain may suffer far more from the village's decline.

kinds of human settlements / the 5 elements	temporary human settlements	villages	town or polis	metropolis	megalopolis	national system of human settlements	international system of human settlements
Nature							
Anthropos							
Society							
Shells							
Networks							

51.   Territorial units and ekistic elements

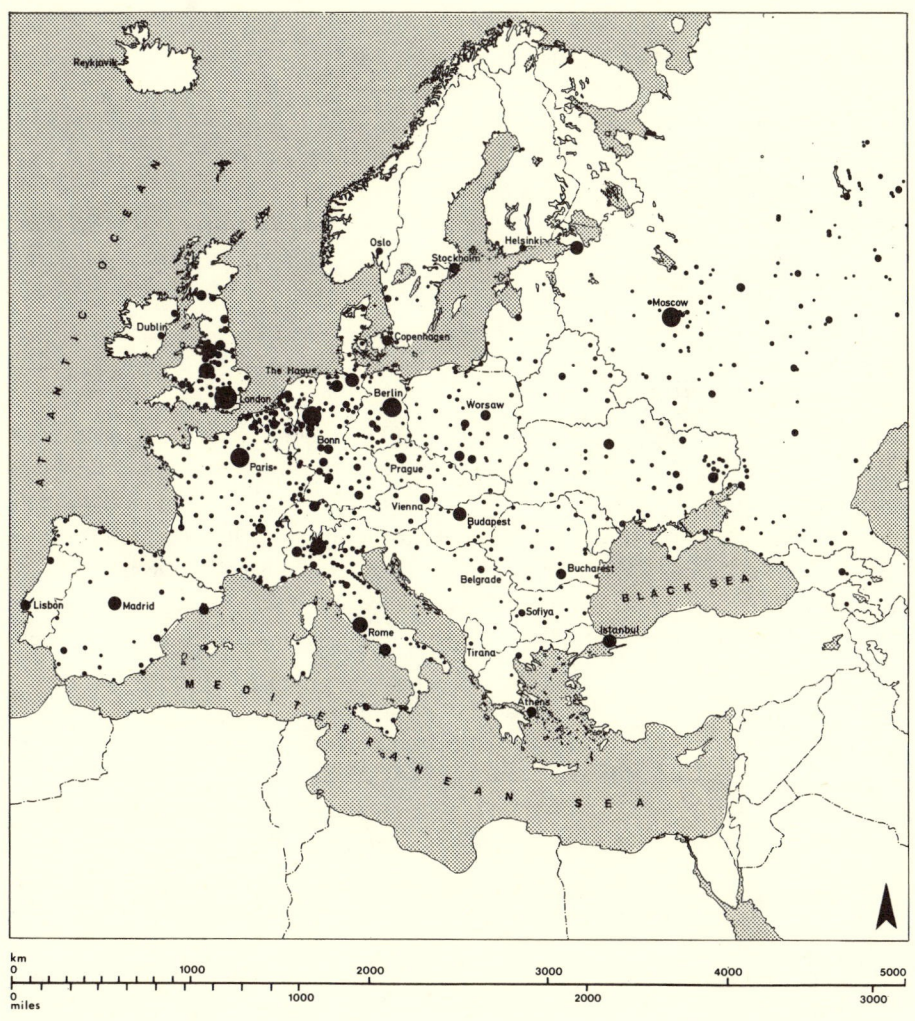

Population:

·	50,000 -	100,000
·	100,000 -	200,000
·	200,000 -	500,000
·	500,000 -	1,000,000
●	1,000,000 -	2,000,000
●	2,000,000 -	5,000,000
●	5,000,000 -	10,000,000
●	10,000,000 and over	

52. Human settlements in Europe

3. By adding the national importance to the number of people affected by a problem we will express the national degree of, for example, village abandonment and inadequate housing.

4. We can then prepare tables, enabling us for the first time to comprehend the overall situation at the national scale. Only then can we discuss goals, policies, and programs.

116. *Classifying and evaluating the problems, and measuring the real numbers of people affected by them, is the only way to form an accurate image of their importance at the national level.*

7. International systems

The situation on the international scale is highly complex because of the vast differences in population size, territory, income, development, political organization, and culture, covering a greater range of problems than in any single nation (Fig. 52). In spite of the difficulty, the international community sooner or later must understand and face the problems on the international scale. It will be difficult, but it must be done.

117. *Classifying and evaluating the problems and measuring the real numbers of people affected by them is the only way to form an image of their relative importance at the international level.*

How can we stimulate international action to define our problems? First we must understand each other; we must accept a systematic approach to be uniformly applied.

118. *We must understand each other before we can successfully undertake any international effort for human settlements. To do this we must accept the statements made so far, for without them there is no hope for international cooperation.*

By this I do not mean that I insist on acceptance of my proposals. I do, however, mean that we need a systematic approach, and I have worked one out. If any points are unacceptable, then they should be replaced by better ones, but we must have a systematic approach if we are to overcome our confusion.

D. A model for problems

To clarify how these ideas about models can be applied, I have selected, as an example, a study of the Detroit Daily Urban System.

The problems of the urban Detroit area can be systematically classified by ekistic units, locating them and identifying them with their population size. Such a classification is needed to set priorities for action and to evaluate the meaning and importance of proposed development plans.

Forty problems related to the urban Detroit area are classified in Figure 53

Figure 53 — Ekistic grid classifying the main problems and needs of the urban Detroit area. Columns: EKISTIC UNITS 1–15 and COMMUNITY CLASS I–XII.

EKISTIC UNITS →				1 MAN	2 ROOM	3 DWELLING	4 DWELLING GROUP	5 SMALL NEIGHBORHOOD	6 NEIGHBORHOOD	7 SMALL TOWN	8 TOWN (CBD's)	9 LARGE CITY (CITIES)	10 METROPOLIS (SUB-REGIONS)	11 CONURBATION (UDA)	12 MEGALOPOLIS (GLM)	13 URBAN REGION (USA AND CANADA)	14 URBANIZED CONTINENT	15 ECUMENOPOLIS
COMMUNITY CLASS → MAIN PROBLEMS & NEEDS							I	II	III	IV	V	VI	VII	VIII	IX	X	XI	XII
NATURE / Natural Environment		N1	UNFAVORABLE CLIMATE IN GLM				◉	◉	◉	◉	◉	◉	◉	◉	◉	◉		
		N2	DESPOLIATION OF LAND RESOURCES AT ALL SCALES					◉	◉	◉	◉	◉	◉	◉	○			
		N3	LACK OF RECREATIONAL AREAS AT ALL SCALES					◉	◉	◉	◉	◉	◉	◉				
		N4	POLLUTION OF WATER AT ALL SCALES					◉	◉	◉	◉	◉	◉	◉	◉	◉		
		N5	POLLUTION OF AIR AT ALL SCALES				◉	◉	◉	◉	◉	◉	◉	○				
MAN / Demography		M1	GROWTH RATES IN GLM AND UDA FALLING BELOW NATIONAL AVERAGE										○	◉	◉			
		M2	DECLINING GROWTH RATE IN CENTRAL REGION									○	◉	○	○			
		M3	DECLINING POPULATION IN CENTRAL AREAS								◉	◉	○	○				
SOCIETY / Socio-Economic Structure		S1	HIGH RELIANCE OF UDA ECONOMY ON A SINGLE SECTOR									○	◉	◉	◉			
		S2	UNDERDEVELOPED SERVICES SECTOR IN UDA									○	◉	◉	◉			
		S3	LOW PERCENTAGE OF WHITE COLLAR WORKERS IN UDA									◉	◉	○	◉			
		S4	LOW EDUCATIONAL ATTAINMENT IN CENTRAL REGION									◉	◉	○	◉			
		S5	DECLINE OF INCOME IN CENTRAL AREAS								◉	◉	◉	○				
		S6	DECLINE OF RETAIL SALES IN CENTRAL AREAS								◉	◉	◉	○				
		S7	DECLINE OF OTHER ECONOMIC ACTIVITIES IN CENTRAL AREAS								◉	◉	◉	○				
		S8	DECLINE OF TAX BASE IN CENTRAL AREAS								◉	◉	◉	○				
		S9	ECONOMIC SEGREGATION							◉	◉	◉	◉	○				
		S10	RACIAL SEGREGATION							◉	◉	◉	◉	○				
		S11	INCREASING GAP OF CHOICES BETWEEN GROUPS OF PEOPLE							◉	◉	◉	◉	◉				
		S12	SEGREGATION OF AGE GROUPS IN CFA							◉	◉	◉	◉	○				
		S13	OTHER PROBLEMS OF SOCIAL IMPORTANCE					◉	◉	◉	◉	◉	◉	◉	●			
NETWORKS / Physical Structure		P1	NEED TO COORDINATE UDA'S LAND CONNECTIONS WITH ITS WIDER REGION											◉	◉	◉		
		P2	NEED TO COORDINATE UDA'S UTILITY NETWORKS WITH THOSE OF THE WIDER REGION											◉	◉	◉		
		P3	NEED FOR BETTER CONNECTION OF WESTERN MICHIGAN AND THE UPPER PENINSULA WITH UDA											◉	◉			
		P4	LIMITED DEVELOPMENT OF WATER TRANSPORTATION									○	◉	◉	◉	○		
		P5	INADEQUATE FACILITIES TO MEET NEW DEMANDS OF AIR TRANSPORTATION									○	◉	◉	◉	○		
		P6	NEED FOR NEW ORGANIZATION FOR THE LAND TRANSPORTATION SYSTEM IN UDA									○	◉	◉	○			
		P7	NEED TO COORDINATE UTILITY NETWORKS WITHIN UDA									○	◉	◉	○			
		P8	DISORGANIZED EXPANSION OF THE URBAN CENTERS OF UDA									○	◉	◉				
		P9	THE DETROIT CENTRAL CITY SUFFERS AS THE CENTER OF A DISORGANIZED SYSTEM								●	◉	◉	○	○			
SHELLS		P10	POOR HOUSING CONDITIONS IN CENTRAL CITIES				●	●	◉	◉	◉	◉	○	○				
		P11	NEED FOR COMMUNITY ORGANIZATION					◉	◉	◉	◉	◉	○					
		P12	INADEQUATE FUNCTIONING OF THE CBD'S OF CENTRAL CITIES								◉	◉	○	○				
		P13	LACK OF SAFETY AND SECURITY IN THE CENTRAL AREAS					◉	◉	◉	◉	◉	◉					
		P14	LOSS OF HUMAN SCALE				◉	◉	◉	◉	◉	○						
GENERAL / Institutional Structure		G1	NEED FOR A GLM AGENCY												◉			
		G2	NEED FOR A UDA AGENCY											◉				
		G3	NEED FOR AN OVERALL DEVELOPMENT PLAN AND PROGRAM FOR UDA											◉				
		G4	NEED FOR SUBREGIONAL PLANS AND PROGRAMS										◉					
		G5	NEED FOR LOCAL PLANS AND PROGRAMS FOR DEVELOPING AREAS							◉	◉	◉	◉	○				
NUMBER OF PROBLEMS ENCOUNTERED AT EACH SCALE							3	10	10	11	14	23	31	30	32	12	5	

NOTE: Generally the problems listed above are related to the physical elements of the settlements. Thus, under Society, only those socio-economic problems related to physical structure are included.

- • units where problem exists
- ○ units where problem is generated
- ◯ units where action should be taken

53. The ekistic grid classifying the main problems and needs of the urban Detroit area

in 6 ekistic elements and 15 ekistic units. A unit may be associated with a particular problem because the source of the problem is located within the unit, because the unit is affected by the problem, or for both of these reasons. The 40 problems shown in Figure 53 are associated with 181 units or groups of units. Of these problems, 5 refer to Nature, 3 to Anthropos (in respect to demographic pheonomena), 13 to Society, 9 to Networks, 5 to Shells, and 5 are considered problems of a general nature. The following pages analyze them in greater detail.

Nature

The climate in the urban Detroit area does not attract population from other parts of the country. Furthermore, it will get worse, for experts predict that the world climate will be coldest 20 to 30 years from now before gradually warming to its hottest in a century's time.

The topographic and geological features of the urban Detroit area have not impeded the expansion of its urban centers, with the possible exception of certain small areas with high water tables and poor drainage. This expansion in virtually all directions, combined with the lack of an adequate conservation policy, has resulted in a reduction of agricultural land and a despoliation of land resources in general, especially in the immediate vicinity of existing urbanized sections. There are, however, ample land resources for urban development.

Although large tracts of land have been reserved throughout the urban Detroit area for recreational activities, the distribution of these areas is uneven. There is a significant lack of park and recreational open space within the residential communities, particularly in the more urbanized counties. Many central areas, in fact, have no land resources left for recreational purposes. This problem is expected to become more serious as the population increases and its demand for such activities multiplies as it increases income, mobility, and leisure time.

Although the urban Detroit area has enough water resources to meet the needs of urban development for the foreseeable future, the quality of this water is threatened by industrial waste. In many areas immediate drastic action is required.

The threat to air is not yet as great as the threat to water, but in the central region the problem is critical. The problem has many aspects, three of which are economic (the cost of the damage caused by air pollution and the cost of its prevention), social (it is more serious in industrial zones adjacent to low income residential areas), and esthetic (damage to the beauty of the environment).

Anthropos

In both the urban Detroit area and in the Great Lakes Megalopolis as a whole immigration was responsible for the fast population growth at rates well above the United States average until the late 1950s. Since then these two areas have been experiencing both emigration and a decline in their natural rate of population increase, causing their population growth to drop below the national average.

Since 1960 emigration has been evident in most metropolitan areas and particularly in the center of Detroit. This recent development causes concern because in the past immigration gave the center of Detroit the highest rate of population growth in the urban Detroit area. The seriousness of this problem is increased by the probability that net emigration involves the loss of some of the strongest elements of the population, especially the young and the educated.

In the heart of the central region decline may be measured in terms of loss in population, income, and business, and is reflected in the deterioration of its physical structure. This deterioration is not only of its physical structure, but is reflected in the isolation of this area from the remaining central city. Indeed, the most characteristic expression of this deterioration are the expressways which have broken up the physical continuity of the central city.

Society

The economy of the urban Detroit area is primarily oriented toward manufacturing, which in 1960 absorbed 39 percent of total employment. The center of Detroit is even more specialized, with 40 percent employment in manufacturing, most of which is automotive manufacturing. This heavy reliance on a single sector of economic activity, manufacturing, and, furthermore, on one, the automobile, industry, disrupts the area's economy. Although the urban Detroit area has been prosperous during periods of national boom, it has been extremely vulnerable to downturns of the economic cycle.

This unbalanced economic structure has stunted development of the services sector. Although there has been a marked increase in service employment in the urban Detroit area since 1950, nevertheless this sector represented only 59 percent of total employment in 1960, compared to 65 percent for the United States as a whole.

In 1960 the percentage of white collar workers in the urban Detroit area was 18.9 percent, lower than the United States average of 19.6 percent.

The manufacturing base has earned the urban Detroit area higher per capita incomes than the national average. Within the center of Detroit, however, the movement of the higher income groups to the suburbs has caused a decline of aggregate income. It also has intensified the decentralization of business and trade and created commercial centers on the periphery of the central region. The rapid development of these regional retail centers, such as Northland on the outskirts of the city of Detroit, has attracted a substantial portion of the city's consumers, reducing the central region's importance as a major retail center.

Deterioration in the physical environment and loss of business in the city of Detroit have caused a steady decline in land values since 1930 (Fig. 54). In 1963 new capital investment in manufacturing in the city of Detroit was 45.9 percent lower than in 1954. In the center the number of retail establishments is declining. Generally speaking, the nearer one gets to the center the fewer activities there are. The closer one comes to the area where one would expect life of high intensity and quality, the lower it actually is.

In the city of Detroit the loss in population and income has caused a sharp decline in its tax base and, consequently, in its ability to provide the services which would strengthen its economy and aid its functioning as the cultural and economic heart of the urban system.

The continuous outward movement of the economically privileged groups from the center to the periphery of the metropolitan areas, combined with the influx of low income families into the core, has caused segregation by income group. This segregation is the main cause of the multiple social problems evident

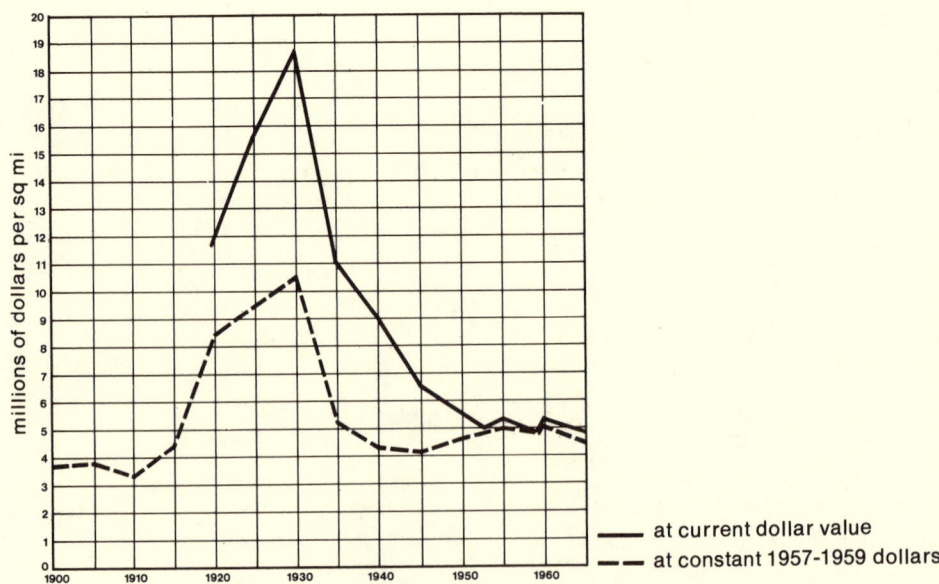

54. Evolution of land values

today in the core. If present trends continue, the low income inner zones of the core are expected to become even more isolated from the rest of the urban system.

In a small settlement all the people, old or young, rich or poor, meet one another on the streets. They all have the same possibilities for contacts and the same possibilities to visit all places within their settlement. In the contemporary large settlement, however, some people are free to make almost any contact they choose, and others are not. This is not caused by racial discrimination alone, but also by economic discrimination as is shown, for example, by a low percentage of car ownership among the population of the urban settlement which does not have readily available mass transit.

Racial segregation and the growing conflict among racial groups is a major problem in all American cities today. The inhabitants of a large settlement come in contact with a great number of other people every day, thereby running a much higher risk of encountering conflict than do the inhabitants of a village. Imbalances and disparities become more evident as people's mobility increases, becoming a major source of conflict when it involves great numbers of people. People avoid contacts they do not like by segregating themselves. The rich create their own ghettos in the suburbs, leaving the poor in ghettos in the city centers.

Among the people moving out from the central areas of Detroit are the younger and most active segments of the population. This is particularly evident in the central functions area, which has become dominated by older people and is being deprived of the services that would cater to a younger population, stimulate greater vitality, and attract people of all age groups.

Many social problems may not, however, be directly related to the structure of the city. These would include problems involving the population as a whole, such as public health, education, welfare, and those referring to special groups, such as the creation of a proper environment for children. Whether directly related to the overall urban system or not, these problems, if not properly dealt with, can harm the city. They also must be included when we deal with the socio-economic structure of the city.

Networks

The urban Detroit area and its connections are more local than regional in structure, making it difficult for Detroit to take advantage of its privileged position within the Great Lakes Megalopolis, even hindering its participation within the megalopolis. They must change, therefore, to another structure. In essence this requires reorganization of the regional axes of land transportation, creating a new framework for the development of other, both local and regional, functions. The lack of an overall development plan to reorganize its connections with the wider region is the urban Detroit area's most important problem.

Regional utility networks are expanding over ever greater areas. The lack of a plan coordinating these regional networks among themselves and with the Great Lakes Megalopolis has caused undesirable effects in the countryside and in many settlements where permanent commitments have been made. Apart from the economic and organizational repercussions, such a lack of coordination often wastes natural resources and ruins scenic areas.

The urban Detroit area is not taking sufficient advantage of the Great Lakes water system, for 90 percent of the tonnage exported from Michigan overseas is routed overland to coastal ports. The use of other Great Lakes ports also is threatened by other means of transportation, even for such usually water-borne commodities as coal. This situation is expected to worsen because considerable dredging is needed before the Great Lakes will be accessible to large containerized ocean-going ships.

The existing airport facilities in the urban Detroit area can not meet the demands of new technological developments or even serve local needs adequately, although the location of the urban Detroit area within the Great Lakes Megalopolis is particularly favorable.

The land transportation network does not function satisfactorily, especially in the more developed parts of the system. Continuation of present trends would mean continued expansion of a system developed in another era for other needs and a much slower pace of development. Moreover, if the land transportation system is left to grow as it has been growing, it will keep pace with technological development with increasing difficulty and will further suffocate the central urban Detroit area.

Utility networks face similar difficulties, particularly in the central urban Detroit area, because of the uncoordinated, haphazard development of the urban system and the regional utility networks. The situation will worsen if all Networks are not coordinated on the basis of an overall development plan.

Growth continues to take place along the periphery of the existing urban centers, particularly of those urban centers along the basic axes of development. Such development, which usually occurs without planning even at the local level, is at a very low density. As a result, the urban centers are being strangled by the multiplying rings of low density development. Basic functions decentralize and spread over the periphery to serve the continually outward moving low density development. This is happening at a time when the urban Detroit area needs strong centers to develop a more service oriented structure.

The effect of the above problems on Detroit has been the breakdown of its urban system into three distinct parts, each isolated from the other two and each with different conditions. These parts are the central area, the remaining area of Detroit, and the outer urban zone. If present trends continue, much of the future growth of the urban Detroit area will continue to be at the periphery of the central area with haphazard, low density development. This will create additional pressures on an already congested urban system, the central areas of which will deteriorate further and become more isolated from the outer areas.

The center of Detroit has the most severe symptoms of decline. It is fragmented by major roads and suffocated by the surrounding industrial rings. The old land uses and the main infrastructure of the core, which were created for a much smaller urban organism, have erected physical barriers between the old center and the rest of the city. The center suffers from its proximity to industry and from industrial traffic flowing through residential streets. Some residential districts have developed near factories and railroads, areas more suitable for industrial use. Some industrial plants, on the other hand, have become isolated by changes in the surrounding land uses, leaving them relatively inaccessible and with no room to expand. Commercial enterprises which follow the alignment of major roads often disrupt the continuity of residential areas and create parking problems on residential streets.

Shells

The quality of housing in Detroit is bad. Few new residential units are being built, and of the 353,000 existing residential structures in the administrative city of Detroit, approximately 50,000, 14 percent, are blighted, and much of the rest is becoming so.

Disorganized development has created problems for the proper distribution of essential community facilities such as schools, commercial centers, libraries, and theaters. Detroit also lacks an internal organization based on a system of self-contained communities with a well-balanced distribution of public services and functions.

Large open parking lots have greatly contributed to the physical decline of the environment by filling the area with ugly gaps which discourage pedestrian circulation and shoppers, and by creating security problems. Such areas cannot be adequately policed, especially after dark, since law offenders have many outlets for escape.

The loss of human scale is particularly evident. The roads and built-up areas are dominated by the automobile, forcing the pedestrian to co-exist with the machine. Another factor which has contributed to the loss of human scale within the urbanized area is the creation of multi-story buildings for residential use. In these buildings people are physically isolated from each other but exposed to one another's noise. Although these multi-story residential buildings are usually created in highly urbanized areas and are supposed to be of high density, usually no effort is made to ensure the continuity of built-up and open spaces which is essential for an attractive urban environment. Instead, high-rise apartment buildings are intermingled with low-rise single-family dwellings isolated from each other, while large open spaces and parking lots are created between them. The result is that people in the city feel isolated, out of place, and insecure, especially at night.

Conclusions

In defining the problems of the urban Detroit area it became obvious that most of them would have to be dealt with at a level higher than that of the urban Detroit area. The study of urban development in the Great Lakes area has revealed the evolution of a megalopolitan formation extending across several states from Illinois to New York and even into Canada. A planning process, therefore, should start at a higher level, but no authority to undertake such an effort exists. If the future growth of the Great Lakes Megalopolis is to be properly guided and its component parts provided with an overall coordinated plan for their functional participation, the establishment of an appropriate institutional framework for this effort is of immediate importance.

While some plans have been formulated covering partial phenomena, such as highways, utilities, and their networks for parts of the urban Detroit area, they do not provide an overall conception of its future organization. This is the most serious overall problem of the urban Detroit area, and it is expected to become more serious as more growth is added to present development.

At the local level, urban growth has in many cases been proceeding without the guidance of comprehensive master plans. In those units in which the planning process has already been initiated, the lack of overall as well as regional plans and programs has impeded coordination among them. The problem is most urgent in those areas now entering the period of urban growth. In such areas, which are not yet extensively developed, excellent opportunities are presented for properly planned growth if immediate action is taken.

Part Three

Goals for Human Settlements

A. Ultimate and immediate goals

When we begin discussing goals we must clarify a very basic question: What goals are we talking about, the goals for tomorrow, for twenty-five years from now, or for one hundred years in the future? If we do not give dimensions to the future we can not hope to make any reasonable statement about it.

What goals should we set in this study of human settlements? If the study were for a certain city or even for a certain nation we could give a specific answer after careful study of the case. But this is not possible at the international level where every problem applies to millions of cases, each with a different timetable for realizing its goal. If some people are homeless because of an earthquake, our goal is to house them immediately. If people have houses but no telephones or poor traffic connections, the time schedule can be different. Unless we have a thorough understanding of each case, we cannot define goals in terms of either time or content.

But what can and must be achieved is to establish the process for setting goals and to give enough examples to illustrate the cases everyone must face everyday. We must start with the dimension of time and be certain that we know what our ultimate goals are. If our goal is to give every family the chance to build a complete house with up to five rooms, there is no hope of ever achieving it if we give them one room in a very small plot. Where will they build the other four rooms? By defining ultimate goals we are also including the dimension of time. If we speak of a family-built one-story house we really mean a one-generation house, because the family may move, and the neighborhood itself may require two- or three-story houses. Our ultimate goals should be long term ones.

119. *The practical way to deal with goals in terms of time dimensions and contents is to set the ultimate and immediate goals.*

The big question is how far ahead we should look when setting the ultimate goals. In 1820 the ultimate goal of human mobility would have been for every family to own a horse-drawn cart. By 1830, after the first railroad was developed, the goal would have been to give every family the opportunity to use a train. Later, the goals would have been shifted to access to a good underground metro, to one car per family or one car per person. The lesson is clear: When we speak of ultimate goals we must set them in terms of the foreseeable future. If we attempt to plan too far ahead we risk employing vague ideas which may be unrealizable or unrealistic.

120.   *Ultimate goals must be set for the foreseeable future in a realistic way.*

This usually involves a process based on proper economic and population projections, leading to accurate estimates of what can be achieved. Since some projections may be affected by unpredictable events, we must proceed with the predictable and be intellectually ready to adjust our goals when the unpredict-

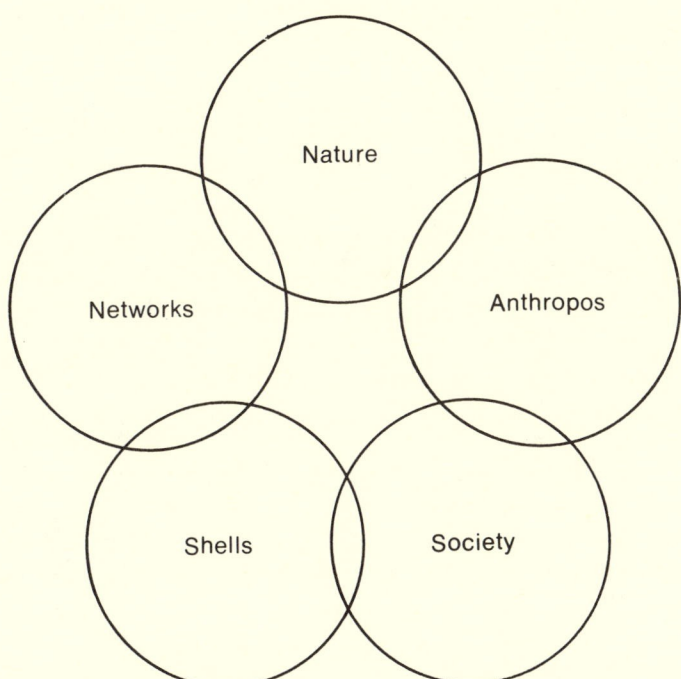

55.   The goal of ekistics is to achieve a balance among the elements of human settlements in order to guarantee happiness and safety for Anthropos.

able happens. Such considerations usually confine us to a time limit of one generation because recent history has clearly shown that within each generation the situation changes greatly.

There are, however, many sectors in which projections must be made for longer periods, even if changes have to be made later. For example, unless long term predictions are made about the direction of growth of a human settlement, many basic functions, such as the installation of power or telephone lines, will develop without any overall guidance. Without guidance a chaotic situation will result, since every authority and company will place its own Networks in a different way.

121.　*Ultimate goals must cover a wide range of time, ranging from one generation to a considerably longer period.*

For example, we do not know how many monuments of the past we will find, so we cannot predict how many will need to be saved. Many countries have a very important past which is still buried underground or exists in the form of later buildings which must be preserved. The ultimate goal should be a general expression covering many areas, from serving the existing generation in a very specific way to providing for general human needs. We can even speak of the eventual realization of dreams if we express them in a way that is not utopian but entopian, that is, in a way that someday can be implemented.

Although ultimate goals are fundamental for long term planning, they can be detrimental to immediate action. Immediate action requires short term goals. The complete effort requires a systematic approach by which both the ultimate and the immediate goals can be properly interconnected (Fig. 56).

When we speak of immediate goals we mean that immediate action is necessary because people or Nature are suffering. When people are homeless, the only reasonable goal is to house them immediately, even if in tents. When a coastal area in which people swim is polluted by the large number of ships entering it, the only reasonable thing to do is to stop the entrance of polluting ships.

122.　*The immediate goal is whatever can start being implemented at once.*

Not every immediate goal can be immediately implemented, but action can be started promptly and the goal achieved quickly. The immediate goal may not be the best solution for the problem, but it is the most practical solution in terms of time. Most problems have various possible goals with small differences in the time they will take to be implemented, the cost, and the services they will provide. Selection of the immediate goal is not easy. Do we prefer a goal that can be completed sooner but serve fewer people, or a goal that may be completed later but serve more people? There is no methodological approach to the selection of goals. While there is plenty of time to consider ultimate goals, there is no such time to consider immediate goals. In some ways the immediate goal is only the beginning of the long process of attaining the ultimate goal.

EKISTIC UNITS

	Designation of Units	1 MAN	2 ROOM	3 DWELLING	4 DWELLING GROUP	5 SMALL NEIGHBORHOOD	6 NEIGHBORHOOD	7 SMALL TOWN	8 TOWN	9 LARGE CITY	10 METROPOLIS	11 CONURBATION	12 MEGALOPOLIS	13 URBAN REGION	14 URBANIZED CONTINENT	15 ECUMENOPOLIS

DESIGNATION OF UNITS AND CORRESPONDING STUDY AREAS — CBD's (9), CITIES (10), SUB-REGIONS (11), UDA (12), GLM (13), USA AND CANADA (14)

COMMUNITY CLASS: I, II, III, IV, V, VI, VII, VIII, IX, X, XI, XII

PROBLEMS REQUIRING IMMEDIATE ACTION FOR VARIOUS REASONS

MAIN PROBLEMS & NEEDS

NATURE — Natural Environment
- N1 UNFAVORABLE CLIMATE IN GLM
- N2 DESPOLIATION OF LAND RESOURCES AT ALL SCALES
- N3 LACK OF RECREATIONAL AREAS AT ALL SCALES
- N4 POLLUTION OF WATER AT ALL SCALES
- N5 POLLUTION OF AIR AT ALL SCALES

MAN — Demography
- M1 GROWTH RATES IN GLM AND UDA FALLING BELOW NATIONAL AVERAGE
- M2 DECLINING GROWTH RATE IN CENTRAL REGION
- M3 DECLINING POPULATION IN CENTRAL AREAS

SOCIETY — Socio-Economic Structure
- S1 HIGH RELIANCE OF UDA ECONOMY ON A SINGLE SECTOR
- S2 UNDERDEVELOPED SERVICES SECTOR IN UDA
- S3 LOW PERCENTAGE OF WHITE COLLAR WORKERS IN UDA
- S4 LOW EDUCATIONAL ATTAINMENT IN CENTRAL REGION
- S5 DECLINE OF INCOME IN CENTRAL AREAS
- S6 DECLINE OF RETAIL SALES IN CENTRAL AREAS
- S7 DECLINE OF OTHER ECONOMIC ACTIVITIES IN CENTRAL AREAS
- S8 DECLINE OF TAX BASE IN CENTRAL AREAS
- S9 ECONOMIC SEGREGATION
- S10 RACIAL SEGREGATION
- S11 INCREASING GAP OF CHOICES BETWEEN GROUPS OF PEOPLE
- S12 SEGREGATION OF AGE GROUPS IN CFA
- S13 OTHER PROBLEMS OF SOCIAL IMPORTANCE

NETWORKS — Physical Structure
- P1 NEED TO COORDINATE UDA'S LAND CONNECTIONS WITH ITS WIDER REGION
- P2 NEED TO COORDINATE UDA'S UTILITY NETWORKS WITH THOSE OF THE WIDER REGION
- P3 NEED FOR BETTER CONNECTION OF WESTERN MICHIGAN AND THE UPPER PENINSULA WITH UDA
- P4 LIMITED DEVELOPMENT OF WATER TRANSPORTATION
- P5 INADEQUATE FACILITIES TO MEET NEW DEMANDS OF AIR TRANSPORTATION
- P6 NEED FOR NEW ORGANIZATION FOR THE LAND TRANSPORTATION SYSTEM IN UDA
- P7 NEED TO COORDINATE UTILITY NETWORKS WITHIN UDA
- P8 DISORGANIZED EXPANSION OF THE URBAN CENTERS OF UDA
- P9 THE DETROIT CENTRAL CITY SUFFERS AS THE CENTER OF A DISORGANIZED SYSTEM

SHELLS
- P10 POOR HOUSING CONDITIONS IN CENTRAL CITIES
- P11 NEED FOR COMMUNITY ORGANIZATION
- P12 INADEQUATE FUNCTIONING OF THE CBD'S OF CENTRAL CITIES
- P13 LACK OF SAFETY AND SECURITY IN THE CENTRAL AREAS
- P14 LOSS OF HUMAN SCALE

GENERAL — Institutional Structure
- G1 NEED FOR A GLM AGENCY
- G2 NEED FOR A UDA AGENCY
- G3 NEED FOR AN OVERALL DEVELOPMENT PLAN AND PROGRAM FOR UDA
- G4 NEED FOR SUBREGIONAL PLANS AND PROGRAMS
- G5 NEED FOR LOCAL PLANS AND PROGRAMS FOR DEVELOPING AREAS

NUMBER OF PROBLEMS ENCOUNTERED AT EACH SCALE: 3, 10, 10, 11, 14, 23, 31, 30, 32, 12, 5 | 15, 12, 21, 9

NOTE: Generally the problems listed above are related to the physical elements of the settlements. Thus, under Society, only those socio-economic problems related to physical structure are included.

- ● units where problem exists
- ○ units where problem is generated
- ◯ units where action should be taken

- ■ to relieve human distress
- ▨ to create new system of future development according to concept plan
- ▣ to utilize ongoing efforts within new development frame of concept plan
- ▨ to secure balanced overall development

56. The ekistic grid indicating the programs needed to achieve the immediate goals in the urban Detroit area

Although the ultimate goal could be described as another step to the future, such a view can delay real action.

123. *The immediate goal is of the greatest importance and is the first step in the long development process.*

Because the immediate goal is the first step, we must pay great attention to its connection with subsequent goals. If, in order to house villagers made homeless by an earthquake, we move them to a nearby metropolis while we reconstruct the village, we may find that several families will prefer the new way of life in the metropolis. In such a case the immediate goal was successful in that it did provide housing, but it failed since it reduced the population of the village and probably contributed to its decline.

124. *The immediate goal must be the foundation for a sound development process connected with the ultimate goal.*

I repeat that it is of the greatest importance that the two types of goals be connected into one system. If the ultimate goal for the village discussed above is to revive the village because the productivity of the land is promising, it would be a great mistake to rehouse the villagers in the metropolis. It would be much better to bring any kind of shelter to them. On the other hand, if there are signs that the area will cease to prosper, then this is the right occasion to move the people into whatever human settlement is foreseen as the center of the future.

125. *Both the immediate and the ultimate goals are simply two points of a long development process.*

From goals we must move to development processes, programs, and policies, which will be discussed in Part Four. We must set goals instead of proceeding directly to development because we need clear images in our mind. Our actions are much more sound if these images represent specific numbers and not just certain tendencies. A statement that new housing for the poor must be increased at a high rate may not mean much either to the poor without housing or to the people who are in a position to take action. But if we say that at the end of this year there must be 3,000 new houses ready for occupation and that everybody must be housed within thirty years, then specific programs can be put into action.

126. *Although at the end we deal with development processes, we must first express them as goals to be achieved by specific dates, beginning with the immediate and ending with the ultimate goals.*

B. Ekistic elements

1. Nature

When we begin to design goals for Nature we must remember that we cannot think in terms of Nature alone but in terms of Nature in relation to human settlements. Ten thousand years ago human settlements had little effect on Nature, but today human settlements and Nature have to live together.

127. *Our ultimate goal for Nature is to bring it into balance with human settlements.*

The immediate goal should be to stop human aggression against Nature, but this cannot be done. We cannot, for example, immediately stop air pollution caused by motor vehicles, but we can reduce it in the immediate future. It is also impossible to present the exploitation which threatens to eliminate natural resources, for we cannot stop growth.

128. *Our immediate goal for Nature is to control the use of its limited resources.*

The first of the four categories of problems given in Part Two is the elimination of some natural resources. The subject of this study is not how to replace them, but how to deal with the impact of this elimination upon human settlements. The problem is most clearly seen in the effects of various types of mining upon the surface of the land. The ultimate goal in such cases is to plan land use in such a way that, when the mines are abandoned, the land can be used for agriculture, wildlife, human settlements, or as an industrial zone.

129. *In the case of the elimination of natural resources, the ultimate goal is to prepare an environment that can survive forever and the immediate goal is to plan for it. This requires a radical change in our attitude for such cases, a real belief in the future.*

Our goal concerning the temporary elimination of natural resources is the same, but it can be attained much more easily if proper action is taken in time.

130. *The ultimate goal concerning the temporary elimination of natural resources is to plan for a constant, desirable, and feasible environment. The immediate goal is to prepare an action plan in this spirit.*

Next comes the problem of the permanent pollution of natural resources. If the pollution is really permanent, or at least long term, such as is caused by throwing away machines and industrial products which cannot now be recycled, the only reasonable goal is to set apart areas for such pollution until the day when recycling will be possible, at least to the degree that the polluting materials will be turned into non-polluting ones, even if they cannot be reconstituted and

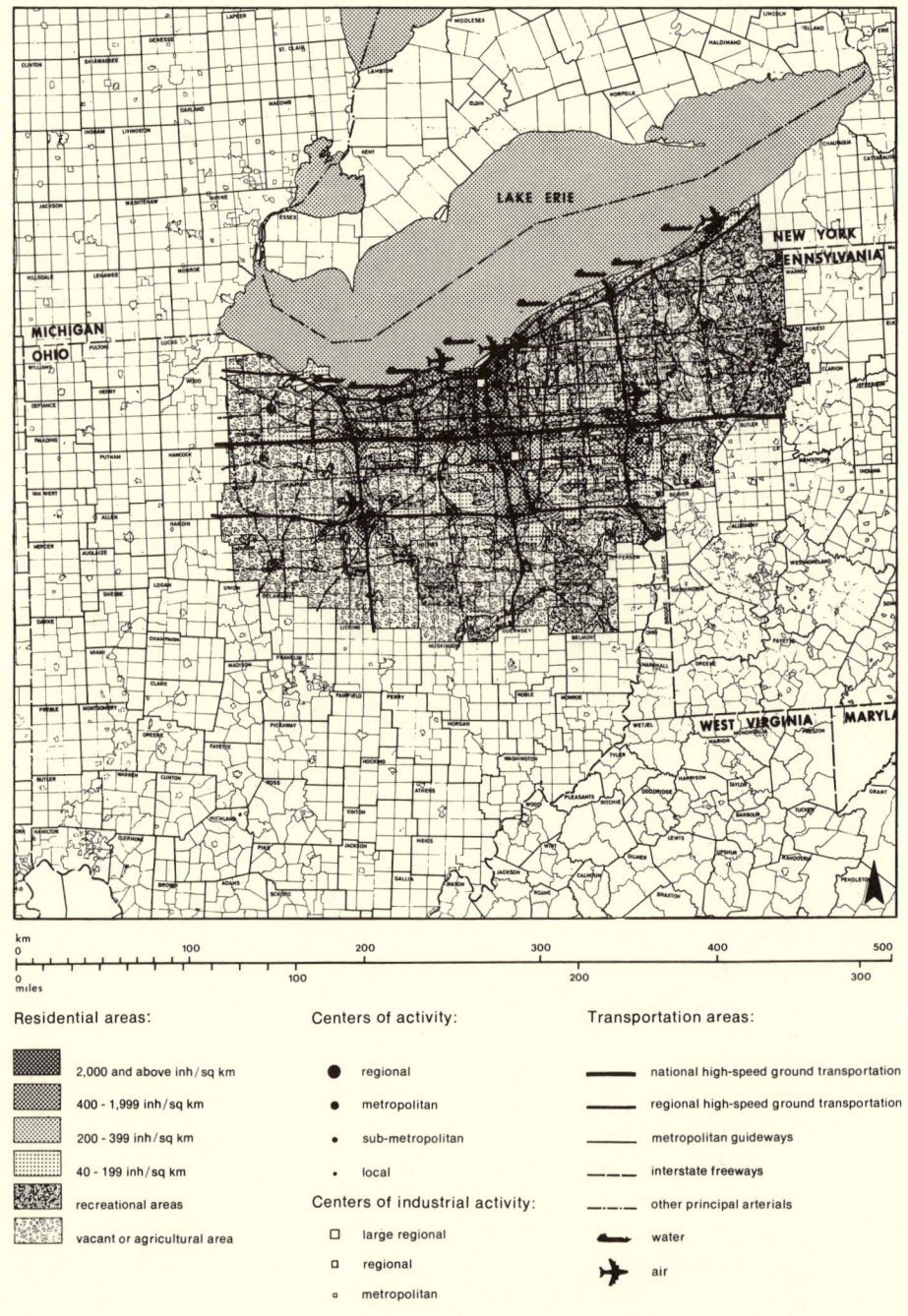

Residential areas:

- 2,000 and above inh/sq km
- 400 - 1,999 inh/sq km
- 200 - 399 inh/sq km
- 40 - 199 inh/sq km
- recreational areas
- vacant or agricultural area

Centers of activity:

- ● regional
- ● metropolitan
- • sub-metropolitan
- · local

Centers of industrial activity:

- ☐ large regional
- ▢ regional
- ▫ metropolitan
- · local

Transportation areas:

- ——— national high-speed ground transportation
- ——— regional high-speed ground transportation
- ——— metropolitan guideways
- – – – interstate freeways
- –·–·– other principal arterials
- ⬤ water
- ✈ air

57. Relationship between urban development and Nature in the Northern Ohio Urban System, U.S.A.

become useful. Large areas of the globe, such as deserts, are non-productive and, although there are many reasons why such areas should remain virgin and never be polluted, we could use a small part of their area, considerably less than one percent, to create special zones for waste disposal. These special zones will remain isolated and create no problems over breader areas. Some day in the future science, technology, and economy will enable us to use these waste disposal zones as industrial or even natural zones, but in the meantime we should avoid the great dangers of permanent pollution by taking the right decisions.

131. *The ultimate goal concerning permanent pollution is the creation of special zones in isolated areas for waste material. The immediate goal is to study these possibilities and prepare the waste zones.*

Problems of temporary pollution are easier to face. Of course, by temporary pollution we are not referring to situations that temporarily affect a given human settlement (where, for example, wind will carry the pollution away), but those pollutions which are temporary for our biosphere because they will change chemically and become harmless.

132. *The ultimate goal concerning temporary pollution is the creation of the technology to relieve us from it. The immediate goal is to start the process now.*

If factories produce smoke that is not dangerous, but simply annoying, there is no reason why a network of underground pipes should not be built in which air currents can carry the smoke miles away to an area where the natural winds will blow it away from human settlements. Humans did this to remove smoke from their homes when they first created fireplaces. Thousands of years ago when people had an income of $ 70 per capita, they solved their smoke pollution problem by creating pipes five and ten meters long. Today the income in many metropolises is $7,000 per capita, so it should be even easier to eliminate temporary pollution by building long pipes to remove the smoke. A similar solution for automobile emissions would be to turn many highways into deepways with the polluted air being absorbed along the channels and set free outside the inhabited areas.

2. Anthropos

The ultimate goal for Anthropos, as Aristotle defined it, is to be happy and safe in his city and to have his polis assist his human development.[1] Though most important, these are general goals. To proceed to action we must be more specific and turn to the two views of Anthropos presented in parts one and two: to consider Anthropos as an individual in terms of the four parts of the human being: body, senses, mind, and psyche. This is the only way to proceed systematically.

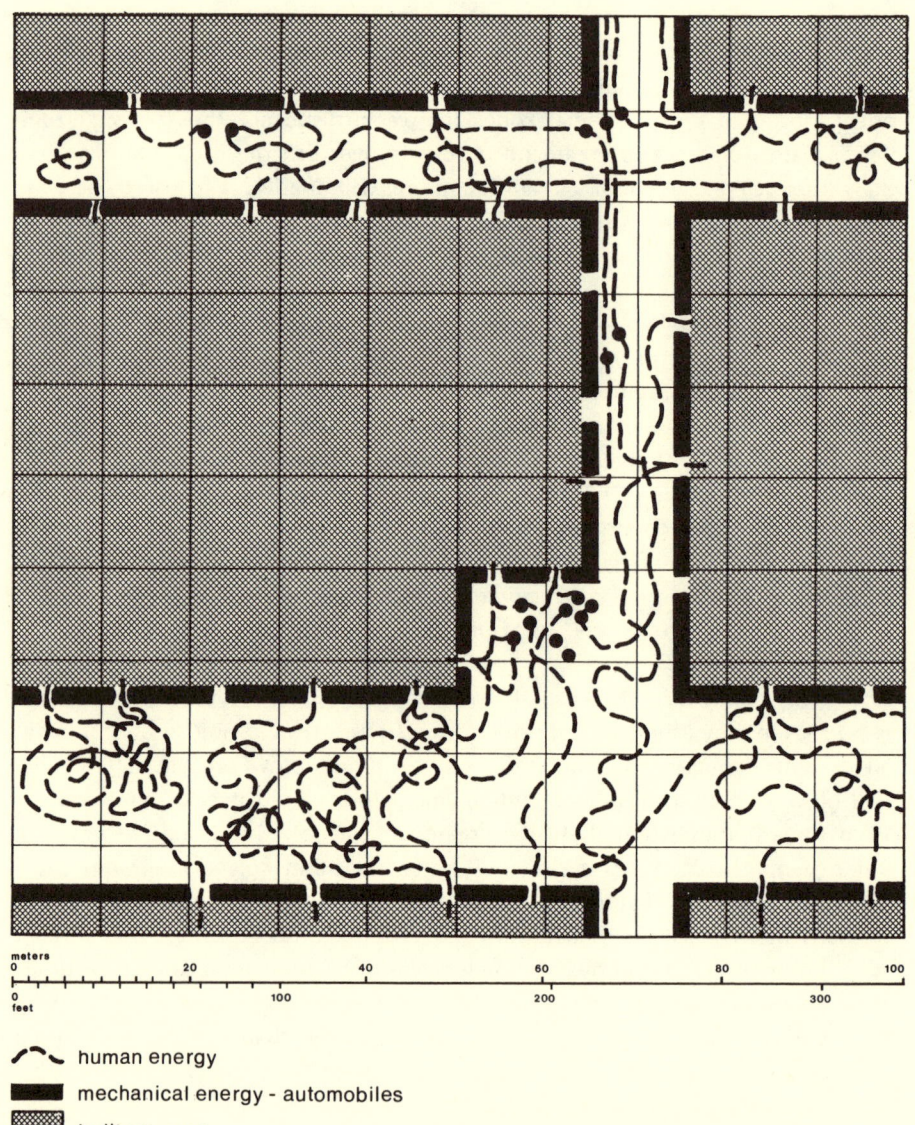

meters
0 · · · · · 20 · · · · · 40 · · · · · 60 · · · · · 80 · · · · · 100

0 · · · 100 · · · 200 · · · 300
feet

⌒⌒ human energy

▬▬ mechanical energy - automobiles

▓▓ built-up area

58. Our goal is to help Anthropos regain the ability to move freely and to communicate in the street.

The term Anthropos includes each individual human being. We must also keep in mind the twelve development phases through which each Anthropos, at least each lucky one, passes (See Fig. 8). Thus we begin to be realistic in setting our goals.

133. *The ultimate and, as far as possible, immediate goal is to create human settlements which protect and develop Anthropos.*

When we examine the four parts of the human system we must begin with the body's physiological needs, which shows us that both the immediate and the ultimate goal is to provide Anthropos with all the basic elements necessary for survival. If this goal is not fulfilled immediately, there is no human life.

134. *The immediate and ultimate goal for survival in human settlements is the fulfilment of all basic biological and physiological needs, starting with oxygen and temperature and ending with all other needs defined by experts in this field.*

Another demand of the body is access to appropriate space. Of course, many people have managed to live long lives confined in cells, but our goal for human settlements is not to care for prisoners but for people who are happy and safe. We need to provide all types of spaces and the freedom to use them. These spaces range from the room to the whole globe because really happy and safe people may want to travel long distances to find the place which is best for them, whether permanent or temporary. Such unlimited opportunities for travel should not be set as a goal, however, because humanity is not yet ready for a concept of freedom extending beyond national boundaries, sometimes not even within them. When speaking of space for Anthropos we must limit our concern to the daily urban systems. Beyond these limits the problem is political.

135. *The ultimate goal of human settlements is to give to every Anthropos adequate space, starting with the room and extending to the area of his daily urban system.*

The need for space is not only a need of the body but also of the senses, the mind, and the psyche, which makes it difficult to determine why an individual may want a particular space in which to live. Does the particular space satisfy the demands of his body or does it fulfill other sensual, intellectual, or psychological requirements? Scientific research one day will clarify these questions; now we can merely make different hypotheses.

After considering the dimensions of the space needed by Anthropos we must consider its characteristics and its qualities, which are closely related to the structure of each human settlement. A large, wide avenue like the Champs Elysées in Paris is highly satisfactory in Paris, but if it were in a small town it would simply be a chaotic space. Our bodies would tire of crossing it several times daily, our senses be disturbed, and our mind and psyche would reject it as a crazy solution for the small town.

136. *Another ultimate goal of human settlements is to give high quality to*

the spaces made available to their inhabitants. This high quality must be related to the biological and physiological needs of the inhabitants, their history, culture, and civilization.

We must be certain that when we consider a space we rely on those people who will use it, provided they have adequate experience and judgement. This is difficult in our era of change because few people fully understand the impact of new technology on the quality of life. When the first automobiles invaded the cities everyone admired the new choices they made available, but it took two generations to understand the pollution they created. Formerly, plans for the future were based on a continuity with the past. Today, everything is subject to changes and judgements are not so absolute, but we must endeavor to base them on safe and sound foundations.

137. *This is another reason why we need a science, without which there is no hope for a clear definition of goals and, therefore, of their achievement.*

3. Society

The most important goal for Society as an element of human settlements is for all people to have equal rights. Although this is an ancient goal, we must understand what it means in terms of human settlements. A good example of equality expressed in spatial terms is the right to enter all public and private institutions without reservations or distinctions. No segregation of any kind is justified in any human settlement anywhere on our globe.

138. *The ultimate, but also the immediate goal in terms of importance and urgency, is to make everyone equal inside all areas of human settlements.*

From the goal of equality in human settlements derives the next goal, the need for equal choices for everyone. Theoretically, everyone should be able to go wherever anybody else can go. This would only be possible if everyone were able to travel on a bus, boat, or airplane without paying, which would be far too costly to realize in the foreseeable future. What we can set as a realistic goal is to enable all people to go to all places, but in different ways and at different costs, by using different means of transportation. If, for example, only private cars can reach a beautiful national park, public buses should be provided in sufficient numbers to serve those who do not own a private car or cannot drive. Everyone must be able to visit any place in his own way.

139. *Another ultimate goal for all human settlements is to give all people equal opportunities to visit any place they choose.*

Even in the streets many people do not have equality of movement, such as people who do not drive, who have fewer choices than do drivers. Such a situation leads to the new and age-old principle to have streets for humans, which we call hustreets.[2] We also need separate streets, which we call mecstreets, for machines. These machines should be automatic so that everybody may use them.[3]

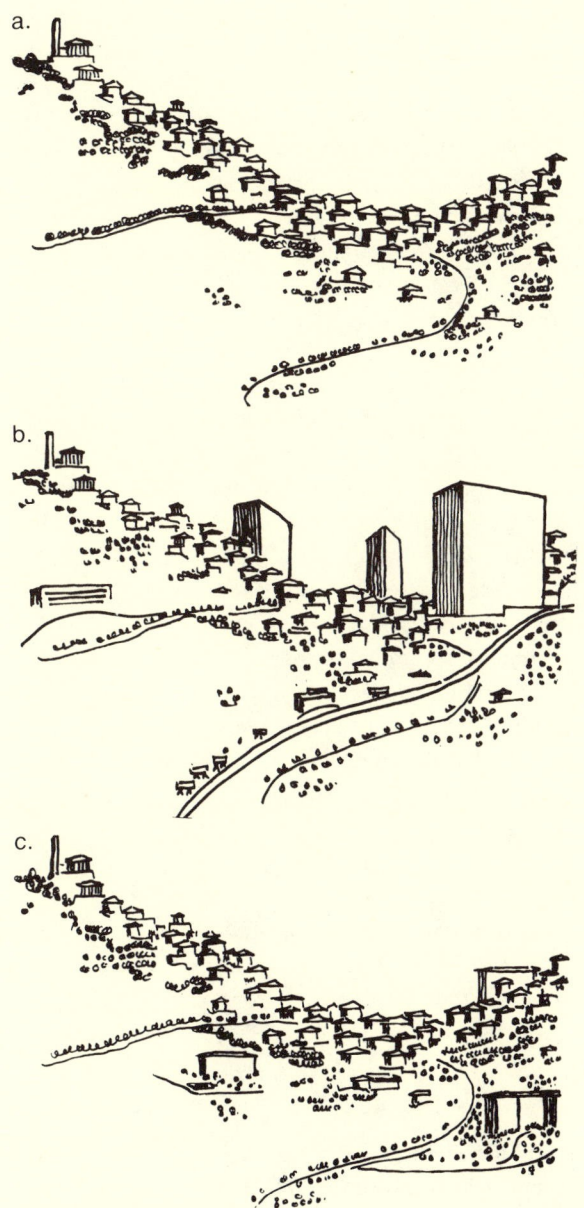

a. In the past, Anthropos created a balance with Nature and Society in his cities.

b. Anthropos is now spoiling what he managed to create in the past by allowing some owners to rise above the city.

c. In the future, there is an imperative need for social balance which is also the basis for a balance between Nature, Society, and Anthropos.

59.   Balance in human settlements

140. *An ultimate but distant goal is to separate all pedestrians from machines and to make machines automatic in order to serve everybody in exactly the same way.*

We move next to the problem of safety and security, which is related to many elements. Nature can kill us with an earthquake or a hurricane, and a human mistake in Shells and Networks can also kill us. The greatest dangers, however, are those related to the operation of Society. Its successful operation depends on the organization of all security forces, in the broadest sense of the word.

141. *An ultimate goal of Society in human settlements is to guarantee safety and security to all humans, and an immediate goal is to guarantee this to the maximum possible extent.*

The achievement of these goals requires an organized Society. There are many aspects in organization which need a detailed analysis, but what is important for human settlements is the spatial organization of Society as a whole system. This vital subject has been overlooked because of the exploding cities, but it must be studied with great care. Humans, as do other animals, survive best when they have well defined territories which do not create conflicts with their neighbors. When national boundaries are not respected, tension and strife inevitably break out. The same is true for cities of all sizes, even neighborhoods. The conflicts between them are not as apparent as they are between nations, since they do not result in wars, but they cause confusion that often leads to chaotic and tragic situations within our polises. When we expect the mayor of a metropolis to decide on the status of a small neighborhood square, we cannot hope for a timely and satisfactory decision. The only hope is to organize human settlements into neighborhoods with authority to take decisions that correspond to their level, and to express opinions on other issues to a higher authority which must take the overall decisions.

142. *The ultimate goal is the spatial organization of all human settlements in a hierarchical way, and the immediate goal is the definition of at least some levels of local authorities and agencies for special tasks without overlapping boundaries.*

4. Shells

It is difficult to define the goals for Shells, as we have already seen in Part Two, because there are no internationally accepted values or standards to guide us. In addition, the ultimate goals and the immediate goals are likely to be very different. For example, there is the case of housing. The ultimate goal can be very ambitious, and remote, for many countries. But the immediate goal can be extremely close. If an earthquake destroys the houses of a town everyone must immediately be given some kind of temporary shelter, no matter how crowded. Humans first need protection from danger, and only when they are safe can we discuss ways to improve the overall situation.

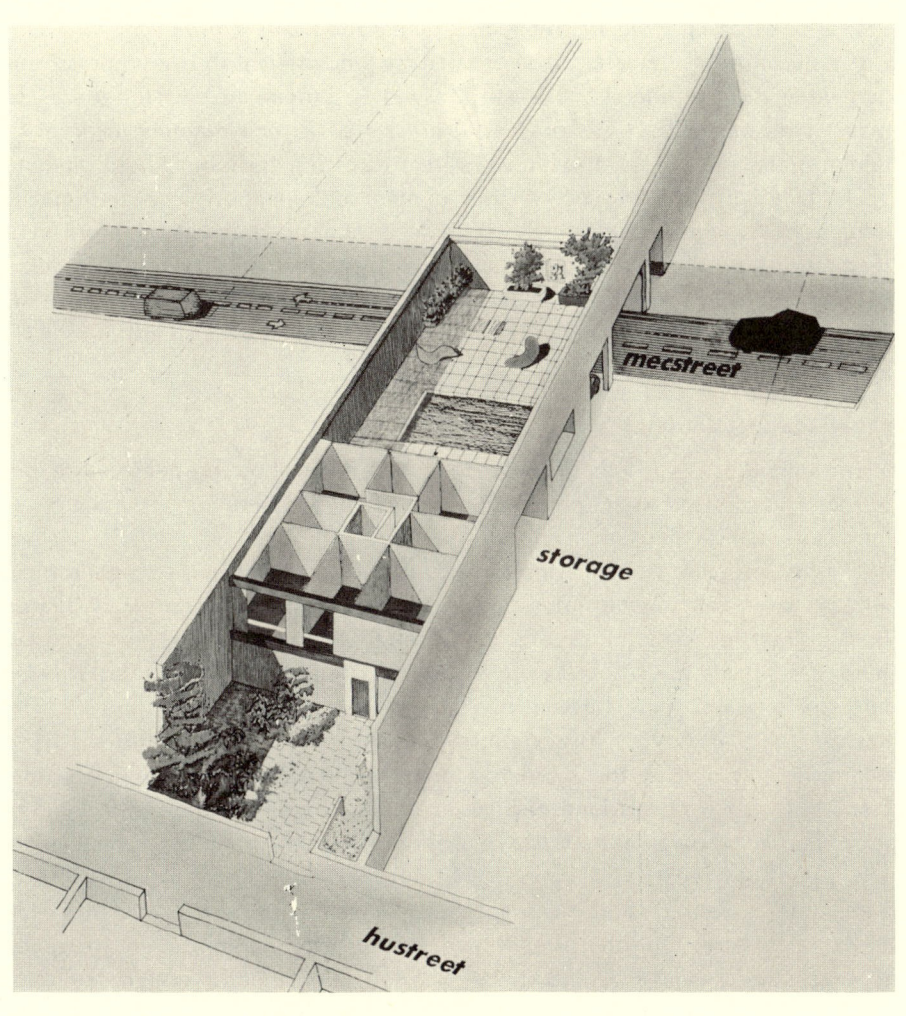

60. A house type of the future

143. *The ultimate and the immediate goals for Shells can be very different.*
The question of ultimate goals for Shells is fundamental to every human settlement under consideration, but an answer is difficult to give for there are
many types of Shells. I will present in greater detail one example in order to
demonstrate how we must move with great care to choose our future ultimate
goals for Shells, as all aspects of our human settlements will be enormously
influenced by our decisions. My example is housing, for which, surprisingly,
there are no precise international standards. I will deal with the house in detail
to help us make some decisions concerning it and also to demonstrate how,
when the time comes, we should think about the other types of Shells.

What is proper housing?

Throughout the world there is much concern today about proper housing, but
we have not defined what "proper housing" really is. There are two basic problems causing this confusion.

The first problem concerns the notion of proper standards, their significance,
and the laws which would impose them. When I visited the capital of a large
nation twenty years ago, I was amazed to see that most of its workers had to live
ten miles outside the city and were obliged to commute daily, using overloaded
buses or bicycles. Why, I asked, don't they live closer, or within the city? The
answer was that they could not afford to build, or pay the rent for, the types
of houses required by the standards for the capital city. This astonished me,
and I said that with this kind of logic another law could be passed forbidding
those people who can not afford 2,500 calories per day (the international standard of average needs) to eat.

Obviously, we must both stress the need for standards as well as clarify what
the standards are. Our obligation however, is to help people who are struggling
to reach these standards, and if they cannot reach them overnight we must
help them do so in stages. Our policies should not be aimed primarily at determining what should be stopped, as often happens, but at what our goals should
be and how we can reach them.

The second problem concerns the definition of the complete house. There is
a tendency to limit the term to the area covered by the house itself, which may
be correct theoretically but is usually incorrect practically. The house is one
spatial unit, but it is not independent, since its function and quality depend on
the housegroup of which it is a part as well as on its neighborhood and city.
On the other hand, the house is really one overall unit consisting of subunits,
such as rooms, and their subunits, such as the furniture, furnishings, and deco-
ration.

One-room units

When we talk about housing, we use such terms as "housing units" or "dwelling," but forget two basic facts: first, that the smallest unit is the room, and that a system cannot be built properly unless its basic unit is built properly; and second, that although the family is an important social unit, the individual is fundamental. We should start the process of housing by conceiving the room as an independent unit, and then connecting it with other rooms to form the unit of one house; then the houses into a housegroup, and so on.

The basic room should consist of:

1. The room itself,
2. a shower or bath and WC,
3. kitchen facilities,
4. storage space,
5. open space (balcony, veranda, courtyard, or garden, depending on climate and location),
6. connecting space (corridor, hall) with the broader unit to which the room belongs.

One-room units are already being built, mostly in or near universities, but the concept of the one-room unit has not yet won formal recognition, either technically or socially. One case worth mentioning is that of the Housing Foundation for Working Youth in the Netherlands, which has already completed its first apartments in Leiden, and is working on its second project, in which boys and girls as young as 16 can rent a unit ($55 per month) with parental permission.[4]

The standard need for everyone to have a "room" is comparable to the requirement of 2,500 calories of food per day for each person. This does not mean that the family will not need an additional common living room or that the neighborhood will not need more space, but it clearly defines the basic human needs in a built-up housing space.

144. *The basic unit in any effort concerning houses should be the room.*

The dimensions of the human room

We must decide upon the dimensions of the basic room. When considering dimensions we must start with the statement by Protagoras that "man is the measure of all things, of the existence of the things that are and the nonexistence of the things that are not."[5]

If any spatial dimensions are important for humans, the mother's womb and the room are the most so. Our birth depends upon the first and our survival upon the second. We spend 40% of our time in our own room, more than in any other space, built-up or open. Children and old and sick people spend even more time in their room (Fig. 62).

Long experience in building and living in rooms, which started without any theories or prejudices more than 10,000 years ago, has led to specific conclusions regarding the minimum and maximum dimensions of the common average room.

The minimum dimensions for a normal room are 9 sq m (100 sq ft) for the room itself and double this i.e., 18 sq m (200 sq ft), for the room and its auxiliaries (bath, kitchen, storage), with a height of 2.40 m (8 ft). The maximum dimensions of the normal room are 23 sq m (324 sq ft). These figures do not contain the open and connecting spaces belonging to each room, because these factors are determined by such variables as climate, culture, habits, location, type of inhabitants (families or old people, students, etc.). The open space dimensions must first be decided by region or locality and for the specific case, and then become part of special standards.

Another factor influencing final dimensions is the need for both isolated and interconnected rooms. If we establish that the infant should have his own room, then this room must be connected with the his parents' bedroom. Later on these rooms will have to be separated from each other, and perhaps someday belong to different apartments.

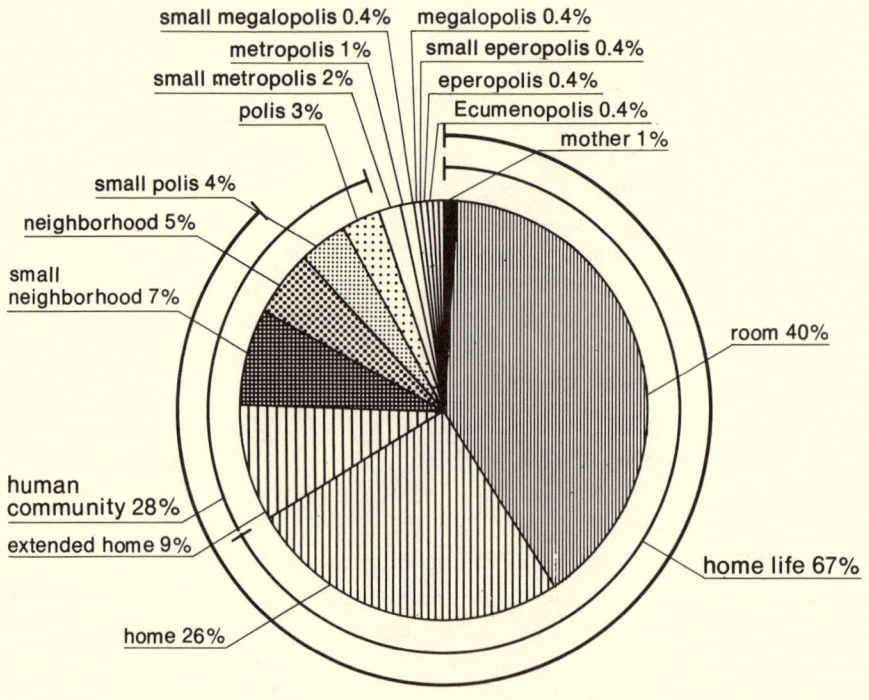

61. Lifetime spent in different units of space

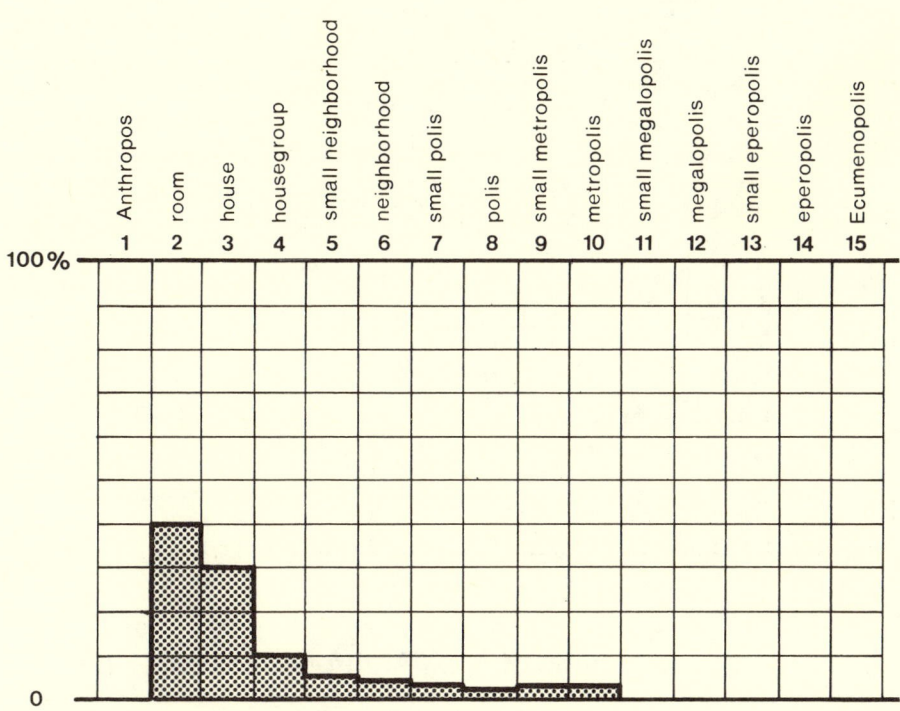

a. time spent in each ekistic unit by a child

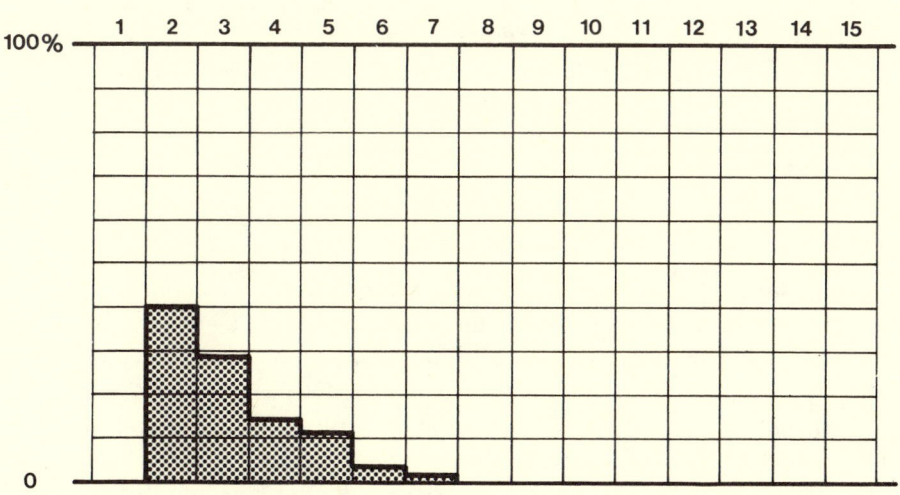

b. time spent in each ekistic unit by an elderly person (76 to 100 years old)

62. Much more time is spent in the room by an infant and an old man than the average person

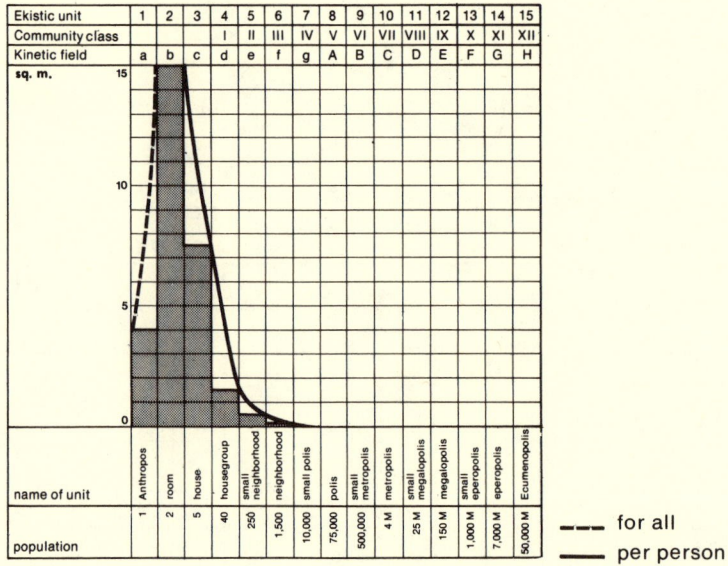

Ekistic unit	1	2	3	4	5	6	7	8	9	10	11	12	13	14	15
Community class				I	II	III	IV	V	VI	VII	VIII	IX	X	XI	XII
Kinetic field	a	b	c	d	e	f	g	A	B	C	D	E	F	G	H

sq. m.

15 — 10 — 5 — 0

name of unit	Anthropos	room	house	housegroup	small neighborhood	neighborhood	small polis	polis	small metropolis	metropolis	small megalopolis	megalopolis	small eperopolis	eperopolis	Ecumenopolis
population	1	2	5	40	250	1,500	10,000	75,000	500,000	4 M	25 M	150 M	1,000 M	7,000 M	50,000 M

—— for all
——— per person

63. Approximate needs of each Anthropos for built-up space

Naturally, the total built-up space for one human includes far more than the basic unit of the room. For example, a family may have a living room, or a library, or a workshop, providing additional space per person (Fig. 63).

145. *The dimensions of the human room will tend, in the long run, to meet assumed international standards.*

The shape of the human room

An understanding of the importance of the shape of the room is especially needed today because there is something of a fashionable tendency to seek new and different shapes. I have carefully studied the human experience about the room's formation and use and have reached the following conclusions:

First: Anthropos started forming and building rooms in many more ways than is usually thought and with almost each new archaeological excavation we find additional ways. This was natural, for humans did not know what they needed and had to experiment. As far as we know, gorillas live in more than thirty different kinds of habitation. If one kind of ape tries so many solutions, it is natural that Anthropos tried many more. These human solutions included round, elliptical, square, orthogonal, and nongeometric shapes.

Second: Humans experimented with different room shapes even within one area, and they did so both during different phases of their evolution and within a given phase. This is shown particularly clearly on Easter Island, perhaps the most isolated area on earth, where we see great differences in room shapes (Fig. 64). Some rooms are only 2 meters in diameter while others are almost 100 meters long. Some have very thick stone walls in relation to their interior space; others do not. Some are independent structures; others are extensions of caves.

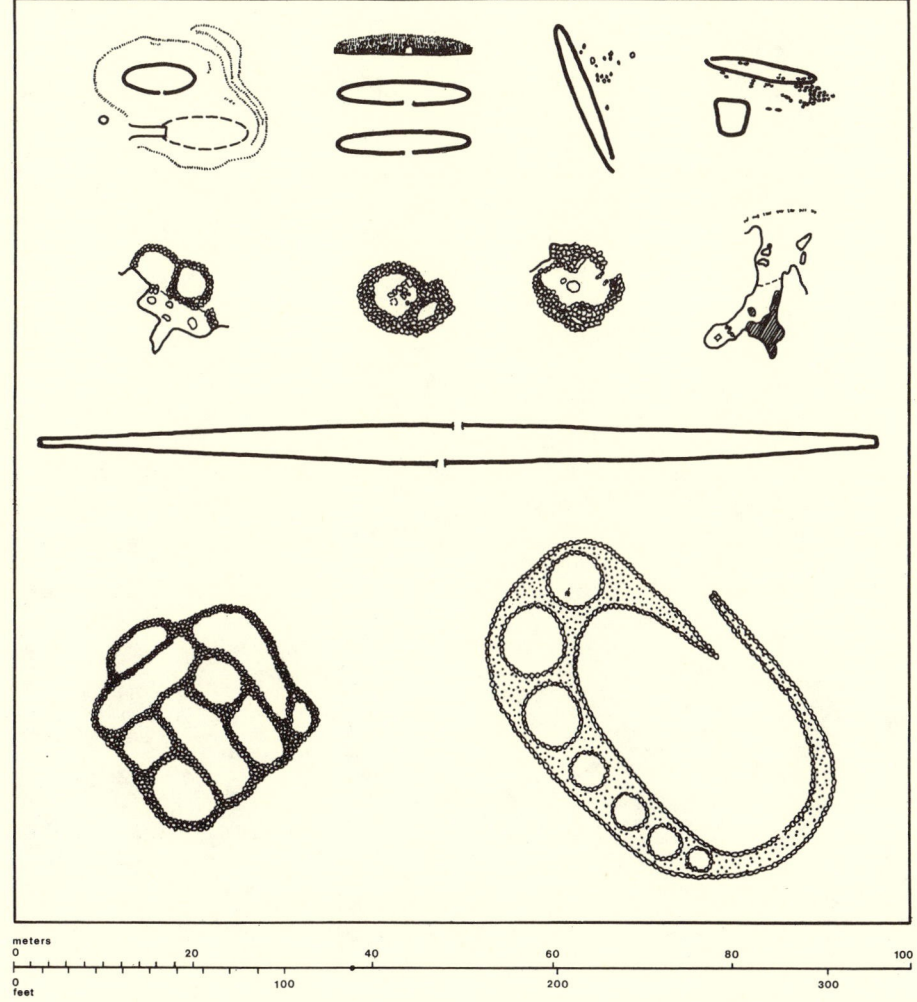

64. Different types of rooms and houses on Easter Island

Third: After the orthogonal room was discovered, however, the other room shapes were gradually abandoned, with the exception of a few cases in isolated settlements, such as in some parts of Syria (Fig. 65).

The same happened with ceilings. Horizontal ceilings gradually replaced all other types, especially after the second story was invented. Floors certainly had to be as horizontal as possible from very early on.

Since archaeology continues to give us new information, we do not know in detail how the room evolved, but we do know well its general evolution on a global scale. Humans started in many cases with isolated rooms, comparable to isolated cells (Fig. 66). After much trial and error Anthropos selected the orthogonal room as a cell of the urban system. This process in ancient Greece is well documented (Fig. 67).

The orthogonal room Anthropos selected, with a horizontal floor and ceiling, was, with some variations for differing local conditions, a global solution.

146. *The shape of the room tends to be orthogonal, with a flat horizontal ceiling and floor.*

65. Traditional village on the national road between Damascus and Homs, Syria

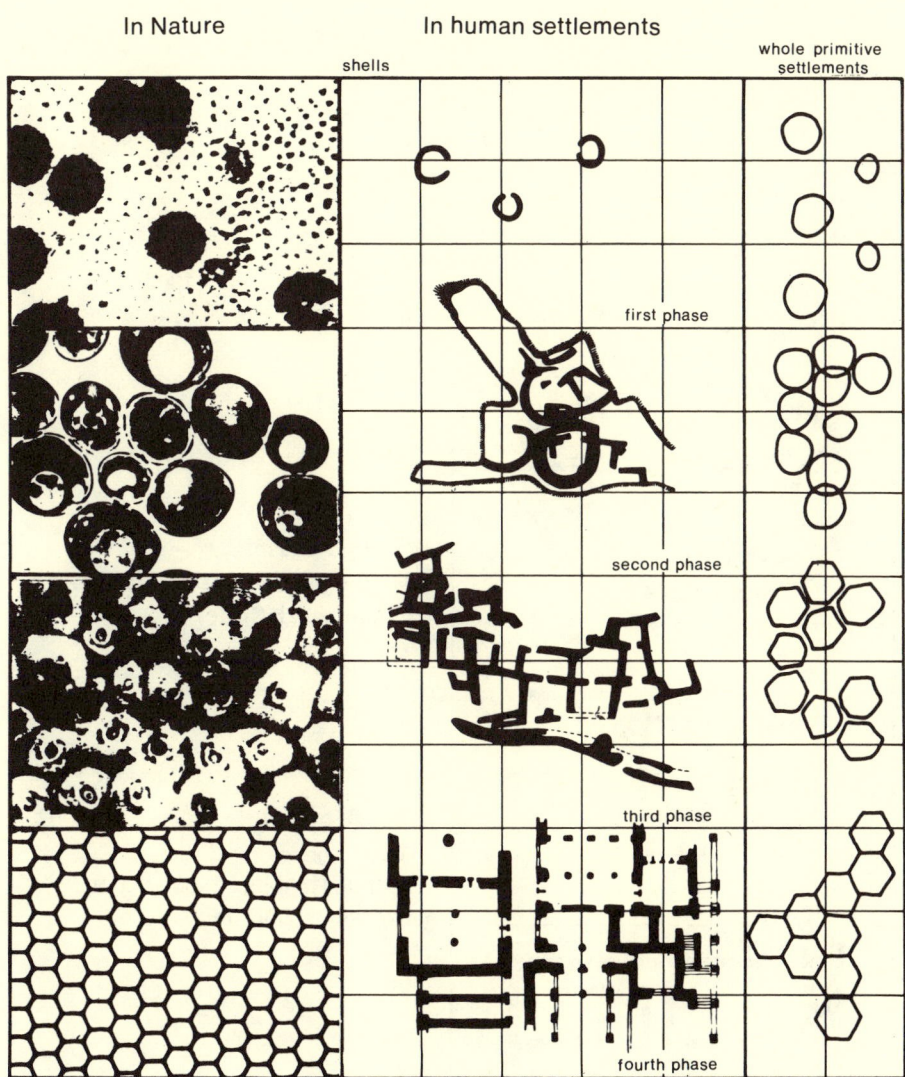

| In Nature | In human settlements | | whole primitive settlements |
| shells | | |

First phase

second phase

third phase

fourth phase

First phase: Volvox colony; Kumasa, Crete
Second phase: Cells of brewer's yeast; Orchomenos, Boeotia
Third phase: Cells of sunflower seed; Malthi, Messinia
Fourth phase: Honeycomb; Knossos, Crete

66.   The evolution of rooms is comparable to the evolution of cells.

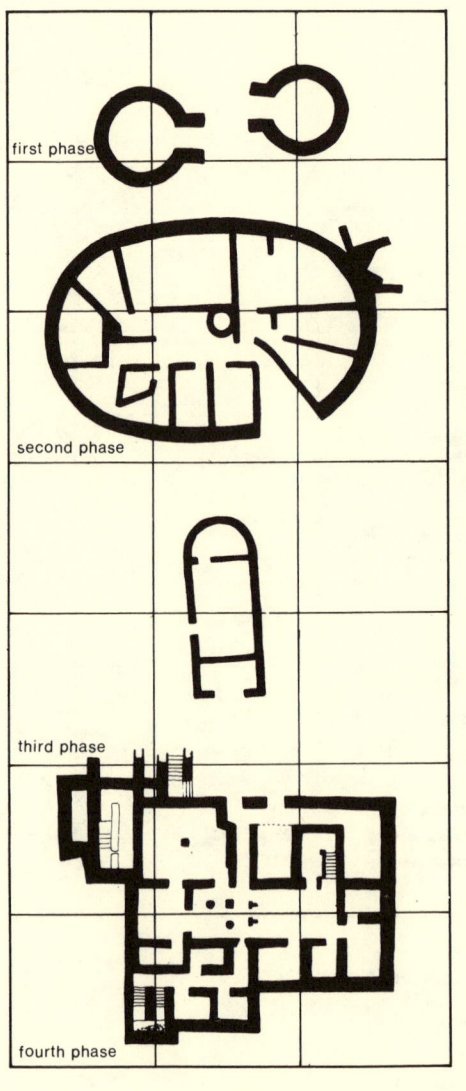

First phase:
Early Minoan, 2800-1900 BC
(Kumasa, Crete)

Second phase:
Middle Minoan I, 1900-1750 BC
(Chamoezzi, Crete)

Third phase:
Middle Helladic, 1900-1600 BC
(Korakou, Corinthia)

Fourth phase:
Late Minoan, 1600-1125 BC
(Tylissos, Crete)

67.   Development of the Greek house type

The quality of the human room

Dimension is the most important factor to a room, then shape, but without quality as well a room can serve only some physiological needs. In order to be completely satisfied we must serve all other physiological, such as visual and tactile needs, as well as psychological and other needs. There are five basic characteristics of quality.

First is the need for isolation and privacy, from protection from noise to complete security. Many societies have managed to live with the front door unlocked, and some cultures have set this as a goal, as has China which, in its *Book of Rites*, has written "the front door need not be closed, day or night. This is the Great Society."[6] But whether the door is open or closed, if people do not feel secure then we have not offered them the kind of quality they truly need.

The second characteristic of quality is the opposite of the first; that it should be possible to open up the room to Nature, tó let in as much sun and air as possible. It must be able to offer good connections with natural areas, such as planted areas, and also good views of Nature. This can be achieved now by opening doors and windows, but in the future we must be able to open whole walls and even the roof. A new technology must develop automated walls and roofs thereby giving us the maximum number of choices. Is this not the goal of freedom, to increase our choices to the maximum? In the same way, the room should open up to the other rooms of the house, to the corridors, even to the streets. Only a room that can be closed, isolated, and secure and also opened and connected with the other elements of the human settlement can give the maximum number of choices to human beings, making them happy and safe. Aristotle set this goal for the city; I propose that we set it also for the room.

The third characteristic of quality is ownership. Animals and humans have always felt happier and safer in territory they owned, even if this ownership only lasts for certain periods. People who have dealt with the animal world and the origins of Anthropos, like Robert Ardrey, emphasize that "when you own some place that's yours you've got something to be proud of."[7]

The fourth characteristic of quality is separation from areas controlled by machines. A room should not open directly onto mecstreets, only onto hustreets. They should, however, be served by machines in the best possible way. They should be connected to but completely separated from machines, which can be accomplished if the machines are placed underground.

The fifth characteristic of quality is related to the optical relationship between Anthropos and the polis. If we continue to believe that we can live inside buildings that give us but two views of the city, either that we are birds and see it from above (Fig. 68) or mice and see it from below (Fig. 69), then there is no hope of becoming normal humans who respect Nature and human values as we did in the past. We need to give the room a really human character by guaranteeing that, when we open our windows and doors and later the "auto-walls," we will be in contact with our environment at levels and distances in keeping with it.

By trying to give the room these basic characteristics we set the foundations

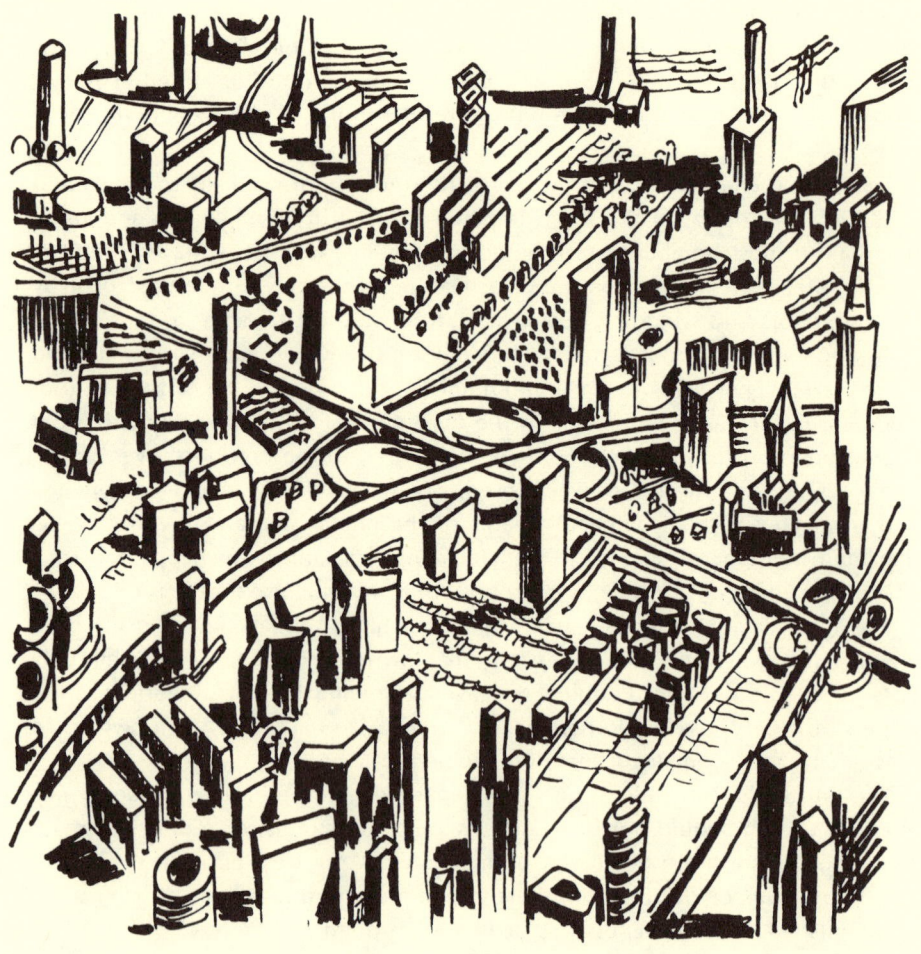

68. A bird's eye view of the city transmits one message: There is no order in our life system.

for quality, the elaboration of which depends on the completion of many details. For instance, the reason why ownership contributes so much to quality is that each room owes much of its character to the user of the room and not only to the builder. If we want real quality we have to ensure that the user is really the owner. Then details are up to them, and not a global problem at all.

147. *The quality of the room depends on many factors, only some of which have been mentioned here.*

69. When we see the city from lower floors we notice that there are no people, and that machines are our only neighbors.

Our total needs for rooms

We must estimate the total number of rooms we need. We should estimate in rooms rather than houses, because people are easier to count than families and we can work more accurately.

Unfortunately, we cannot determine the number of rooms there are on earth, both because no data exists for many countries, such as China, and because much of the data we do have is inaccurate. We suggest that a special effort be made for a census so that calculations can proceed accurately. In the meantime we must work with the reasonable assumption that there are now two billion rooms of all kinds and qualities, out of which one billion may be satisfactory.

The estimate of the number of satisfactory rooms can only be an extremely rough guess because of the lack of global criteria for quality. Recent reports for England, for example, show that 20% of the existing housing stock lacks basic amenities,[8] while in the U.S.A. the latest estimate by the Harvard-MIT Joint Center for Urban Studies states that 7 million people, only 3.5% of the U.S. population, live in physically inadequate households.[9] The great difference in these two estimates of quality show how we can speak of quality only in terms of very rough estimates.

On the basis, however, of our assumption that there are two billion rooms in the world and that approximately one billion may be satisfactory, we can estimate that by the year 2000 we will need 5 billion new rooms and replacements for another billion, that is, we will need three times as many rooms as we have now. Fulfilling this need seems impossible, so we should make estimates as well for the years 2025, 2050, and 2075 for a total global population of 15 billion, which is the probable leveling off point for our exploding population. This means that we have to prepare ourselves to build 13 billion rooms and replace one billion more. This will not be easy to do, but we must undertake it in a realistic way.

With an awareness of the ultimate goal for rooms, we must define the immediate goals, considering existing conditions and conditions foreseeable for one generation ahead. If the economic situation indicates that in one generation's time we can reach the ultimate goal and supply every single person with a room, we must build houses with this in mind. Some people will have rooms immediately with the best standards, but other people will have to wait. To make the goal realistic for those people who cannot have rooms immediately, we must plan appropriately so that they will have the space and the proper technology to add their rooms. This case demonstrates how we can connect the ultimate with the immediate goals.

148. *We must coordinate the ultimate and the immediate goals as well as possible.*

Other types of Shells

We must now study all other types of Shells. This is difficult, but for many Shells it can be done. For example, we cannot do so for a research laboratory, because new discoveries will make several of its parts unnecessary and many new ones indispensable. The ultimate goal in planning for a research laboratory is to plan for all possible changes. On the other hand, we do have enough experience with hospitals to let us set ultimate goals for them. Clearly, about some Shells we know enough to set ultimate goals, and about others we do not.

149.   *When defining the ultimate goals for Shells, we must be aware that there are sectors where we can be very specific and others where we must remain prepared for all kinds of changes. It may or may not be possible to coordinate the immediate with the ultimate goals.*

This is also true of the goals in terms of quality; but in some places ideas about quality can change frequently if people are influenced by fashions, while elsewhere they can remain the same for long periods of time. Some people prefer to live in very old, sometimes centuries old houses, after adding modern technology. These cases show that quality has some permanent values, at least for certain people and certain environments. The esthetic aspects of quality vary with each individual and cannot be imposed.

150.   *The goals concerning quality can be defined only for the immediate future and for a certain proportion of the total needs, because we can never be sure whether there is full agreement on matters of quality. Technological are universally valid, but only for the immediate future and not as ultimate goals, because new demands will arise.*

The next question is how to set goals for the organization of Shells. Long experience tells us that certain types of buildings, such as schools or hospitals, must correspond to a definite number of people, which presupposes a relationship between the number of houses and other types of buildings. We cannot be sure of the standards applicable to all types of relationships among all kinds of buildings, nor can we speak of a permanent organizational goal. But this is not necessary, since with time many changes occur, especially at higher organizational levels. A few decades ago no one could have foreseen today's need for supermarkets nor the great number of colleges and universities now needed. It is much easier to speak of the need for a small-sized temple, mosque, or church because these are connected with traditional neighborhoods. In the same spirit we can speak of needs for corner stores and other small facilities.

151.   *The ultimate goal for the organization of all kinds of buildings cannot be defined. But since Society must be organized and people should be prepared for new demands in buildings, we must estimate space which should be conserved for all types of future Shells.*

Another goal for Shells is the saving of the old Shells of historical or cultural value. I mention this in particular because there is a tendency to separate this saving of valuable old Shells from the subject of Shells as a whole. Traditional buildings are often placed under a special authority which may overlook their importance or treat them as dead relics. It is much more constructive to consider the old buildings as representing certain values in the total system of Shells and to use them in the spirit in which they were created.

152. *Both an ultimate and an immediate goal is to enable old buildings of historical or cultural value to survive as living parts of the whole system of Shells and not as dead relics; in which case they are in great danger of being permanently lost.*

After looking at the different aspects of past, present, and future Shells we can see that we need to develop a system incorporating the past, present, and future as one aspect of a developing world.

153. *Both an ultimate and an immediate goal for Shells is to examine all existing buildings, including those which must die and those which should be helped to live forever, and then to foresee the new Shells necessary for tomorrow and the more distant future. Only by making this overview can we unify old and new demands into a living system of Shells.*

Networks

The ultimate goal for Networks is a coordinated system for all the Networks taken together (Fig. 70). The immediate goal for Networks is the provision of whatever services, such as water supply or sewage, are urgently needed, with an understanding of the ultimate coordinated system of which these services should form a part.

154. *The ultimate goal for Networks is a coordinated system. The immediate goal is to serve urgent needs in the spirit of the ultimate goal.*

This coordinated system will never be properly understood if we do not study the evolution of Networks in terms of their sizes and dimensions. We must also relate the Networks to population and income distribution according to sound predictions. Networks are the physical expressions of developing technology. Unlike the case with Shells, there is no sign that either people or governments retain an old in preference to a new technology.

155. *To lead the whole system of Networks towards implementation we must conceive it as a truly modern technological system related to the anticipated population and income level.*

An early concept of the complete system does not increase the cost because, when the moment comes for its realization, the settlement is prepared to implement it.

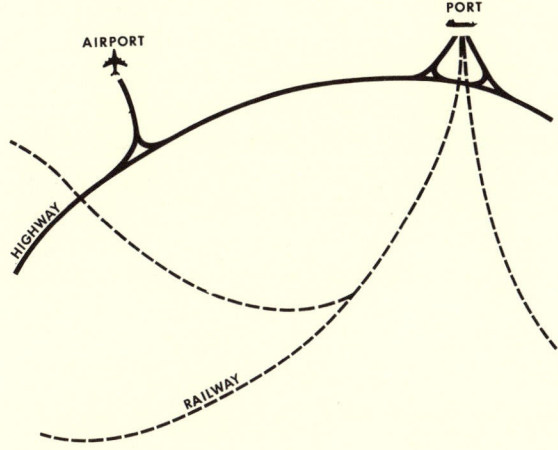

A. Present type

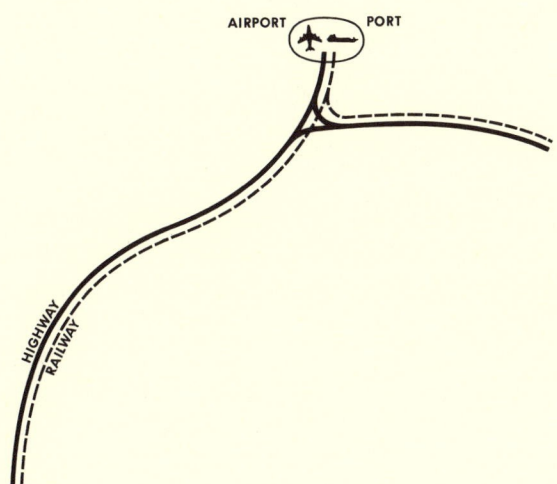

B. Desirable type

70.   The LANWAIR knot

There are dangers, however, in overestimating some of the future needs. A frequent example of this is the planning for wider streets than are actually needed, especially in the suburbs. Although a number of roads will have to serve a larger flow of traffic, many will and should remain only wide enough to serve limited flows of local traffic. Unless the function and use of each road is defined and adhered to, confusion will result as the roles of roads change.

156. *In order to succeed, the goal of a coordinated system of Networks must be rational and must define the future role of each part of the system. This means that the whole human settlement must be very well planned for present and future needs.*

The need for an overall concept of coordinated Networks brings us back to the danger we identified in Part Two, that of the elimination of the Networks of the past because they were considered useless for the future. The most characteristic example is the elimination of the small roads of the past, which is the elimination of the human scale. We must not make this mistake through a lack of consideration of the total situation from the past to the present and to the future.

157. *To achieve the goals set for Networks we must consider all needs of the past, present, and future, and connect them all into one balanced system.*

C. Ekistic units

1. Temporary human settlements

The existence of temporary human settlements is a tragedy in our time. No living conditions are as bad as those described in the section on temporary human settlements in Part Two. Both ultimate and immediate goals could justifiably aim at the elimination of temporary human settlements, but there are two reasons why this is not now either possible or advisable. The first and most important is that no preparation has been made for the transformation of a nomad or a hunter into a permanent inhabitant of a given area. Such a drastic change in life style needs systematic preparation. The second reason is that we are learning and must learn even more from surviving bands of nomads about human evolution and ecology.

158. *The ultimate goal for temporary human settlements is the settling of their inhabitants as permanent residents of a given area as soon as this is reasonably possible.*

The immediate goal is related to the conditions under which the inhabitants live. If they experience a crisis such as a drought, the immediate goal is to help them survive. If, on the other hand, their living conditions are "normal," the immediate goal is to prepare them for permanent settlement (Fig. 71).

159. *The immediate goal for temporary human settlements is to select a plan of action. This plan may be for urgent and immediate aid for survival or a long term plan to assist the people to become residents of permanent human settlements.*

The notion of "long term" should be as limited as possible. It may be reasonable to set twenty-five years for the realization of the ultimate goal, but this may be difficult to do in the case of certain countries and tribes. Only by creating a special international program with proper funds and scientific mobilization can the ultimate goal be achieved within the next fifty to seventy-five years.

71. Trailer residents attempt to settle permanently.

2. Villages

Most (51.3%) of the world's population live in villages, but there are no villages in which the tendency to move to the polis does not exist. It is very hard, therefore, to set the goals for villages. It is unrealistic to decide to eliminate them, but we do not believe they should exist forever in a world of equal people.

The solution to this difficult problem is to help both old and new types of villages to exist but at the same time to give their inhabitants all the advantages available to urban dwellers. Villages with no future because of their land's low productivity will be abandoned or turned into second home areas for relaxation and entertainment. Productive or potentially productive villages will continue to be used, but their inhabitants will live in nearby cities and commute to their fields.

160. *The ultimate goal for villages is to give their inhabitants choices equal to those of the urban dwellers by making them parts of daily urban systems.*

The cells which created and were created by agriculture are no longer necessary in their old form based on pedestrian people. If we were obliged to re-create agricultural human settlements without any commitment to the past, we would find other types of solutions, such as agricultural towns in sizes corresponding to the degree of land productivity, income levels, and social and political systems. We are dealing, however, with human settlements that have existed for thousands of years. Our solution for the future must be sought in a balanced combination of old and new. The goal for the villages will always be the same — to save the villagers from isolation and lack of equality with urban dwellers — but different local conditions will dictate different methods and approaches.

The different solutions will all tend to replace the old notion of village with the notion of urban neighborhood. Those villages which remain will be strengthened in population and mobility by becoming parts of the daily urban system of a polis, metropolis, or megalopolis. This means that the village children could go to urban schools, that major shopping could be carried out in the urban area, that some people could work in the urban area while the majority could drive to work fields.

An extreme solution is the abandonment of villages as permanent human settlements. Villages may survive as weekend homes for urban dwellers, but the cultivation of outlying fields will become an urban profession. Today, when major projects are built outside urban areas, they are built by urban dwellers who commute to the projects. In the same way major cooperatives or major private companies will mobilize their members or employees for agriculture. The only difference from the present will be that agricultural workers will commute over much greater distances than they do today.

These two different solutions demonstrate that, ultimately, villages will cease to exist. Human mobility will increase greatly and we will enter a new phase of human history in which all people will, for the first time, be equal.

161.   *The ultimate goal for villages will bring us a completely new urban system of human settlements which will house agricultural workers as members of an urban profession.*

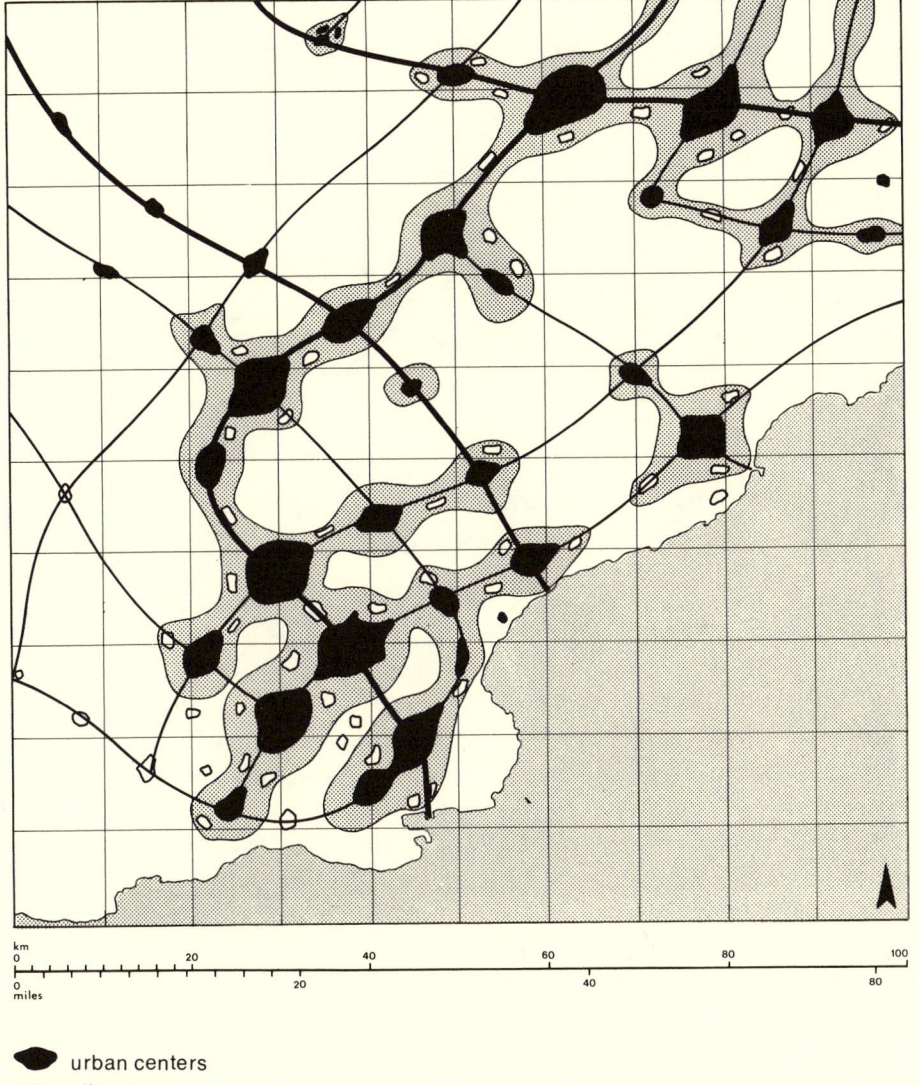

72.   The goal of a village is to become part of an urban system.

The ultimate goal, although lacking a precise time schedule for all cases, is clear, but the immediate goal will vary from case to case. Every situation has its own characteristics, many of which change with the passing of time, with increasing incomes, and with new technological developments such as the opening of a new traffic route. There is no single solution for such a complex situation nor any specific method to be followed.

162. *The immediate goal for each village requires acceptance of the ultimate goal and a realistic analysis of its particular situation. The immediate goal may change if the situation changes.*

3. Polises

The future of a village mainly depends on developments in an area a few tens of kilometers square, but the future of a polis depends on developments in an area thousands of kilometers square. Many more activities take place and many more unexpected changes can occur in such a large area. Most polises will continue to live and probably will explode in size and activities, but a few polises, in remote areas with no economic future, will die. The future of any polis depends on the broader system to which it belongs.[10]

163. *The ultimate goal for most polises is to become an organic part of the broader urban system. A few polises will be allowed to decline and die if there is no place for them in the changing system of human settlements around them.*

The immediate goal is obvious in the rare case of a polis which will die in 25 years: let the polis disappear. It is more difficult to set the immediate goal for the polis which will disappear not in 25 but in 50 or 100 years. In such a case we must take care in setting immediate goals. Negative measures should not be taken for this polis simply because its death is foreseen. The time it is expected to die is so distant that many things may happen to alter the ultimate goal from negative to positive. The death of a polis is a major loss.

164. *When the ultimate goal for a polis appears to be negative, we must set the immediate goals with particular care because through them we may change the ultimate goal into a positive one, thereby saving the polis and all its values.*

A development which could change a negative ultimate goal could be the creation of a specialized industry that is missing from the region and does not require a special location, especially if it uses small quantities of material and much labor, which always can be trained in a new sector. Another positive change which might be used in combination with the new industry could be a specialized technical college and school which could train the people needed for the new industry. We need so many things in our increasingly complex systems of life that we almost always can find solutions to save polises from elimination, turning them into lively centers of the broader systems of human settlements.

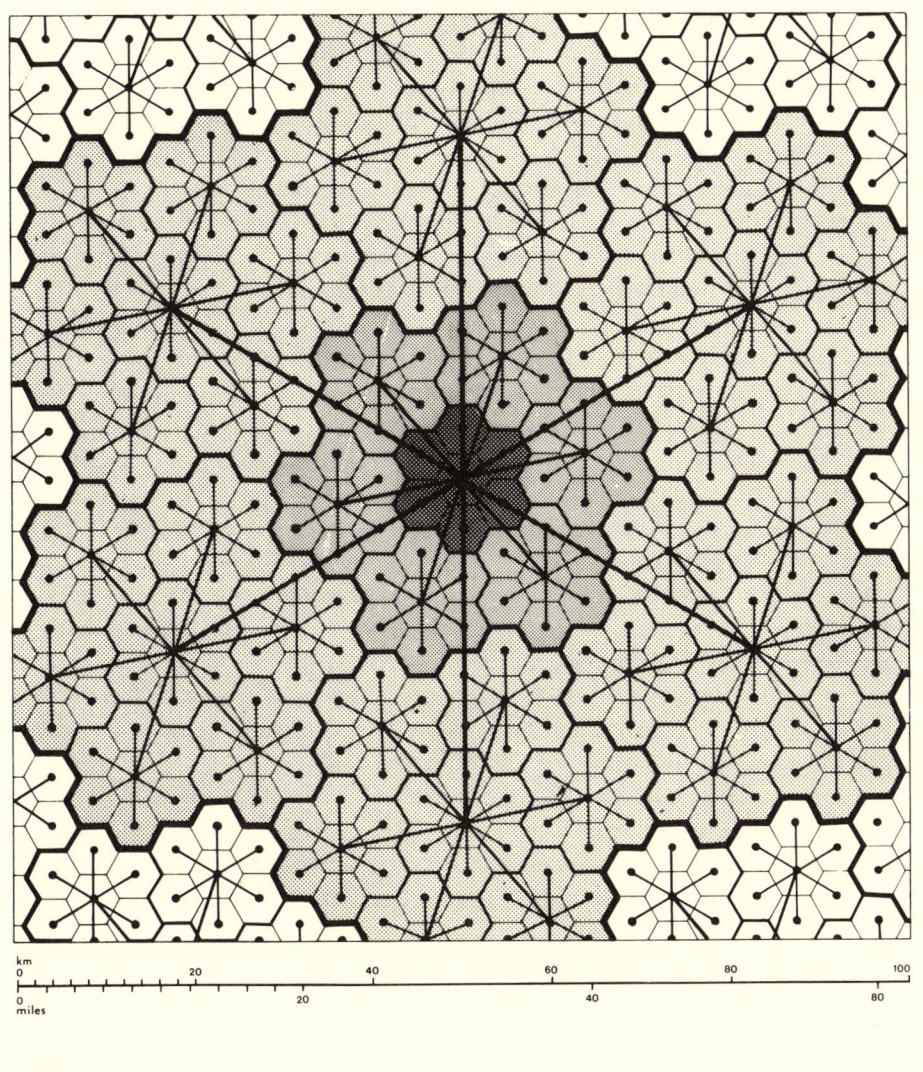

center of a polis

territory of a polis

territory of a large polis

73. Hierarchical organization of a human settlement

4. Metropolises

Metropolises are here to stay, live, and grow. The common negative attitude regarding the growth of metropolises is usually wrong and is in fact often the main cause of the impending disaster, the disaster of unprepared growth. Although they now contain only 12.6%, in the future metropolises will absorb a high percentage of the global population. The invasion of cities by machines transformed villages and polises into metropolises, and this invasion is not going to stop. Metropolises are the main human settlements of the future. Many will be united into megalopolises, and all of them together will eventually become one Ecumenopolis. This development, however, will not mean the elimination of the individual characteristics of each metropolis any more than the creation of polises eliminated the neighborhoods they absorbed.

Today no real goals, except for negative ones, exist for metropolises. They must be set with skill, courage, and imagination. I speak of courage for the first time here because we need a real change in our attitudes about the cities of the future.

165. *The ultimate goal for metropolises is acceptance of the facts about their existence and preparation for appropriate development and growth without any negative attitudes.*

How can we achieve this ultimate goal when we know well that metropolises threaten many aspects of our system of human settlements? One example of this threat is the elimination of land suitable for cultivation. Our only hope of avoiding the disastrous growth of many existing problems and the appearance of new problems is to face them in advance. If we guide the growth of metropolises we can see that some areas should remain Naturareas or Cultivareas and not be turned into Anthropareas or Industrareas (Fig. 74).[11]

166. *To achieve our ultimate goal for metropolises we must plan for proper land use, taking into consideration the need for two new types of areas, Anthroporeas for humans and Industrareas for industry, as well as the need to save and develop existing Naturareas for wildlife and Cultivareas for agriculture.*

To do this planning we must act immediately. One reason we have so many problems from metropolitan growth is that many people pretend that we must stop metropolitan growth. Plans are often drawn up for areas and numbers of people smaller than the actual growth will require. We must have accurate calculations about future needs.

167. *The immediate goal for metropolises is to prepare accurate calculations of future growth and the physical plans to guide it.*

It is better to overestimate future growth than to let things happen haphazardly. Planned Networks are a good example of how predictions can help us.

In Part Two we saw the confusion created by uncoordinated Networks (See Figs. 47, 48). When we plan for the future we should envision a total system of coordinated Networks as an immediate goal.

168. *Implementation of immediate goals should be steps toward achieving the ultimate goal.*

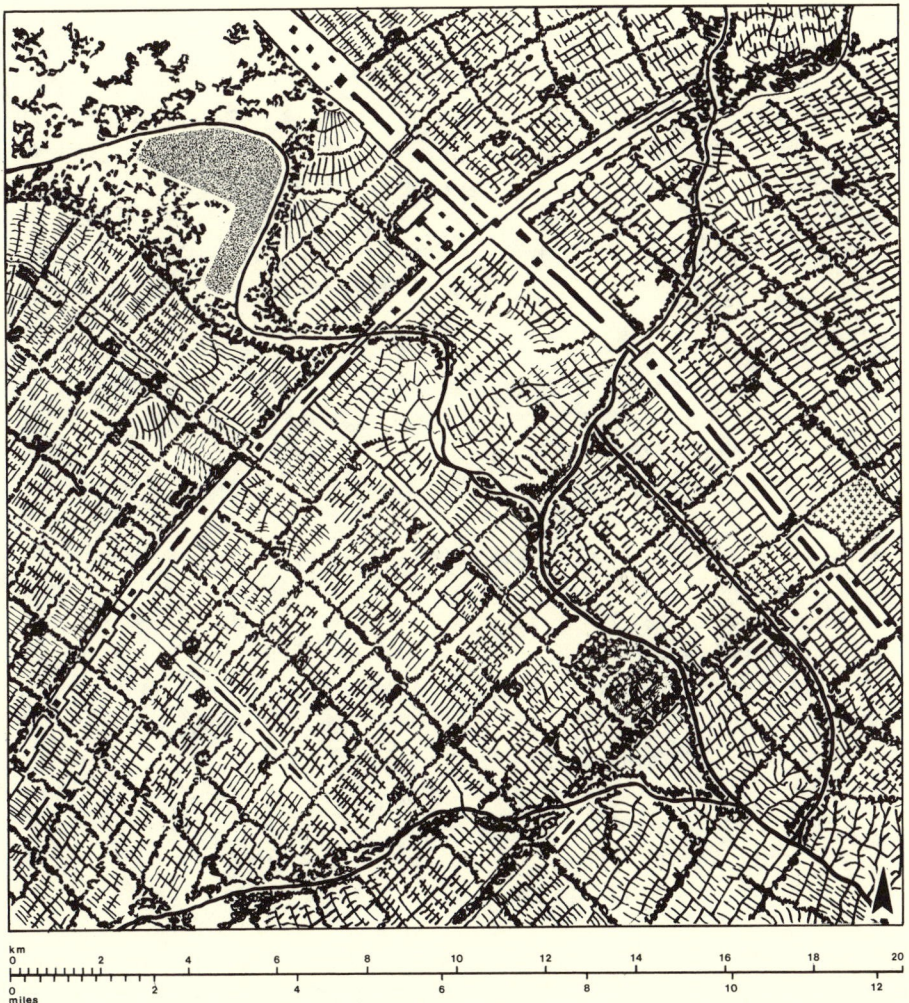

74. The metropolis of the future

5. Megalopolises

We know little about metropolises, which are only 150 years old, and almost nothing about megalopolises. Since only 30 years have passed since they were born, not one of them has grown with guidance, even incorrect guidance.

169. *The immediate goal for megalopolises is to understand them.*

There are three ultimate goals, corresponding to the three great problems of megalopolises given in Part Two. The first ultimate goal for megalopolises is to come to terms with its existence and to face its organization at the proper scale. Without understanding and organization there is no hope of determining and acting upon their real needs.

170. *The first ultimate goal for megalopolises is understanding their territorial organization.*

For example, how can we avoid the chaotic situation created by confusing systems of Networks if we do not know that our megalopolis consists of a certain number of metropolises covering a certain amount of territory with a certain number of people inhabiting each metropolis, and that the needs of these people are a certain amount in terms of energy, water, movement, etc.?

171. *The second ultimate goal for megalopolises is to coordinate their total systems of Networks with the total territorial organization.*

Finally, we can deal with the elimination of natural resources, which is the greatest danger posed by megalopolises. What can we do to achieve a balance of Nature with the other elements? Why do we not begin by setting our goals for the salvation of Nature? This would be the proper method if we were dealing with a new megalopolis in a virgin area, but this is not the case for the megalopolises which exist today. Much of their territory has already been developed, committing Nature over very large areas. We cannot, then, start with Nature, but must recognize the existing commitments for all elements of the megalopolis. We must acquire an accurate picture of the total situation, and then begin with our plans for the future. We must start with the total megalopolis, organize its administration, organize its Networks, and then deal with Nature.

172. *The third ultimate goal for megalopolises is to save their natural resources and form a system with them. Nature is needed as a system.*

Lest there be any misunderstanding about saving Nature being given here as the third ultimate goal, let me point out that saving Nature is always the first ultimate goal in terms of priorities, but here we are dealing with a realistic process of setting the goals. First we must understand the situation and its problems, second we must deal with administrative and territorial organization and the system of Networks, and only third can we deal with saving Nature because only then do we know what really can be done in the very complex system of the megalopolis (Fig. 75).

173. *Saving Nature is the first ultimate goal in terms of importance, but in terms of execution it is the third. First in importance, last in execution illustrates how we can deal with the ultimate goals.*

km
0   20   40   60   80   100   120   140   160   180   200

0   20   40   60   80   100   12
miles

Anthroparea
Industrarea
Cultivarea
Naturarea

75. Balance among the four types of areas leads to the proper conception of the megalopolis of the future.

6. National systems

We should use the same method for defining the national goals for human settlements as that we use for defining their problems: by analyzing all human settlements on a national scale in a manner which takes into account all the different types as well as the five elements of human settlements. The four steps needed to do this are: 1) classifying each human settlement problem, 2) measuring the number of people who are suffering from each human settlement problem, 3) multiplying these two estimates to learn the meaning of each problem at the national level, and 4) comparing all human settlement problems on the national level.

It is, however, difficult to compare the different problems. Let us assume that one million people suffer from a problem to which we give the value of one. This means the total problem equals 1,000,000. On the other hand, there may be 1,000 people who have lost everything because of an earthquake. Their problem is given the value of one hundred, making a total problem value of 100,000. The first problem may be said to be ten times larger than the second. But what is our goal? Which problem should we solve first? Obviously, evaluating problems differs from setting goals. A humanistic approach has taught us that we must first help the suffering few, although we must help both.

174. *To set national goals we must understand all the problems and the degrees to which humans are affected by them. Only in this way can we establish proper goals and the proper priorities.*

Unless we have clarified the goals we cannot proceed with a national program for human settlements. In our experience, the most difficult stage of the whole process (understanding and analyzing the subject, defining the problems, setting the goals, defining the policies and programs) is the stage related to goals.

175. *Our greatest and most difficult obligation is to set the national goals. Without national goals the overall effort for human settlements will fail.*

Our obligation to set goals is enormous, but there is little more to say about them now because, in fact, this whole book deals with them. When we tried to analyze what human settlements are, when we tried to show what their problems are and how we can recognize them, and when we outlined what goals we can set for each element and type of human settlement, we were really working towards setting national goals for human settlements. We have seen much work throughout the world analyzing cities and regions which came to nothing because it was not connected with national goals.

176. *The setting and achieving of national goals is the only justification of other action for human settlements. This is our ultimate goal. The immediate goal is to begin working toward it.*

7. International systems

We can define the international goals by following the same process we used when setting the national goals. We cannot, however, do so immediately. National goals have not yet been set, so the setting of international goals is impossible. The ultimate international goal must incorporate all goals presented so far for the five elements and the different types of human settlements, as well as other problems of general human concern.

177. *The ultimate international goal is to fulfill all goals set by all nations and inspired by the principle of a global system of human settlements with equal rights.*

It will take generations, probably centuries, to fulfill this goal. We must, therefore, concentrate on the immediate international goals. The immediate international goals are those which will help start the process for international action, to reach an agreement among nations that will permit us to understand the total situation of human settlements, their problems, and their goals. This study is an attempt to lay the foundations for the international effort which will begin at the United Nations 1976 conference in Vancouver.

178. *The first immediate international goal is for all people dealing with human settlements to accept a methodology for the understanding of human settlements, their problems, and their solutions.*

Once it is accepted that an international methodology for the understanding of human settlements is an essential first step, then an agency must be established to be responsible for the methodology and for training the experts. Although we did not start with the purpose of setting up an agency, it appears as the solution for our other immediate goals.

179. *The second immediate international goal is to train and develop experts on human settlements all over the globe.*

Since the implementation of these goals requires regular financing, an agency will be needed with the power and the money to act on a scale greater than is being done today by the International Bank for Reconstruction and Development (IBRD) and some other banks.

180. *The third immediate international goal is the provision of the capital needed to begin and continue action for human settlements.*

Capital alone is not enough, however, even if it is coordinated with knowledge and experts. The materials and the industry which will make implementation possible are also necessary. At the beginning of a new effort in a new area the necessary materials must be imported and industrial plants must gradually be created at the right places in order to supply the area with its needs. Since ancient times we have always begun by importing materials and technology, then gradually learning technology, and finally taking over production on our own.

181.   *The fourth immediate international goal is twofold: first, to create the mechanism for supplying materials and, second, to create the necessary industry so that human settlements will be dependent on outlying areas as little as possible.*

We cannot hope to realize any one of these goals at an international level without an agency to do the task. This statement raises problems, as there are already two United Nations offices, a temporary office preparing the 1976 Vancouver conference and a permanent office, dealing with human settlements. The International Bank for Reconstruction and Development (IBRD) is also involved in some few aspects of human settlements. The question arises if we also need a new agency and, if so, what will be its relationship with the existing agencies. The answer is that one international agency is needed to absorb all the existing agencies and organizations in order to meet all needs and help us attain all our goals. The only agency of those mentioned which should not be absorbed is the IBRD, which deals with many more problems than human settlements alone and should remain as independent as possible. The new agency should either have its own bank for human settlements or the IBRD should create a special office and take over all financing of the human settlement sector.

182.   *The fifth international goal in terms of orderly thinking and the first international goal in terms of time and importance is the creation of the International Agency for Human Settlements (IAHS) and a bank, part of either the IAHS or the IBRD, for human settlements. By their creation and collaboration we will be on the road to action.*

Part Four

Policies and Programs

1. The most difficult task

Defining policies and programs is the most difficult task of all because it requires immediate implementation. Our role is not to theorize, but to formulate specific policies and programs in detail. This is easiest for small human settlements, such as a neighborhood or a village, for the lower the ekistic unit, the easier it is to carry out a program of action. There is much less differentiation between the elements and problems, policies and programs in a small unit.

For example, if we wish to build a single house for a particular family, we have only to understand what it is they desire and how much they can afford to pay for it. In the case of a neighborhood the differences in demands increase enormously, and the situation becomes more complex with each successive ekistic unit. In addition, a new human settlement presents far fewer problems than does one which has developed over the centuries. We cannot deal here with any specific example of policies and programs, for even a single village requires long study, but must limit ourselves to a general view of policies and programs, letting the reader apply them to specific cases. We begin by studying and trying to understand human settlements, continue with the precise definition of their problems, and conclude with a description of their ultimate and immediate goals. Only then can we define policies and programs.

183. *To proceed to policies and programs we must begin by defining the term human settlements, then define the problems, and conclude by defining ultimate and immediate goals.*

To do this we must be specific. Generalizations are not helpful; we cannot discuss policies and programs for the five elements and the different types of human settlements if we do not define the specific metropolis, the policy, and the program with which we are dealing. It is the same in medicine; we can talk about it as a science, we can discuss particular diseases and general goals related to them, but unless we define the specific case of the individual patient we cannot determine a specific treatment.

184. *To define the policies and programs we must deal with one human settlement or a specific group of human settlements.*

The more clearly the problem can be defined, the more easily it can be dealt with. If we deal with one polis we can detail policies and programs, but if we deal with a region with tens of polises and hundreds of villages dependent on them, we cannot enter into the same detail. In some sectors we can be more specific, but in others we can speak only in general terms.

185. *The larger the area of human settlement involved, the more general will be the policies and programs.*

We must now consider the territorial considerations of where we act. If a river passing through a polis is polluted by industry outside the polis we should not, however possible theoretically, clean the river within the polis's territory. To do so would make the small polis pay to solve a problem belonging to the entire metropolitan area.

186. *To carry out the programs we need we must define the human settlement within which the problems are created and the responsibilities this human settlement has for their solutions. We cannot limit the implementation of programs to the administrative boundaries of the human settlement suffering from a particular problem.*

For these reasons we will not deal in Part Four with the different types of human settlements as in the other parts, but will give only national and international examples of a practical approach which help guide action at lower levels as well. A practical example can be the room.

2. Considerations on the room

I will use the example of the room to illustrate how we can move from setting ultimate goals to action and implementation.

Our goal of one room for every human is shown in Figure 76 as given by the line of rooms needed which follows the probable population curve. When the stage of implementation has been reached it will have to be worked out in further detail, but the dynamic curve sets a clear goal.

How this goal can be achieved differs from country to country. But, as we hope the day will come when the rich countries will really help the poor, not only with impressive sounding advice, it is important that the right policies be used throughout the world so that people, after covering their own needs, may be able to help others.

As the *first* step, we must formulate policies for the just and economic use of land, so that everyone can acquire land corresponding to his real needs. We waste land and energy on the rich while leaving the poor without the land on which to build even the simplest houses.

The *second* step is to provide for the gradual creation of all community facilities, beginning with water and ending with telecommunications.

The *third* step is proper financing on the basis of one room per person. The occupant should pay no taxes on his room even if the room is used by two people. Only when we offer the proper incentives can we hope to mobilize private initiative to start on such a small scale. We should not forget, however, that most cities were built by private initiative, and in most cases not through big projects but by families acting for their own benefit.

The *fourth* step is the creation of a system of taxation based on the following principles:

1. The person owning one room should not be taxed on that room.
2. If a family of five owns two houses, one house with three rooms and one house with two rooms, the family should not pay taxes on its houses.
3. If a family of three owns a six-room house, it should pay taxes on only three rooms.
4. Taxation should be at a higher rate when the number of rooms is more than double the number of persons owning them.

Conclusion: One room for every human is a fundamental goal. We must work toward it with courage and imagination with a proper scale of time and dimension. We must set global goals and programs and help every country and every human to reach their goals in their own way. We give practical help only when we create the proper frames for action, not when we impose our own plans.

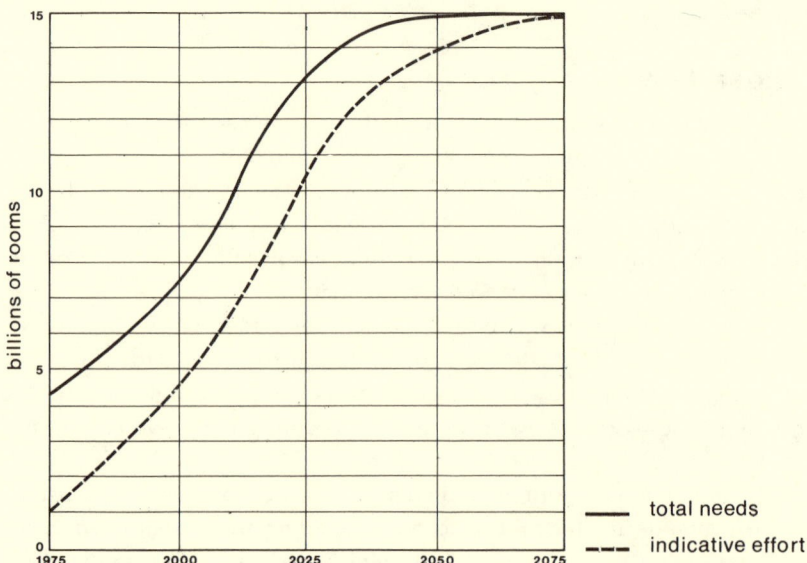

76. Our goal is to secure the rooms needed throughout the world.

3. National policies and programs

Implementing national policies and programs is the most difficult task in the general field of policies and programs we can undertake now. There has been no preparation for international policies and programs so it is, simply, impos-

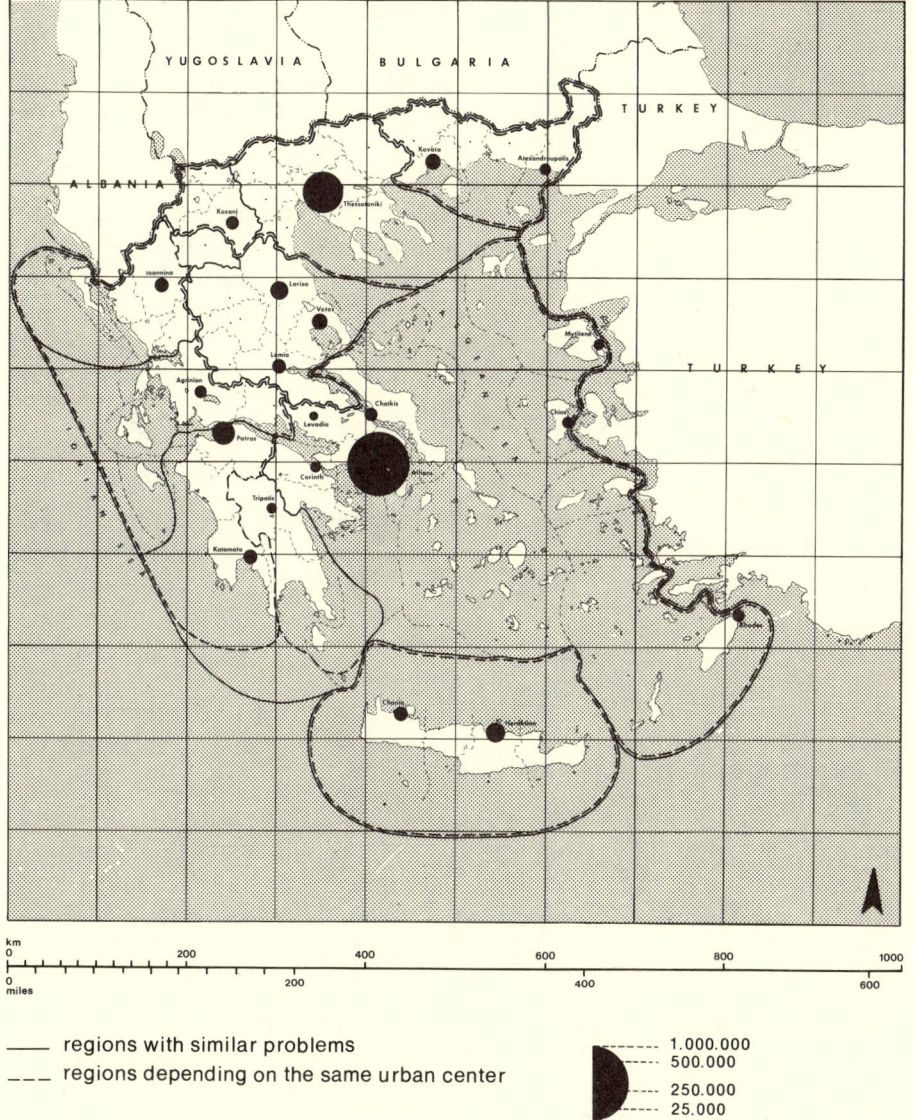

regions with similar problems

regions depending on the same urban center

1.000.000
500.000
250.000
25.000

77. Greece subdivided by cohesive regions and areas with similar problems

sible for us to implement them now. National governments do have agencies which could undertake the great responsibility of carrying out policies and programs, but no such agencies exist at the international level.

At the national level we deal with all sorts of human settlements. Even some of the so-called "advanced" countries still have nomads, and their human settlements may range from temporary ones to megalopolises. National policies and programs, therefore, must include almost all types of human settlements and must deal with each one separately.

At the national level we must first determine whether the nation is small enough to be dealt with as one unit or if it should be subdivided into several units.

In almost all cases the nation should be divided into parts, because policies and programs cannot be the same throughout a territory with major differences in human settlements. The practical method is to divide the territory into units so that policies and programs can be unified. This can be done in two ways: by cohesive units (megalopolis, metropolis, polis, etc.) or by units with similar characteristics and problems (declining villages, growing cities, etc.). We should use both methods, because otherwise we will not be able to check the programs and policies. Only when we have the ability to reckon that a given nation is subdivided into, say, seven metropolitan regions can we think of the proper policies and programs for each region. At the same time, we must estimate the number and population of the declining villages in the seven regions and test whether the nearby towns can or cannot be expanded to absorb this new population.

187.   *To develop the proper national policies and programs we must divide the nation into cohesive regions and into areas with similar problems.*

Figure 77 shows this dual division of Greece.

4. International policies and programs

We now reach the most difficult aspect of all, not only because it is the largest one, not only because it contains the greatest spectrum of variations, but also because it has no permanent authority to deal with its problems. We have already discussed the process we must follow in order to achieve our international goals, and concluded that a strong international agency, which we called the International Agency for Human Settlements (IAHS), is essential. Now that we have reached the stage of actual implementation we must restate that we badly need such an international agency, and that it can only be established within the framework of the United Nations. The agency, then, should not be called the International Agency for Human Settlements but the United Nations Agency for Human Settlements or UNAFHS. This is the only thing we can recommend at the international level. Without UNAFHS we cannot hope for any action at the international level. Thus, although this task is immense, we are obliged to conclude the discussion about international policies and programs with the only recommendation that can help us achieve our goals.

188. *To move toward international action for human settlements we must create the United Nations Agency for Human Settlements.*

Part Five

The Radical Changes We Need

When dealing in the present book with human settlements, problems, goals, policies, and programs we did not enter into details or give examples because to do so would require hundreds of volumes. There is, however, the lesson I learned by dealing with all these subjects throughout my lifetime, that, in the explosion through which we are passing, we have made many mistakes and have not understood the changes being made. We have made and are still making many great mistakes, such as allowing the exploitation of the higher levels of space by a few people in a way that creates inequalities in the ownership of land.

For these reasons I feel obliged to present some of the radical changes that we need. These radical changes are not all the radical changes we need. There remain several more, especially if we also consider political, organizational, administrative, and other aspects of human settlements.

We must have the courage to formulate these changes, but based on an exact knowledge of the subject. Various proposals have been made, but they are simply "great ideas" without practical meaning if they are not based on knowledge but simply on good intentions. For these reasons I introduce the radical changes that we need with the following basic statement:

189. *To begin proper action for human settlements and to make the necessary changes we must acquire precise, scientific knowledge of our subject and then act with courage to take the necessary measures which serve human goals.*

1. First Proposal: twelve global zones

Trying to save land, water, and air resources without defining the reasonable uses and the basic resources of the global surface is meaningless. The villages which survived for centuries or thousands of years properly defined the land they cultivated, the land they built on (usually unproductive or less productive soil), and the land they left untouched for natural resources, such as wildlife, timber, and proper water balances. There is no hope for us unless we achieve the same goals.

The proposal: Since our systems of life are much more complicated today, we need to establish twelve zones ranging from the most natural zone to the zone of the greatest human intervention. These twelve zones should be expressed in the following ways:

1. Twelve zones for land uses.
2. Twelve zones for water uses.
3. Twelve zones for coastal area uses.
4. Twelve zones for air uses.

Since air is always in motion, without boundaries, our action is restricted almost to the surface of our globe alone, so we have to express our goals and policies in terms of land and water. The same is valid for other phenomena such as the climate, the flora and fauna; they are all important, they all have to be considered as goals, but they have to be coordinated into a total system expressed in the above zones. We cannot save natural fauna, for example, if we do not save the whole natural environment of a given area (land, water, air, climate, and flora), because everything depends on the whole ecological balance.

2. Second proposal: ownership of global space

The problem of ownership of global space did not exist before the twentieth century — ownership of land was sufficient because humans could not fly and could build nothing higher than a few stories. Thus the notion arose that ownership of land surface also meant the ownership of all resources below it and of all space above it.

Now that we can build tall buildings landowners tend to exploit space. The result is continuous pressure for higher buildings, which is, in many ways, some of which I mention here, disastrous.

1. Lower income countries building multi-story buildings have to import materials and equipment at a large cost which could otherwise be saved both in terms of expense and in terms of foreign exchange.
2. All cities which build buildings higher than is justified by their general urban structure create huge problems of transportation, overcrowding, equality

(what happens to the neighbor with a small piece of land, appearance of the city, etc.).

3. All values of the past are lost because of a disastrous change of scale. Huge hotels destroy the beautiful villages the tourists came to admire, towers destroy natural landscapes, etc.

The proposal: There is no hope for the solution of all these problems if we do not shift from landownership to space ownership, so that everyone owning land can use up to a certain height above it, beyond which the space will have to be bought from the local, national, and even some day international authorities which will own it in a hierarchical way. Only with such a system will the pressures for higher buildings be stopped and landscape, tradition, culture, and human settlements regain the balance they have lost.

3. Third proposal: human space

If there is any real limit to human development and growth on our globe it is not directly related to resources, which change with technology, but to the relationship of humans to space, as we have learned from the relationships of all living organisms to space. Strangely enough, this has been overlooked recently, but it is a basic problem we have to face, and if we do not face it with specified dimensions we cannot proceed to action.

For many thousands of years humans lived as urban dwellers with average optimum densities of 200 persons per hectare, except when danger forced them to live in higher densities inside city walls or when security and high incomes enabled them to spread out in lower densities as in the case of the Roman villas. Today, because of the exploding forces and the understandable inability to deal with them meaningfully in the middle of the explosion, people live at a great variety of densities, from very low to very high. This is a great mistake and we know very well that the areas where people suffer the most in many ways (insecurity, social problems, energy waste, etc.) are those with extreme densities: either very low or very high.

The proposal: Our experience is enough to lead to specific figures for the best relationship of humans to space for every type of human settlement. I limit here the proposal to the basic units which already exist or must be created today which give the framework for the other types of human settlements as well.

	sq meters per person	persons per hectare limits	average
ekistic units 7, 8; polis	50.0 – 33.3	200 – 300	250
ekistic units 9, 10; metropolis	66.6 – 50.0	150 – 200	175
ekistic units 11, 12; megalopolis	100.0 – 50.0	100 – 200	150
ekistic units 13, 14	125.0 – 66.6	80 – 150	115
ekistic unit 15	166.6 – 83.3	60 – 120	90

These figures of spatial needs should be multiplied by 3 (densities have to be divided by 3) to include the area humans need for their leisure. This gives us a clear picture of the best amount of space for normal living conditions inside the so-called built-up area, which is really the human space or Anthroparea.

4. Fourth proposal: human scale

Since 1825 when the first railway appeared modern technology has been serving many human needs which had not been served before, but at the same time creating new problems in human space, which ceased to be human. The human scale began to disappear. This process is continuing in all human settlements because the invasion of the machine and the imposition of its own scale (dimensions, speed, noise, pollution) creates new conditions.

The proposal: The only reasonable solution is not to complain about machines, nor to allow human life to be dominated by them, but to attain the best development and use of machines for Anthropos. This means the separation of humans from machines and the re-creation of the age-old human scale.

5. Fifth proposal: equal choices and rights

One of the greatest problems of the emerging new types of human settlements is the creation of conditions which increase the differences between their inhabitants. This has always been a problem but, instead of being reduced now that we pretend we are civilized, it is being increased enormously. It is also being ignored. We have already mentioned such examples as the unequal use of space in heights of buildings or in densities, but there are many other aspects also. I will mention one characteristic example. In the past people felt equal in the streets regardless of age or income, but this is no longer true. The people who use automobiles are the masters of the streets and the people who do not use cars do not have the same freedom, speed, mobility, or choices.

The proposal is precise: We have to give people equal chances in all aspects and expressions of the social system in space. An example is our obligation to establish the age-old system of human streets and to keep the machines inside the mechanical streets (related to the fourth proposal). In this way the problem of equality in public human space can be solved and there is again hope for proper human development. This solution is not sufficient for equality in mobility. To solve this problem we must establish proper public transportation systems, first by using our existing technology and later on we can establish a more important public transportation system combining the advantage of the private car (any point to any point connection) with the advantage of public transport (everyone can use them). This proposal has been explained in detail in the Urban Detroit Area Study.[1]

6. Sixth proposal: territorial organization

Once upon a time, that is before 1825, the territorial organization of human settlements was meaningful and functional. Their birth and growth was based on the daily movements of people. Since the speed was constant (5 km per hour), life and organization were based on the same principle: that people belonged to communities (villages and polises) whose centers, services, and administration could be reached in no more than an hour.

Often, when the population became too big and the city could no longer serve tens of thousands and in some cases hundreds of thousands of people, a new subdivision was created which enabled everybody to belong both to the big city (one hour's maximum distance) and to a community or neighborhood inside it (shorter distances). This happened, for example, in ancient Greece, the Arab world, and in China.

Now the speeds are increasing every day, and many more people come together, but there is no principle for territorial organization. We must, therefore, organize human settlements on the basis of principles which are age-old but adjusted to our times.

The proposal is the following:
1. Recognition of the existence of twelve functional territorial units based on population and distances.
2. Creation of basic units on the principle of one hour's distance. There are now daily urban systems, ranging from a radius of 5 km (where no machines yet exist) to 250 km as in some extreme cases in the U.S.A.
3. Subdivision of these units on the basis of population units and physical characteristics based on both geographic units and technological units created by Networks.

7. Seventh proposal: housing for everybody

There is great confusion about housing today, and this in turn causes many more problems. This confusion can be understood if we recognize some basic mistakes, the two most important of which are the following:

1. We think that housing has to be of a certain standard to be built. I know of a country which has a regulation that unless a house is above a certain standard it cannot be built in its capital. This is like saying that unless a poor person has 2,500 calories per day to eat he should not be allowed to eat.
2. We think that governments should build houses for the poor, forgetting that even in the highest income countries this has not yet been achieved. People have always built their own houses in many ways.

The proposal is to be realistic and to help people acquire the proper houses at the proper time by giving them as much as possible in the following order:

1. The land, which is a minimum of 150 sq m, for a proper house. Without it there is no hope.
2. Water.
3. Sewage.
4. One room.
5. More rooms.
6. Electricity.
7. Other facilities.

Unless we follow this natural and realistic policy there is no hope of housing the people on a global scale for many generations. Instead, all types of problems (economic, social, political, technical, cultural) will increase because of overcrowding, the creation of slums which cannot be saved, and the waste of private efforts.

8. Eighth proposal: community services

The same problems of housing also exist for all types of community services, ranging from the simplest corner shop to the most elaborate cultural center and including every possible service. As there is usually no money for them right from the beginning, no provisions are made for the land which will be needed, and when the time comes for them to be built the difficulties increase enormously because of the lack of land. Implementation then does not take place or it takes place at a much lower level than desirable and at a higher cost than reasonable.

The proposal is similar to the one for housing, but requires much better planning and organization because, while for housing the situation is simpler (so many families, houses, plots), for community services we need proper calculations of what will exist in the next two to three generations.

The proposal is to implement the process in the following way:

1. Proper territorial organization (sixth proposal).
2. Calculation of the needs in community services for every type and size of

community and the corresponding land in terms of location and size.

3. Retain this land for the community.
4. Provide water, sewage, electricity, and other facilities as for housing (seventh proposal).

In this way the land can be used even without buildings as people can have an open air market and use the land for a school with or even without tents for any possible educational activity.

9. Ninth proposal: LANWAIR systems

When we deal with movement we make many mistakes. I will concentrate here on two basic errors.

The first is that we speak of "transportation." We assign tasks to transportation experts, forgetting that Anthropos does not live by transportation, but by movement. Transportation is only a part of Anthropos's movement and by overlooking this truth we benefit the machines and harm Anthropos.

The second error is that the existing transportation Networks lack coordination. They have not been conceived as integrated systems coordinating, for example, airlines with ferryboats. I have not found any case in any country where the transportation Network has been conceived, realized, and operated as an overall system for the most economic uses of time, energy, and money.

The proposal: We must adópt a new approach to deal with these problems as follows:

1. We need to eliminate such words as street and square from our vocabulary and replace them with hustreet and husquare as well as with mecstreet and mecsquare, the former meaning human and the latter mechanical. We cannot survive as humans unless we separate the huspace from the mecspace (fourth proposal).
2. We need a new concept of LANWAIR (Land-Water-Air) systems.[2] We must realize that in the future there will be an even more pressing need for. much closer coordination among all Networks moving people and goods. They must be conceived as unified systems.

10. Tenth proposal: utilities and movement corridors

The word "transportation" implies only persons and certain goods. We forget the existence of water (clean or otherwise) moving in pipes; of gas, oil, and electricity; of the movement of messages. As a result we waste space and Networks. This has been shown by many studies, especially in Europe and the U.S.A.[3]

Before the last world war there were few dense Networks outside the major cities. The only coordination needed then was between seaports and railways and to some degree with highways. After World War II, however, everything expanded very quickly beyond the cities. Each public or private agency for all sorts of utilities developed its own particular Network to suit its own purposes, without consideration of the other Networks.

The proposal is the creation of coordinated transportation and utility corridors. We can call them transutilidors or moveridors. By doing so we can save more than 80% of the total area of land occupied today, as was shown to be possible in the Urban Detroit Area Study, which was carried out in detail with full coordination of all agencies and companies concerned on both the United States and Canadian sides. The savings in the quality of the environment and in the quality of life in the countryside would be even greater.

11. Eleventh proposal: living human settlements

Even if we apply the first ten proposals there is no hope for solving our problems if we do not understand that our human settlements are living organisms. We do not recognize that many human settlements are declining or even dying, others are static, and others are growing dynamically, exploding. If we miss this diagnosis of real situations we cannot act properly with our first ten proposals because we do not know where and how to act. We need houses but we have to be sure where and when they are needed, otherwise our action may not serve our goals. Action is insufficient and may be disastrous if it is misdirected.

The proposal is the following:

1. Analyze the total situation for every human settlement and never one aspect only.
2. Proceed with the diagnosis which will help us to define the problems.
3. Decide on the proper action.
4. Begin with only one goal in mind: to serve Anthropos and not any technical or other isolated aspect.
5. Do this as quickly as possible without justifying any delays because of research work. A real doctor gives first aid even while the analysis is going on and before the final detailed diagnosis is completed.

Such a road requires courage for decisions at the top and avoidance of every escape because the experts in a certain field are delaying their opinions. It is the whole system of our life as expressed in human settlements that has to be served. We need courage and a scientific approach to tie all the parts together and to form the program of action.

12. Twelfth proposal: healthy and clean human settlements

Although it is now more fashionable to concentrate on pollution, we must recognize that what matters to any organism is to be complete and to develop properly. To achieve this it must be healthy and clean. The eleven proposals are related to the existence, growth, and development of the total human settlements, and the twelfth proposal is to keep them healthy and clean.

We must give the proper priority to health and cleanliness because what matters most in a low income area is to give people the proper food, water, and services which help them to develop in the best possible way, even if some factories have to continue or even if new factories have to be built close to them in spite of the creation of new pollution problems.

The proposal includes the following parts:

1. Save all natural values such as landscapes and their elements (land, water, climate, air, flora, fauna), because if we lose them their revival is very difficult if not impossible (first proposal).

2. Where these values have been destroyed, plan for the creation of new values. When the rock in the center of Athens, the Acropolis, was turned into a fortress, it was not turned back into a natural rock, but Pericles used it as the basis for the creation of the symbol of Athens, and the Athenian Confederation. As such, it is still respected today as the most important feature of Greece.

3. Save all those values humanity created in the past because they are irreplaceable. We can turn a changed landscape into a new monument, but we may not replace any work of value of the past by one of our own. It is like killing some people or some animal species because we think that we are better or that there are better ones.

4. Help to protect human beings by selecting the technological solutions which create the minimum disturbance and pollution, as is already beginning to happen.

5. Replace, in the broadest possible way, all those technical solutions which exist and are dangerous for Anthropos, with a proper time schedule and priorities.

6. To achieve the above goals we must plan the total system and give the proper priorities in terms of projects and time to be achieved (eleventh proposal).

13. Conclusion

We have ten proposals to save the five elements of human settlements (Nature, Anthropos, Society, Shells, Networks) but there is no hope of carrying them out unless we conceive the whole system of life and its total needs and choices (eleventh proposal) and try to save all its values (twelfth proposal) in a co-ordinated way.

A therapy and development is what we need for human settlements, as for every simple organism, and to achieve this we need a prevention, therapy, and development program, or a PRETHEDE.

Appendix 1 The ekistic scales

From the start of the effort to find a systematic approach to human settlements an attempt has been made to create an ekistic scale which could include all types of human settlements — ancient, present, and future, from the smallest to the largest. The basis for such a classification was the population of each human settlement, for people are the most important element of human settlements.

Very early we concluded that we must deal with 15 units, from the individual Anthropos to the several billion people of Ecumenopolis (Fig. 1). The same scale includes the 12 classes of communities. Later, when I studied the kinetic fields, these were also included in two categories influenced by the existence of a real city or polis as a full urban system.[1] The nomenclature and the population figures of the scale recently have been changed slightly. The change in nomenclature was necessary to develop a better glossary. A number of people could not clearly envisage a conurbation, or distinguish between a large city, which means megalopolis, and the megalopolis itself. Another weakness was the use of the terms town and city in several units only. Most people call any type of urban human settlement a city, and apply the term town to several categories.

For these reasons a glossary which avoids any ambiguity was developed for all types of human settlements. This glossary is different when referring to rural instead of urban human settlements, and I use it here for urban settlements. It starts with Anthropos (instead of Man which is sexually oriented), continues with room, house, housegroup, small neighborhood, and neighborhood, and from then on uses one root term, polis, for the remaining units, ending with Ecumenopolis (Fig. 2). Such terms as room and neighborhood are well understood. The root term polis has been successfully used for a very long time, and two new terms (eperopolis or continental city and Ecumenopolis or global city) are based on this successful experience.

I have also changed the population figures related to each unit. These changes are the results of an attempt to use the Ekistic Population Scale (EPS) and the Ekistic Territorial Scale (ETS) in conjunction, during which it became clear that in order to make proper comparisons between people and their territory we had to use a more accurate scale.[2]

To classify properly all human settlements by size we should start with the smallest unit, the individual Anthropos. This spatial unit includes the individual, his clothing, and certain furniture, like his chair. The second unit is equally well defined; it is the space belonging to him alone or shared with a few others — that is, his personal room. The third unit, the family home, is well defined also, as long as we have families. The fourth unit is a group of homes corresponding to the old patriarchal home and probably to the extended family of our day. This is the unit that children need most, mothers need mainly because of their children, and fathers need, if perhaps not directly for themselves, then because they are interested in the satisfaction and happiness of both mothers and children. The first three of these four units are clearly defined, physically and socially, and the fourth can be conceived as a social unit.

Beyond this point we have no clear-cut definition of any unit until we reach the largest one possible on earth, the global system of human settlements. We have, then, five basic units, four at one end of our scale and one at the other. No other well defined unit exists today, except for statistically defined units which are arbitrary, as may be seen from the differences in the official definitions from country to country. Throughout the long evolution of human settlements, however, people in all parts of the world tended to build an urban settlement which reached an optimum number of 50,000 inhabitants and physical dimensions which enabled each person to reach the center within ten minutes.[3] For people who depend on walking as a means of locomotion, this unit is the optimum one from the point of view of movement and social interaction through direct contacts between people. It is also the best unit from the standpoint of esthetics. Creation of the Place de la Concorde in Paris, for example, reduced by 2,100 meters the length of the Champs Elysées. This left 1,400 meters, which one can walk from the Place de la Concorde to reach, and enjoy, the Arc de Triomphe. This unit may also be best from the social point of view. Pericles in ancient Athens, for example, could get a reasonable sample of public opinion by meeting 100 to 150 people while walking from his home to the Assembly. Now we have four units at the beginning of the scale, one larger one somewhere beyond them, and one at the end — a total of six. How can we complete the scale?

We can do so if we think of units of space measured by their surface and increase their size by multiplying them by 7. Such a coefficient is based on the theory, presented by Walter Christaller, that we can divide space in a rational way by hexagons — that one hexagon can become the center of seven equal ones.[4] Similar conclusions can be reached if we think of organization of population, movement, transportation, and so on. Such considerations lead to the conclusion that all human settlements can be classified into 15 units.[5] With the basic units defined as No. 1 (Anthropos), No. 2 (room), No. 3 (house), No. 4 (group of houses or housegroup), No. 8 (traditional town or polis), and No. 15 (universal city or Ecumenopolis), we can define the others by systematic subdivision. All these units can also be classified in terms of communities (from I to XII), of kinetic fields (for pedestrians, from a to g; for motor vehicles, from A to H; and so on) (Fig. 3).

The scale thus defined has to be used for any very careful comparisons, but it has the disadvantage that it cannot easily be remembered. To correct this,

I reformed the scale in two ways. First, I used round figures which can be more easily understood and remembered. Second, apart from the single figure for every EPS unit, I gave the whole range of populations belonging to each unit (Fig. 4). In this way we may classify every human settlement, and we create the basis for a statistical classification of all human settlements in the EPS.

What is not answered here is the relation of the EPS to the Ekistic Territorial Scale, but this is another much more complicated subject, which can be used as a more elaborate method for the analysis of the characteristics of the ekistic units.[6]

Ekistic unit	1	2	3	4	5	6	7	8	9	10	11	12	13	14	15
Com. class				I	II	III	IV	V	VI	VII	VIII	IX	X	XI	XII
Kinetic field	a	b	c	d	e	f	g	A	B	C	D	E	F	G	H
name of unit		Man	room	dwelling	dwelling group	small neighborhood	neighborhood	small town	town	large city	metropolis	conurbation	metropolis	urban region	urbanized continent	Ecumenopolis
population		1	2	4	40	250	1,500	9,000	50,000	300,000	2 M	14 M	100 M	700 M	5,000 M	30,000 M

1. Ekistic logarithmic scales and grid: old nomenclature

Ekistic unit	1	2	3	4	5	6	7	8	9	10	11	12	13	14	15
Com. class				I	II	III	IV	V	VI	VII	VIII	IX	X	XI	XII
Kinetic field	a	b	c	d	e	f	g	A	B	C	D	E	F	G	H
name of unit	Anthropos	room	house	housegroup	small neighborhood	neighborhood	small polis	polis	small metropolis	metropolis	small megalopolis	megalopolis	small eperopolis	eperopolis	Ecumenopolis
population	1	2	4	40	250	1,500	9,000	50,000	300,000	2 M	14 M	100 M	700 M	5,000 M	30,000 M

2. Ekistic logarithmic scales and grid: new nomenclature

Ekistic unit	1	2	3	4	5	6	7	8	9	10	11	12	13	14	15
Com class				I	II	III	IV	V	VI	VII	VIII	IX	X	XI	XII
Kinetic field	a	b	c	d	e	f	g	A	B	C	D	E	F	G	H
name of unit	Anthropos	room	house	housegroup	small neighborhood	neighborhood	small polis	polis	small metropolis	metropolis	small megalopolis	megalopolis	small eperopolis	eperopolis	Ecumenopolis
ekistic population scale	1	2	5	35	245	1,715	12,005	84,035	558,245	4,117,715	28,824,005	201,768,035	1,412,376,245	9,886,633,715	69,206,436,005

3. Ekistic logarithmic scales and grid: new nomenclature and ekistic population scale

Ekistic unit	1	2	3	4	5	6	7	8	9	10	11	12	13	14	15
Com. class				I	II	III	IV	V	VI	VII	VIII	IX	X	XI	XII
Kinetic field	a	b	c	d	e	f	g	A	B	C	D	E	F	G	H
population range				3 - 15	15 - 100	100 - 750	750 - 5,000	5,000 - 30,000	30,000 - 200,000	200,000 - 1.5 M	1.5 M - 10 M	10 M - 75 M	75 M - 500 M	500 M - 3,000 M	3,000 M - 20,000 M	20,000 M and more
name of unit	Anthropos	room	house	housegroup	small neighborhood	neighborhood	small polis	polis	small metropolis	metropolis	small megalopolis	megalopolis	small eperopolis	eperopolis	Ecumenopolis
ekistic population scale	1	2	5	40	250	1,500	10,000	75,000	500,000	4 M	25 M	150 M	1,000 M	7,500 M	50,000 M

4. Ekistic logarithmic scales and grid: final version

Appendix 2
Population of human settlements

Data on population

In this appendix some aspects of population, to which there is frequent reference in the main text of this book, have been assembled. This data is also given in Appendix 1 of *Ecumenopolis: the Inevitable City of the Future*.

Tables 1, 2, 3, and 4 give various types of breakdowns for number and size of settlements in the period 8500 B.C. to 1970 A.D., together with the corresponding total population and percentage distribution of past population. They have been updated to 1970 under the realistic assumption that the same global yearly growth rates of population of the 1950-60 period for each category of settlement will also hold for the 1960-70 period.

Table 5 gives the present distribution of settlements by size categories, both in numbers and in population, partial and cumulative up to 1970. This table is based on estimates made by the Athens Center of Ekistics in a comparative study of data from a large number of sources.

Daily Urban Systems — urban and rural population

Tables 1, 3, and 4 provide data on the urban and rural population of the earth based on the size of these settlements. They do not take into account, however, those settlements which, though rural in character and size, are so close to big urban centers as to be a part of their daily urban systems.

Lack of analytical data by country makes a detailed estimate of the *real* urban population impossible. The estimate of the earth's real urban and rural population is based, therefore, on a more general method. Areas near urban centers, including all settlements no matter how small, were classified as urban because their inhabitants are in close communication with the neighboring urban centers and live and behave more or less like urban dwellers. Rural population is estimated on the basis of rural inhabitable land and the amount of inhabitable land in the vicinity of urban centers. If we assume that the average population density of rural settlements is approximately the same in all the inhabitable areas of the earth we can arrive at alternative estimates of the rural population by calculating on the basis of several distances from each urban center with a given size.

Table 6 gives various alternatives for the inhabited area in sq km from the center of settlements with a given size and distance from their center. Assuming that by 1970 the smallest urban size which can create a daily urban system is

50,000, we arrive at an area of 11.1 million sq km which is related to a rural area of 9 million sq km. Since the non-urban inhabitable land is around 54 million sq km it follows that 9/54 of all the rural settlements can be practically considered as parts of daily urban systems. Since from Table 5 the population of rural settlements (below 5,000 inhabitants) is 1,845 million, it follows that 307

Dates	Settlement Categories						
	over 1 million inh.	over 100,00 inh.	over 20,000 inh.	over 5,000 inh.	ca. 3,300-5,000 inh.	over ca. 3,300 inh.	2,000-ca. 3,300 inh.
				urban 1		urban 2	
8500 B.C.	—	—	—	—	—	—	—
8000	—	—	—	—	—	—	—
7500	—	—	—	—	—	—	.002
7000	—	—	—	.01	.004	.014	.005
6500	—	—	—	.03	.01	.04	.007
6000	—	—	—	.05	.01	.07	.009
5500	—	—	—	.06	.01	.07	.014
5000	—	—	—	.06	.01	.07	.02
4500	—	—	—	.06	.02	.08	.02
4000	—	—	—	.07	.02	.09	.03
3500	—	—	—	.13	.04	.17	.04
3000	—	—	.2	.60	.08	.68	.08
2500	—	.6	2	3	.2	3	.2
2000	—	.9	3	4	.3	4	.3
1500	—	.6	2	4	.4	4	.4
1000	—	.1	2	3	.4	4	.5
500	—	3	6	9	.7	10	.8
B.C./A.D. ± 0	1	8	13	17	1	18	1
A.D. 500	1	6	10	13	1	14	1
1000	9	18	24	28	1	29	1
1500	6	19	25	30	1	31	2
1650	6	18	25	30	2	32	2
1750	4	18	26	33	4	37	6
1800	5	21	29	56	14	70	14
1850	6	34	56	110	25	135	25
1900	35	117	191	290	45	335	45
1950	225	448	604	783	78	861	77
1960	370	702	936	1,164	85	1,250	85
1970	612	1,108	1,457	1,752	93	1,815	94

Table 1. Past global population by broad settlement categories (also urban and rural)

million people participate in the characteristics of daily urban systems and can be considered in some ways as already urban. As a result the total population of the earth in 1970 is constituted by 1,538 million of purely rural population (43%) and 2,059 million of urban population (57%). These estimates would be different if other assumptions about the average radius of the daily urban systems and the minimum populations of their nuclei were made.

Settlement Categories							Total population of the earth
over 2,000 inh.	1,000–2,000 inh.	over 1,000 inh.	under 5,000 inh.	under ca. 3,300 inh.	under 2,000 inh.	under 1,000 inh.	
urban 3		urban 4	rural 1	rural 2	rural 3	rural 4	
—	—	—	14.5	14.5	14.5	14.5	14.5
—	.002	.002	16.0	16.0	16.0	15.598	16.0
.002	.01	.012	19.000	19.000	18.998	18.988	19.0
.019	.03	.049	22.990	22.986	22.981	22.951	23.0
.047	.05	.097	28.970	28.960	28.953	28.903	29.0
.079	.06	.139	37.940	37.930	37.921	37.861	38.0
.084	.07	.154	50.940	50.930	50.916	50.846	51.0
.09	.09	.18	61.94	61.93	61.91	61.82	62.0
.10	.12	.22	71.94	71.92	71.90	71.73	72.0
.12	.15	.27	79.93	79.91	79.88	79.73	80.0
.21	.25	.46	85.87	85.83	85.79	85.54	86.0
.76	.5	1	92.40	92.32	92.24	92	93.0
3.2	1	4	98	98	98	97	101
4.3	2	6	106	106	106	104	110
4.4	2	7	116	116	116	114	120
4.5	3	7	129	128	128	125	132
10.8	4	15	137	136	135	131	146
19	5	24	148	147	146	141	165
15	6	21	182	181	180	174	195
30	7	37	217	216	215	208	245
33	9	42	365	364	362	353	395
34	12	46	515	513	511	499	545
43	32	75	697	691	685	653	728
84	75	159	850	836	822	747	906
160	140	300	1,050	1,025	1,000	860	1,160
380	220	600	1,320	1,275	1,230	1,010	1,610
938	320	1,248	1,710	1,632	1,555	1,245	2,493
335	330	1,665	1,796	1,710	1,625	1,295	2,960
1,909	340	2,250	1,845	1,782	1,688	1,347	3,597

Population figures in millions

Dates	Settlement Sizes					
	million inhabitants				thousand inhabitants	
	10—20	5—10	2—5	1—2	500—1000	200—500
8000 B.C.	—	—	—	—	—	—
7500	—	—	—	—	—	—
7000	—	—	—	—	—	—
6500	—	—	—	—	—	—
6000	—	—	—	—	—	—
5500	—	—	—	—	—	—
5000	—	—	—	—	—	—
4500	—	—	—	—	—	—
4000	—	—	—	—	—	—
3500	—	—	—	—	—	—
3000	—	—	—	—	—	—
2500	—	—	—	—	—	—
2000	—	—	—	—	—	.3
1500	—	—	—	—	—	.3
1000	—	—	—	—	—	—
500	—	—	—	—	1	1
B.C./A.D. ± 0	—	—	—	1	3	2
A.D. 500	—	—	—	1	1	2
1000	—	—	5	4	3	3
1500	—	—	5	1	4	5
1650	—	—	2	4	3	5
1750	—	—	—	4	5	4
1800	—	—	—	5	5	6
1850		—	2	4	10	10
1900	—	5	11	19	23	29
1950	23	62	59	81	69	85
1960	41	97	107	125	96	130
1970	73	152	194	193	134	199

Table 2. Past global population by settlement sizes over 5,000 inhabitants (quasi-logarithmic scale based on multiples of 1, 2 and 5)

Settlement Sizes					Total
thousand inhabitants					over 5,000
100—200	50—100	20—50	10—20	5—10	—
—	—	—	—	—	—
—	—	—	—	—	—
—	—	—	—	.01	.01
—	—	—	.01	.02	.03
—	—	—	.03	.03	.06
—	—	—	.03	.03	.06
—	—	—	.03	.03	.06
—	—	—	.01	.05	.06
—	—	—	.01	.06	.07
—	—	—	.03	.10	.13
—	—	.2	.2	.2	.6
.6	.5	.6	.4	.4	2.5
.6	.6	1	.6	.6	3.7
.3	.7	1	.8	.7	3.8
.1	.6	1	.7	.7	3.1
1	1	2	2	1	9
2	3	2	2	2	17
2	2	2	2	1	13
3	3	3	2	2	28
4	3	3	3	2	30
4	4	3	3	2	30
5	4	4	4	3	33
5	4	4	10	17	56
8	9	13	20	34	110
30	36	38	39	60	290
69	71	85	73	106	783
106	108	126	107	121	1,164
163	162	187	157	138	1,752

Population figures in millions

Dates	Settlement Categories									
	over 1 million inh.	over 100,000 inh.	over 20,000 inh.	over 5,000 inh. (urban 1)	c. 3,300-5,000 inh.	over 3,000 inh. (urban 2)	2,000-c. 3,300 inh.	over 2,000 inh. (urban 3)	1,000-2,000 inh.	over 1,000 inh. (urban 4)
8500 B.C.	—	—	—	—	—	—	—	—	—	—
8000	—	—	—	—	—	—	—	—	1	1
7500	—	—	—	—	—	—	1	1	3	4
7000	—	—	—	1	1	2	2	4	8	12
6500	—	—	—	4	2	6	4	10	18	28
6000	—	—	—	6	3	9	5	14	22	36
5500	—	—	—	7	4	11	6	17	29	46
5000	—	—	—	7	5	12	7	19	32	51
4500	—	—	—	8	7	15	10	25	37	62
4000	—	—	—	10	9	19	13	32	62	94
3500	—	—	—	16	16	32	24	56	105	161
3000	—	—	6	47	29	76	43	119	215	334
2500	—	4	30	117	53	170	80	250	440	690
2000	—	5	40	170	80	250	110	360	870	1,230
1500	—	3	47	208	90	298	150	448	1,150	1,598
1000	—	1	39	194	110	304	200	504	1,650	2,154
500	—	16	96	388	180	568	300	868	2,500	3,368
B.C./A.D. ± 0	1	27	141	500	215	715	315	1,030	3,300	4,330
A.D. 500	1	26	122	435	250	685	330	1,015	4,300	5,315
1000	5	43	165	551	290	841	420	1,261	5,000	6,261
1500	3	52	210	711	350	1,061	700	1,761	6,500	8,261
1650	4	51	215	731	500	1,231	850	2,081	8,700	10,781
1750	3	57	239	969	1,000	1,969	2,330	4,299	23,000	27,299
1800	4	66	251	3,471	3,500	6,971	5,550	12,521	53,000	65,521
1850	4	113	664	7,114	6,350	13,464	10,200	23,664	97,000	120,664
1900	19	361	2,132	23,762	11,700	25,462	18,800	44,262	150,000	194,262
1950	90	960	4,800	25,600	20,500	46,100	32,500	78,600	210,000	288,600
1960	141	1,460	7,200	32,700	23,000	55,700	36,500	92,200	222,300	314,500
1970	221	2,220	10,800	41,770	25,800	67,570	40,990	108,560	235,320	343,880

Table 3. Past number of settlements by broad categories (also urban and rural)

Dates	Settlement Categories										
	over 1 million inh.	over 100,000 inh.	over 20,000 inh.	over 5,000 inh.	over c. 3,300 inh.	over 2,000 inh.	over 1,000 inh.	under 5,000 inh.	under c. 3,300 inh.	under 2,000 inh.	under 1,000 inh.
				urban 1	urban 2	urban 3	urban 4	rural 1	rural 2	rural 3	rural 4
8500 B.C.	—	—	—	—	—	—	—	100	100	100	100
8000	—	—	—	—	—	—	.0125	100	100	100	99.985
7500	—	—	—	—	—	.0105	.063	100	100	99.9895	99.937
7000	—	—	—	.043	.061	.083	.21	99.957	99.939	29.917	99.79
6500	—	—	—	.104	.138	162	.334	99.896	99.862	99.838	99.666
6000	—	—	—	.158	.185	.208	.392	99.842	99.815	99.792	99.608
5500	—	—	—	.118	.137	.165	.302	99.882	99.863	99.835	99.698
5000	—	—	—	.097	.113	.145	.290	99.903	99.887	99.855	99.710
4500	—	—	—	.083	.111	.139	.306	99.917	99.889	99.861	99.694
4000	—	—	—	.088	.113	.150	.337	99.912	99.887	99.850	99.663
3500	—	—	—	.151	.198	.224	.535	99.849	99.802	99.776	99.465
3000	—	—	.215	.64	.73	.82	1.07	99.36	99.27	99.18	98.93
2500	—	.59	1.68	2.48	2.67	2.87	3.85	97.52	97.33	97.13	96.15
2000	—	.82	2.27	3.36	3.64	3.91	5.72	96.64	96.36	96.09	94.28
1500	—	.50	1.84	3.17	3.50	3.84	5.50	96.83	96.50	96.16	94.50
1000	—	.076	1.29	2.35	2.65	3.03	5.30	97.65	97.35	96.97	94.70
500	—	2.06	4.11	6.17	6.64	7.20	9.93	93.83	93.36	92.80	90.07
B.C. A.D. ∓0	.61	4.85	7.88	10.3	10.9	11.5	14.6	89.7	89.1	88.5	83.4
A.D. 500	.51	3.1	5.1	6.7	7.2	7.7	10.8	93.3	92.8	92.3	89.2
1000	3.7	7.4	9.8	11.4	11.9	12.3	15.1	88.6	88.3	87.7	84.9
1500	1.5	4.8	6.3	7.6	7.9	8.1	10.6	92.4	92.1	91.9	89.4
1650	1.1	3.3	4.6	5.5	5.9	6.2	8.4	94.5	94.1	93.8	91.6
1750	.55	2.5	3.6	4.5	5.1	5.9	10.3	95.5	94.9	94.1	89.7
1800	.55	2.3	3.2	6.2	7.7	9.3	17.6	93.8	92.3	90.7	82.4
1850	.52	2.9	4.8	9.5	11.6	13.8	25.9	90.5	88.4	86.2	74.1
1900	2.2	7.3	11.9	18.0	20.8	23.6	37.2	82.0	79.2	76.4	62.8
1950	9.0	18.0	24.3	31.5	34.7	37.7	50.1	68.5	65.3	62.3	49.9
1960	12.5	23.7	31.7	39.3	42.2	45.1	56.3	60.7	57.8	54.9	43.7
1970	17.0	30.8	40.5	48.7	50.5	53.1	62.6	51.3	49.5	46.9	37.4

% of the global population

Table 4. Structure of past global population of broad settlement categories (also urban and rural)

| Size categories (inh.) | Estimates by the Athens Center of Ekistics | | | | |
| | Number of settlements | | Average population (inh.) | Total population | |
	Partial	Cumulative		Partial	Cumulative
in millions:					
10-20	5	5	14.6	73	73
5-10	22	27	6.91	152	225
2-5	59	86	3.29	194	419
1-2	135	221	1.43	193	612
0.5-1	209	430	0.641	134	746
0.2-0.5	648	1,078	0.307	199	945
0.1-0.2	1,142	2,220	0.143	163	1,108
in thousands:					
50-100	2,363	4,583	68.5	162	1,270
20-50	6,217	10,800	30.1	187	1,457
10-20	10,190	20,990	15.4	157	1,614
5-10	20,780	41,770	6.64	138	1,752
circa 3.3-5	25,800	67,570	3.60	93	1,845
circa 2-3.3	40,990	108,560	2.29	94	1,939
1-2	235,320	343,880	1.41	332	2,271
0.5-1	604,500	948,380		410	2,681
0.2-0.5	1,118,000	2,066,380		390	3,071
0.1-0.2	1,723,000	3,789,380		250	3,321
in units:					
50-99	1,940,000	5,729,380	74.2	144	3,465
20-49	1,480,000	7,209,380	33.8	50	3,515
10-19	1,050,000	8,259,380	15.2	16	3,531
5-9	2,600,000 ⎫	10,859,380	7.31	19	3,550
2-4	5,570,000 ⎨ 1,970,000	12,829,380	3.05 ⎫ 4.67	6	3,556
1	1,000,000 ⎭	13,829,380	1.0 ⎭	1	3,557
nomads	400,000	14,229,380	100	40	3,597

Table 5. Present distribution of human settlements by size categories (1970) for the entire globe

From center of settlement (km)	Over 100,000	Over 50,000	Over 20,000
5	17,348.5	174,270	847,800
10	69,394	697,080	3,391,200
15	156,136.5	1,568,430	7,630,200
20	277,576	2,788,320	13,564,800
25	433,712.5	4,356,750	21,195,000
30	624,546	6,273,720	30,520,800
35	850,077	8,539,230	41,542,200
40	1,110,304	11,153,280	54,259,200

Table 6. Settlement categories: occupied area in sq km

Table 7, giving the estimated population and number of settlements by type of human settlement, has been estimated on the basis of the above Tables 1-5.

Type of human settlement	Population range	Estimated population	%	Estimated no. of settlements	%
very small settlement	1-100	276 million	7.7	10,440,000	73.4
village	100-5,000	1,569 million	43.6	3,747,610	26.3
polis	5,000-200,000	807 million	22.4	40,692	0.3
metropolis	200,000-10 million	455 million	12.6	560	—
megalopolis	10-500 million	490 million	13.6	19(518)*	
					—
total		3,597 million	100.0	14,229,380	100.0

* This 518 is an average estimate of the number of settlements included in the 19 megalopolises. This number has been subtracted where applicable from the preceding types of human settlements.

Table 7. Distribution of types of settlements by number and size

Table 8 shows the estimated population by type of human settlement, taking into account the urban population of the very small settlements in the vicinity of the urban centers and belonging to their Daily Urban Systems.

Type of human settlement	Population range	Estimated population	%
very small settlements	1-100	230 million	6.4
villages	100-5,000	1,308 million	36.4
polis	5,000-200,000	1,003 million	27.9
metropolis	200,000-10 million	566 million	15.7
megalopolis	10-500 million	490 million	13.6
total		3,597 million	100.0

Table 8. Types of human settlements by size

Glossary

Anthroparea: Term coined by C.A. Doxiadis from the words *Anthropos* (human being) and *area,* meaning the so-called built-up area or area mostly used by Anthropos in his daily life.

Anthropocosmos: Term coined by C.A. Doxiadis from the Greek words *anthropos* and *cosmos,* (human being and world), meaning world of Anthropos as distinguished from the great world or cosmos beyond Anthropos's reach.

Anthropos: One of the five ekistic elements, it is the Greek word for human being, used instead of the English word, "Man," since it has no connotation distinguishing sex or age but means men and women equally, belonging to all age groups. See Preface note 3 for further clarification.

Community class: Based on a systematic classification of human communities expressed in the Ekistic-Logarithmic Scale (ELS), starting from class I, which corresponds to housegroup, and ending with class XII, corresponding to Ecumenopolis.

Cultivarea: Term coined by C.A. Doxiadis, meaning the cultivated areas.

Dynapolis: Term coined by C.A. Doxiadis and used since the early fifties in his teaching and writing; meaning dynamic city or dynamic "polis." The ideal dynapolis is the city with a parabolic uni-directional growth which can expand in space and time.

Ecumenopolis: Term coined by C.A. Doxiadis from the Greek words *ecumene,* that is, the total inhabited area of the world, and *polis,* or city, in the broadest sense of the word. It means the coming city that will, together with the corresponding open land which is indispensable for Anthropos, cover the entire earth as a continuous system forming a universal settlement.

Ekistic elements: The five elements which compose human settlements: Nature, Anthropos, Society, Shells, and Networks.

Ekistic logarithmic scale (ELS): A classification of settlements according to their size, presented on the basis of a logarithmic scale, running from Anthropos (ekistic unit 1), as the smallest unit of measurement, to the whole earth (ekistic unit 15). The ekistic logarithmic scale can be presented graphically, showing area or number of people corresponding to each unit, etc., so that it can be used as a basis for the measurement and classification of many dimensions in human settlements.

Ekistics: Term coined by C.A. Doxiadis from the Greek words *oikos,* and *oikō,* "settling down," to mean the science of human settlements. It conceives of the human settlement as a living organism having its own laws and, through the study of the evolution of human settlements from their most primitive phase to megalopolis and Ecumenopolis, develops the interdisciplinary approach needed to solve its problems.

Ekistic unit: A classification of parts of whole human settlements, starting from unit 1 corresponding to Anthropos, and ending with unit 15, corresponding to Ecumenopolis. From unit 4, which corresponds to community class I, to unit 15, which corresponds to community class XII, the ekistic units coincide with the classification of human communities expressed in the ekistic logarithmic scale (els).

Entopia: Term coined by C.A. Doxiadis from the Greek words *en* and *topos*, "in" and "place," to mean place that is practicable — that can exist.

Eperopolis: Derived from the Greek words *eperos*, "continent" and *polis*, "city," it replaces the old term "urbanized continent," which corresponded to ekistic unit 14 and community class XI, with a population of 5,000 million.

House and housegroup: These terms replace "dwelling" and "dwelling group," which corresponded to ekistic units 3 and 4, with a population of four and 40 people respectively. Housegroup corresponds to community class I.

Hustreet (husquare, hu-avenue, etc.): Term coined by C.A. Doxiadis to signify the division of the human from the mechanical. A hustreet is a street reserved for human beings only, and prohibited to machines.

Industrarea: Term coined by C.A. Doxiadis meaning the industrial areas.

Kinetic field: The distance Anthropos can move within a certain period by walking, by using animals, or by using vehicles.

LANWAIR: Land, Water, Air. Term coined by C.A. Doxiadis to mean the transportation Network conceived as a unified system, in which ports, airports, etc. are brought together as LANWAIR knots, enabling people (and goods) to move from airplanes to boats, cars, and trains without any extra formalities or difficulties.

Mecstreet (mecsystem, mecarea, etc.): Term coined by C.A. Doxiadis to denote the mechanical from the human. A mecstreet is a street reserved for machines only.

Megalopolis: Term used since ancient Greek times when the small city of Megalopolis was created in Arcadia. Jean Gottmann gave a special meaning to this ancient term in 1961 in his book, *Megalopolis: the Urbanized Northeastern Seaboard of the United States.* A megalopolis is a greater urbanized area resulting from the merging of metropolises and cities into one urban system. Its population is calculated in tens of millions. It corresponds to ekistic unit 12 and community class IX.

Nature: One of the five ekistic elements corresponding to the natural environment of Anthropos as it exists before he starts remodelling it by cultivation and construction. It provides the foundation upon which the settlement is created and the frame within which it can function.

Networks: One of the five ekistic elements corresponding to the Anthropos-made systems which facilitate the functioning of settlements, such as roads, water supply, electricity.

Prethede: Acronym coined by C.A. Doxiadis to mean a PRevention, THerapy and DEvelopment program for human settlements.

Polis: Corresponding to ekistic unit 8 and community class V, it has a population of 50,000 and replaces the term "city."

Shells: One of the five ekistic elements corresponding to all types of structures within which Anthropos lives and carries out his various functions.

Society: One of the five ekistic elements corresponding to human society with all its characteristics, needs, and problems, where each individual is examined as only one of its units.

Transutilidors (or moveridors): Coordinated transportation and utility corridors.

Bibliography

Christaller, W., *Central Places in Southern Germany*, trans. by C.W. Baskin from the German edition of 1933, Prentice-Hall, New Jersey, 1966.

Cuénot, Claude, *Teilhard de Chardin*, Collection Microcosme, Le Seuil, Paris, 1962.

Fitzgerald, C.P. and The Horizon Magazine eds., *History of China*, American Heritage Publishing Co., Inc., New York, 1969.

Gottmann, Jean, *Megalopolis: the Urbanized Northeastern Seaboard of the United States*, MIT Press, Cambridge, Mass., 1961.

Hall, E.T., *The Silent Language*, Doubleday, New York, 1959.

Hall, E.T., *The Hidden Dimension*, Doubleday, New York, 1966.

Hayek, F.A., *The Counter-Revolution of Science*, Allen & Unwin, London, 1952.

Huxley, Sir Julian, *The Uniqueness of Man*, Chatto & Windus, London, 1941.

Mayer, Harold M. and Clyde F. Cohn, eds., *Readings in Urban Geography*, University of Chicago Press, Chicago, Illinois, 1959.

Schmidt, K.P. and Alfred E. Emerson, "Taxonomy," *Encycopaedia Britannica*, Vol. 21, University of Chicago Press, Chicago, Illinois, 1970.

Simpson, G.G., *Principles of Animal Taxonomy*, Columbia University Press, New York, 1961.

Sokal, Robert R. and Peter H.A. Sneath, *Principles of Numerical Taxonomy*, Freeman, San Francisco, 1963.

Toynbee, Arnold, *A Study of History*, one-volume edition, Oxford University Press in association with Thames & Hudson, London, 1972.

Books and publications by the author

Between Dystopia and Utopia, Trinity College Press, Hartford, Conn., 1966; Faber & Faber, London, 1968; Athens Publishing Center, Athens, 1974.

Urban Renewal and the Future of the American City, Public Administration Service, Chicago, Illinois, 1966.

"Water and Human Environment," *Water for Peace*, U.S. Government Printing Office, Washington D.C., 1967.

Emergence and Growth of an Urban Region: the Developing Urban Detroit Area, The Detroit Edison Company, Detroit, Michigan; Vol. I, 1966; Vol. II, 1967; Vol. III, 1970.

Ekistics: an Introduction to the Science of Human Settlements, Oxford University Press, New York, 1968.

"The Future of Human Settlements," *The Place of Value in a World of Facts*, edited by Arne Tiselius and Sam Nilsson, Wiley Interscience Division, John Wiley & Sons, Inc., New York, 1970.

"Ekistics: the Science of Human Settlements," SCIENCE, Vol. 170, October 23, 1970.

"Ecumenopolis: the Inevitable City," "Isopolis: the Desirable, Humane City." "Entopia or the City We Can Build," the Whidden Lectures, McMaster University, February 17, 18, 22, 1971.

"Order in our Thinking: the Need for a Total Approach to the Anthropocosmos," EKISTICS, Vol. 34, No. 220, July 1972.

The Two-Headed Eagle: From the Past to the Future of Human Settlements, Lycabettus Press, Athens, 1972.

"The Formation of the Human Room," EKISTICS, Vol. 33, No. 196, March 1972.

"Human Settlements in Space and Time," *Nature in the Round*, edited by Nigel Calder, Weidenfeld & Nicolson, London, 1973.

The Great Urban Crimes We Permit by Law, Lycabettus Press, Athens, 1973.

"The Structure of Cities," EKISTICS, Vol. 36, No. 215, October 1973.

Anthropopolis: City for Human Development, Athens Publishing Center, Athens, 1974 and W.W. Norton, New York, 1975.

"The Four Explosions of our Cities," EKISTICS, Vol. 38, No. 228, October 1974.

"Movement and City," EKISTICS, Vol. 37, No. 223, June 1974.

"The Ecological Types of Space That We Need," ENVIRONMENTAL CONSERVATION, Vol. 2, No. 1, Spring 1975.

"The Great Danger," EKISTICS, Vol. 39, No. 230, January 1975.

"Human Settlements and Crime," EKISTICS, Vol. 39, No. 231, February 1975.

(with J.G. Papaioannou), *Ecumenopolis: the Inevitable City of the Future*, Athens Publishing Center, Athens, 1974 and W.W. Norton, New York (in press).

"The Symbols We Need," EKISTICS, Vol. 39, No. 232, March 1975.

"Metropolis and Megalopolis," EKISTICS, Vol. 39, No. 233, April 1975.

"Culture and Ekistics," EKISTICS, Vol. 39, No. 234, May 1975.

"The Housegroup," EKISTICS, Vol. 39, No. 235, June 1975.

"Economics and the Ekistic Grid," EKISTICS, Vol. 40, No. 236, July 1975.

"The Changing Systems," EKISTICS, Vol. 40, No. 237, August 1975.

"Wildlife and Human Settlements," EKISTICS, Vol. 40, No. 238, September 1975.

"Learning from the Great Mistakes," EKISTICS, Vol. 40, No. 239, October 1975.

"Athens and its Future," EKISTICS, Vol. 40, No. 240, November 1975.

Notes and References

No. Page

Preface

1   V   C.A.Doxiadis, "The Human Settlements Research Project." Eight reports were prepared under the above title for the International Federation of Institutes for Advanced Study (IFIAS), and were presented in Athens, May 1974.

2   V   The Eleventh Delos Symposion on "Action for Human Settlements," organized by the World Society for Ekistics, took place between July 7 and 12, 1974 at the Athens Center of Ekistics and Apollonion, Porto Rafti.

3   VI   For years I thought that "Anthropos" (the ancient Greek word for human) would be better than the English word "Man" to describe human beings or mankind, because the word "Man" is also confused with the masculine gender. Now the American Anthropological Association has passed a resolution (November 1973) and has taken the following decision: "In view of the fact that the founders of the discipline of anthropology were men socialized in a male-dominated society which systematically excluded women from the professions and thereby prevented their participation in the formation of our discipline, including its terminology; and being trained as anthropologists to understand that language reinforces and perpetuates the prevailing values and socio-economic patterns that contribute to the oppression of women; we move that the American Anthropological Association:

     a. urge anthropologists to become aware in their writing and teaching that their wide use of the term "man" as generic for the species is conceptually confusing (since "man" is also the term for the male) and that it be replaced by more comprehensive terms such as "people" and "human being" which include both sexes;

     b. further urge that members of the Association select textbooks that have eliminated this form of sexism which has become increasingly offensive to more and more women both within and outside the disciplines.

I agree with this basic goal and throughout this book have used the word *Anthropos* (and where necessary the Greek plural *Anthropoi*) as meaning human of both sexes. Unfortunately, however, because of the grammatical structure of the English language, in several instances it has been impossible to avoid the use of masculine pronouns when referring to *Anthropos*.

No. Page

Part One

1   2   C.A. Doxiadis, "A City for Human Development: Eighteen Hypo-
        theses," EKISTICS, Vol. 35, No. 209, April 1973, p. 177.

2   2   C.A. Doxiadis, "Ecumenopolis: the Coming World-City" in *Cities of
        Destiny*, ed. by Arnold Toynbee, Thames & Hudson, London, 1967,
        pp. 336-38.
        C.A. Doxiadis, "Ecumenopolis: Tomorrow's City" in *1968 Britannica
        Book of the Year*, University of Chicago Press, Chicago, Illinois, 1968,
        pp. 16-38.

3   2   "Environment: Pollution Watch," THE FINANCIAL TIMES, February 20,
        1974.

4   3   *Habitat 76*, "United Nations Conference-Exposition on Human Set-
        tlements," Vancouver, Canada, May 31 to June 11, 1976. Report by
        the Preparatory Planning Group submitted to the Executive Director
        of the United Nations Environment Program, December 31, 1973, p. v.

5   3   Sir Julian Huxley, *The Uniqueness of Man*, Chatto & Windus, London,
        1941.
        C.A. Doxiadis, *Ekistics: an Introduction to the Science of Human
        Settlements*, Oxford University Press, New York, 1968, p. 42.

6   10 C.A. Doxiadis and J.G. Papaioannou, *Ecumenopolis: the Inevitable
        City of the Future*, Athens Publishing Center, Athens, 1974; W.W.
        Norton, New York, (in press).

7   15 E.T. Hall, *The Silent Language*, Doubleday, New York, 1959.
        E.T. Hall, *The Hidden Dimension*, Doubleday, New York, 1966.

8   15 C.A. Doxiadis, *Ekistics: an Introduction to the Science of Human Set-
        tlements*, pp. 300-02.

9   15 Claude Cuénot, *Teilhard de Chardin*, Collection Microcosme, Le Seuil,
        Paris, 1962, p. 91.

10 17 C.A. Doxiadis, *Anthropopolis: City for Human Development*, Athens
        Center of Ekistics, Athens, 1975; W.W. Norton, New York, 1975,
        pp. 55-61.

11 18 Arnold Toynbee, *A Study of History*, one-volume edition, Oxford Uni-
        versity Press in association with Thames & Hudson, London, 1972, p. 43.

12 18 F.A. Hayek, *The Counter-Revolution of Science*, Allen & Unwin, Lon-
        don, 1952, p. 34.

13 27 C.A. Doxiadis and J.G. Papaioannou, *Ecumenopolis: the Inevitable City
        of the Future*, p. 393.

14 29 C.A. Doxiadis, "Action for a better scientific approach to the subject
        of human settlements: the Anthropocosmos model," EKISTICS, Vol. 38,
        No. 229, December 1974, pp. 405-12.

No. Page

15   43   Jean Gottmann, *Megalopolis: the Urbanized Northeastern Seaboard of the United States*, MIT Press, Cambridge, Mass., 1961.

16   43   C.A. Doxiadis and J.G. Papaioannou, *Ecumenopolis: the Inevitable City of the Future*, pp. 425-34.

17   53   C.A. Doxiadis, *Ekistics: an Introduction to the Science of Human Settlements*, pp. 21-43, 44-78.
C.A. Doxiadis and J.G. Papaioannou, *Ecumenopolis: the Inevitable City of the Future*, pp. 1-12.

18   58   C.A. Doxiadis, *Anthropopolis: City for Human Development*, p. 86.
C.A. Doxiadis, "Order in our thinking: the need for a total approach to the Anthropocosmos," EKISTICS, Vol. 34, No. 200, July 1972, pp. 43-46.
C.A. Doxiadis, "Action for a better scientific approach to the subject of human settlements: the Anthropocosmos model," EKISTICS, Vol. 38, No. 229, December 1974, pp. 405-12.

19   59   G.G. Simpson, *Principles of Animal Taxonomy*, Columbia University Press, New York, 1961, p. 11.

20   59   Robert R. Sokal and Peter H.A. Sneath, *Principles of Numerical Taxonomy*, Freeman, San Francisco, 1963, p. 3

21   59   Ibid, p. 11.

22   60   Karl Patterson Schmidt and Alfred E. Emerson, "Taxonomy," *Encyclopaedia Britannica*, Vol. 21, University of Chicago Press, Chicago, Illinois, 1970, pp. 728-31.

23   61   Harold M. Mayer and Clyde F. Kohn, eds., *Readings in Urban Geography*, University of Chicago Press, Chicago, Illinois, 1959, p. 239.

24   62   W. Christaller, *Central Places in Southern Germany*, trans. by C.W. Baskin from the German edition of 1933, Prentice-Hall, New Jersey, 1966.
Brian J. Berry and William L. Garrison, "The functional bases of the central place hierarchy" in Harold M. Mayer and Clyde F. Kohn, eds., *Readings in Urban Geography*, pp. 218-27.

Part Two

1   70   C.A. Doxiadis, *Ekistics: an Introduction to the Science of Human Settlements*, pp. 265-80.

2   74   C.A. Doxiadis, *Anthropopolis: City for Human Development*, pp. 140-45.
C.A. Doxiadis, *Building Entopia*, Athens Publishing Center, Athens, 1975, pp. 112-30; W.W. Norton, New York (forthcoming).